UNIVERSITY COLLEGE

Brescia

BERYL IVEY LIBRARY

"Margarita has written a personal masterpiece. Her Heart, Habit, and Harmony dimensions of authenticity are brilliantly simple and useful. Her stories, tools, and frameworks give readers a clear roadmap for the authenticity journey, and her writing style is comfortably informative as she gently guides us into better leadership. Outstanding!"

Dave Ulrich, Rensis Likert Professor, Ross School of Business, University of Michigan; Partner, The RBL Group

"*Yours Truly*, a book on authenticity in leadership, and in life more generally, is a must-read for current and future leaders in all walks of life. Given the current crop of leaders around the world, this book is essential reading for prospective leaders in business, politics and the public sector."

Professor Sir Cary Cooper, CBE, The 50th Anniversary Professor of Organizational Psychology and Health at the ALLIANCE Manchester Business School, University of Manchester, UK

"A highly interesting read, particularly the idea of multiple selves as a means of balancing flexibility and authenticity when navigating our increasingly complex world. Backed up with stories of diverse effective leaders doing just that."

Bronia Szczygiel, Founding Partner, Aspire Leadership

"Margarita has written an engaging book on a crucial topic, filled with wonderful stories and practical next steps for any leader. I appreciate her three-part model for helping authentic leaders flourish."

James C. Galvin, Ed.D., President, Galvin & Associates; Author of *I've Got Your Back*

"The world needs authentic leaders more than ever before. Margarita Mayo provides new and compelling insights into the need for such leaders and what makes them special. For all who lead and aspire to lead, *Yours Truly* should be required reading."

Stuart Crainer and Des Dearlove, Founders, Thinkers50

"Mayo's new book is a powerful guide that helps leaders understand who they truly are and how they can leverage that insight, not just to be more successful at work but also to lead happier and healthier lives. Based on academic evidence and compelling cases, this is a must-read book for all people in leadership positions."

Dr Jochen Menges, Judge Business School, University of Cambridge

"At a time when the actions of leaders of all kinds are scrutinized more than ever, and understanding the nature of leadership continues to pose a great challenge to social and psychology scholars, Dr. Mayo masterfully explores and explains the ingredients of authentic leadership. *Yours Truly* is a must-read, not only for researchers in the field of management and governance, but for anyone interested in the making of successful leaders."

Luis Rojas Marcos, MD., Professor of Psychiatry, New York University; former Executive President of the New York City Health and Hospitals System

"*Yours Truly* is a bold book that approaches the very well known – and sometimes even hackneyed – topic of leadership in a completely different manner, to the point that it helps you to consider and appreciate things that you probably would not expect. In my opinion, a brilliant, fresh and highly recommended read for those of us who are eager to learn from true leaders, and one that you will not find in the front pages of traditional management publications."

José Amoretti-Cordova, Vice President Corporate HR Europe and Middle East, BMW Group

"Margarita projects the high quality of her personality throughout the pages of this book. The book shows her capacity to lead authenticity and fresh ideas but with the brilliant flexibility that is not commonly found in academics. I would really like to make a full recommendation for reading this book."

Diego del Alcazar, Founding President of IE Business School

"In *Yours Truly*, Margarita Mayo helps us understand the paradox we each need to hold as authentic leaders: being true to our values and passions, while growing and evolving to serve the greater good. Her sharing of compelling stories of everyday authentic leaders inspires us to see ourselves in both their challenges and their triumphs."

Henna Inam, author of *Wired For Authenticity*; Top Executive Coach; and former Fortune 500 C-Suite leader

"*Yours Truly* is a creative and ingenious take on leadership in today´s world. Margarita has written a delightful guide full of practical insights and inspirational stories for all of us who want to lead in an authentic way. An eloquent and personal account filled with heart and wisdom, it is a must-read. I will definitely share this powerful and glowing book with other leadership thinkers and executive coaches."

Marshall Goldsmith, The Thinkers50 No.1 Leadership Thinker in the World, and author of the No.1 *New York Times* bestseller *Triggers*

"Margarita has written beautifully on a series of powerful and diverse leadership stories that support her 3Hs model. The book provides original insights from her rigorous studies while at the same time investigating authentic leadership. *Yours Truly* is a very practical guide for anyone interested in becoming a better leader in the digital era. Highly recommended!"

Isaac Hernandez, Country Manager Google Cloud, Spain and Portugal

"Margarita's book addresses the need for current and future leaders to analyse and work on their authenticity. Her 3Hs formula offers them an excellent tool, one that is highly relevant to the legal profession's leaders. The traditional leadership model in law firms must be reviewed and adjusted to the new realities imposed by the legal services' market. *Yours Truly* is a book that must be read by lawyers."

Fernando Peláez-Pier, Past President of the International Bar Association

"*Yours Truly* adds considerably to the body of work on authenticity and leadership. It is underpinned by classic work in psychology and social psychology, combined with compelling stories of leadership and resilience. The examples are novel and illuminating, and the style is accessible. All those who strive to exercise authentic leadership, whatever their positions in organizations, will be inspired by Mayo's work."

Gareth Jones, Visiting Professor at IE, Madrid, co-author of
Why Should Anyone Be Led By you?

"Margarita Mayo dives deep into the analysis of authenticity and why it is so central to strong leadership. Her case studies and personal stories underscore her compelling thesis of 'Heart, Habit and Harmony' as the drivers behind the world's most successful leaders."

Carol Fishman Cohen, CEO, iRelaunch

YOURS TRULY

YOURS TRULY

Staying Authentic in Leadership and Life

MARGARITA MAYO

Bloomsbury Business
An imprint of Bloomsbury Publishing Plc

BLOOMSBURY

LONDON · OXFORD · NEW YORK · NEW DELHI · SYDNEY

Bloomsbury Business

An imprint of Bloomsbury Publishing Plc

50 Bedford Square   1385 Broadway
London   New York
WC1B 3DP   NY 10018
UK   USA

www.bloomsbury.com

BLOOMSBURY and the Diana logo are trademarks of Bloomsbury Publishing Plc

First published 2018

© Margarita Mayo, 2018

Margarita Mayo has asserted her right under the Copyright, Designs
and Patents Act, 1988, to be identified as Author of this work.

British Library Cataloguing-in-Publication Data
A catalogue record for this book is available from the British Library.

ISBN: HB: 978-1-4729-5091-8
        ePDF: 978-1-4729-5092-5
        ePub: 978-1-4729-5093-2

Library of Congress Cataloging-in-Publication Data
Names: Mayo, Margarita, author.
Title: Yours truly : staying authentic in leadership and life / by Margarita Mayo.
Description: New York : Bloomsbury Publishing Plc, [2018] |
Includes bibliographical references and index.
Identifiers: LCCN 2017045505 (print) | LCCN 2017051785 (ebook) |
ISBN 9781472950925 (ePDF) | ISBN 9781472950932 (ePub) |
ISBN 9781472950949 (eXML) | ISBN 9781472950918 (hardback)
Subjects: LCSH: Leadership. | Leadership--Psychological aspects.
Classification: LCC HD57.7 (ebook) | LCC HD57.7 .M3946 2018 (print) |
DDC 658.4/092–dc23 LC record available at https://lccn.loc.gov/2017045505

Cover design by Alice Marwick
Cover image © iStock

Typeset by Refine Catch Limited, Bungay, Suffolk
Printed and bound in Great Britain

To find out more about our authors and books visit www.bloomsbury.com. Here you
will find extracts, author interviews, details of forthcoming events and the option to
sign up for our newsletters.

To Marco and Monica

CONTENTS

PREFACE

Dear Reader

I've been reflecting on the role of leaders in business and society at large for two decades. In that time, I have been encouraged by the many stories I've heard from a variety of leaders, whether they are CEOs of multinationals, start-up founders, leaders of creative organizations, charities or NGOs.

Amid what is often described as a crisis in leadership, it is moving to find that some of the most authentic leaders are often people no one has heard of. One of the purposes of writing this book is to bring these unsung heroes to centre-stage and to learn from them. I hope you find their stories as inspirational as I have. I believe their stories are a mirror in which we can see the best of ourselves.

For me, writing *Yours Truly* became an exercise in self-awareness, allowing me to see parts of myself in the lives and endeavours of these authentic leaders. My hope is that you can also see parts of yourself in the extraordinary lives of these genuine leaders.

All the stories in the book touched me personally.

I met Rafael de la Rubia, whose passion for life and everything he does is contagious. But the thing that struck me the most about Rafael is his planning. It feels he designed his life way ahead of time and everything is falling into place just as he planned it.

When I spoke with Hiroko Samejima, I was impressed by her ethics, courage and self-confidence. She was leaving her job as a designer at Chanel to start her own company in Ethiopia because of her strong beliefs in ethical principles and slow fashion.

Listening to Carlo Volpi telling the touching story of his business and family was a particular source of inspiration and motivation. Everyone should have a personal story to feel proud of. Connecting the dots in our past allows us to grow into the future.

I could easily relate to the fears and hopes that Rakesh Aggarwal faced when moving from his native India to Australia in search of opportunity and a better life for himself and his family. Talking to him revived my memories of moving from Spain to the United States in my mid-twenties.

Those of you with families will surely agree that Dena Schlutz is a hero, even though she talks about her life as though it were like anybody else's. Her ambition and dedication to others when faced with adversity make her a role model for many women who struggle to find a balanced authenticity in work and family.

That Angel Ruiz is a survivor became clear to me when we spoke about the many challenges he had to face in life. But it is his resilient attitude and control over his destiny, along with his willingness to share his vulnerabilities with others, that I admire most.

Perhaps the story of PERI, a multinational construction company, is the most emotive for me because it goes back to my upbringing. Every morning my father left home at seven to work on a construction site, hanging on to unsafe scaffolding. When I heard from PERI's executives about their commitment to safety and the well-being of their workforce, I wished my father could have worked for a company like that.

The respect and admiration that millennial Francisco Rebelo expressed for the history of his family business combined with his responsible and humanistic approach to business as a young consultant gives me confidence in the new generation of leaders to make the world a better place.

Ana Botín is leading a cultural transformation in a legendary bank to leave a legacy of social purpose with strongly committed executives. I hope we can all embark ourselves on something where we can leave our imprint, hallmark or stamp for others to be proud of.

I want to take this opportunity to express my gratitude to the protagonists of this book for giving me their most precious gift – their life stories. It has truly been an honour to speak with them and learn from them how to stay true to our authentic selves in leadership and life.

I have put my most genuine effort to bring you their inspirational experiences interwoven with the results of more than 20 years of academic research. I hope you enjoy reading the book as much as I have enjoyed writing it.

Yours Truly,

Margarita

LIST OF FIGURES AND PHOTOS

Figures

Photos

Introduction

To thine own self be true, and it must follow, as the night the day,
thou canst not then be false to any man.
WILLIAM SHAKESPEARE, *HAMLET*, ACT I, SCENE 3

Yours Truly is used as a closing in a letter to refer to 'myself' as the author – the person who is speaking, doing or writing. It captures the essence of authenticity from its roots in the Greek term '*authentes*' meaning authentic – being true to oneself.

As Shakespeare notes, being true to oneself – or authentic – is a condition of being true to others, and has been a sign of moral authority throughout history. Today, the need for authenticity and authentic leadership is easy to understand: authentic leaders give the people around them a sense of control and agency over their collective future that enables them to feel better about themselves and what they are doing, sparking change and transformation.

At the same time, one of the most pressing issues we face is a lack of trust in our leaders: we are increasingly unlikely to trust someone just because they hold a senior position. Leadership scholars agree that authenticity – or, the lack thereof – lies near the heart of the crisis of confidence in contemporary corporate leadership.[1]

We have a workforce that distrusts leaders. In Edelman's 2017 Trust Barometer survey across twenty-eight countries, respondents reported trust levels in business leaders at 37 per cent, a decline of six points with respect to 2015 and a decline of fifteen points with respect to 2011.[2] 'We see an evaporation of trust,' observes Richard Edelman. After all, it wasn't the financial crisis that caused us to lose faith in leaders; rather it was the leaders' own overly hands-off attitude that led people to scepticism.

I believe those of us looking to lead can find the antidote to this scepticism in authenticity. Leaders are the glue holding our companies together and are part of the fabric of our society. Once, leaders acquired trust based on formal positions, but today they must rely on authentic relationships. *Yours Truly* explores and explains the fascinating psycho-social dynamics behind authenticity and authentic leadership.

Authentic leadership is not just about being yourself, but also about growing into your best self and being true to others. Authentic leadership can never be static or self-interested. If it is to be truly successful it is grounded, but continually evolving and cooperative. Authentic leaders reinvent themselves and their organizations to address the emotional and social demands of their followers while staying true to their authentic self.

In this book, I draw on interviews I have carried out with executives of multinationals, start-up founders, politicians and athletes, building on nearly two decades of research to examine and explain the missing link in research into authentic leadership: how authentic leaders lead for success, collective excellence and constant renewal while maintaining core principles.

Yours Truly: the 3 Hs of authentic leadership

What makes an authentic leader? To answer this question, I have identified three characteristics that set authentic leaders apart: *heart, habit* and *harmony,* depicted in Figure 1.0. I encourage you to explore these areas in your leadership and life to help identify attitudes and behaviours that will enable you to become authentic and remain so over time.

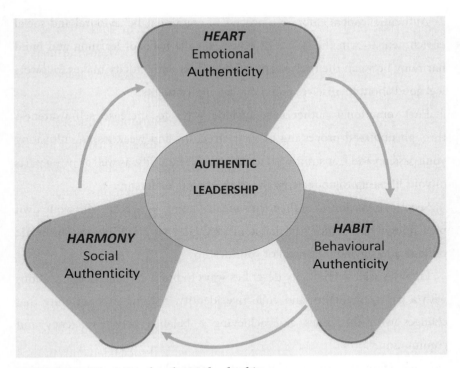

FIGURE 1.0 *The 3 Hs of authentic leadership.*

Heart – This is the emotional factor that characterizes authentic leaders. Learn to look inside yourself to find and cultivate passion. Infect your followers with the passion virus and win over their hearts to find their inner motivation.

Habit – The habit of learning is the key behavioural element of authentic leaders. Seek out honest feedback and develop a growth mindset. Ask for critical feedback to adapt, grow and progress.

Harmony – This is the final characteristic of authentic leaders that guarantees the social enrichment of authentic organizations. Look after others. Seek a harmonious unity between yourself and others to build an authentic context within which to develop followers. This way you will have enduring influence.

Authentic leaders embrace a process of emotional, behavioural and social enrichment to win the hearts of others, set the habit of learning and build harmony between themselves and others. Their authenticity makes followers feel good about themselves and their accomplishments.

First, emotional authenticity include ways to increase self-awareness through unbiased processing of your strengths and weaknesses, cultivating your passion and transmitting it to others with humility, as well as using parts of your life story to underscore the truth of your leadership.

Second, behavioural authenticity means acting in accord with your own principles while setting the habit of changing by fostering an optimistic outlook and staying in control of your destiny.

Finally, social authenticity describes ways to build authentic organizations with a caring mentality and collective identity, creating a community that changes with the times and achieving a balance between agency and communion.

Yours Truly captures the essence of authentic leadership in transforming organizations.

Each chapter tells an inspirational story combined with research-based studies, self-assessment tools and a practical, 10-step guide to help you stay true to your authentic self.

Resolving the three paradoxes of authenticity

Authentic leadership has become a fashionable concept. It argues that leaders must be true to their values and principles if they are to be consistent and succeed. The underlying assumption is that authenticity is unchanging and individual, a matter of personal choice and belief. But my research over the last two decades suggests that behind authenticity lie powerful and largely ignored dynamic social forces and contradictions. Authenticity is not simply being true to oneself, but also means being true to the protean, evolving and social self. If you want to develop and harness your authentic power, understanding the multidimensional, evolving and social process to authenticity is key. Authenticity is not simply about expressing your 'true' self. Instead, it involves identifying and resolving tensions and paradoxes.

The question at the heart of the book is simple but challenging: how do authentic leaders reinvent themselves and still stay true to themselves?

As I show, authenticity and change can go hand in hand:

- How can a company undertake an authentic transformation? The CEO of PERI, a multinational German construction company, called for greater communication to overcome the challenges of rapid international growth with a strong organizational identity: *We are PERI.*

- How can a stay-at-home mom reinvent herself? Dena Schlutz, a rancher's daughter on a Colorado sheep farm, changed roles from being a supportive wife to becoming a top executive at Hewlett Packard and then a successful real estate entrepreneur after her husband had a tragic accident.

- How can a designer produce the most authentic products? Hiroko Samejima left Chanel and her hometown in Japan to start a fashion company in Ethiopia to produce leather bags following her ethical principles of *slow fashion.*

What do these three stories have in common? The CEO of a German multinational, a US real estate entrepreneur and a Japanese fashion designer are all stories of people in search of authenticity. These are examples of authentic leadership during today's difficult times in a business organization that wants to grow internationally, of an entrepreneur true to herself in the face of adversity, and of personal transformation to become a successful authentic designer.

The authentic leaders I talk to in this book pave the way for powerful transformations by resolving three authenticity paradoxes.

First, they resolve the tension between their protean self and being true to their authentic self. They undergo a life review to discover and cultivate their passion, embracing all sides of their story to develop self-understanding and moral steadfastness.

Second, they change over time, finding the balance between growth and authenticity by reaching into the past to create a new future. Connecting the dots drives them forward to learning and experimenting with their possible selves.

Finally, their impact is enduring because they find harmony in the tension between their personal and social self. They build platforms, craft norms and advance social goals that thrive after they are gone.

By learning from these inspiring stories you can deal effectively with the three paradoxes of authenticity: how to stay true to your protean, possible and social self.

PART ONE

THE *HEART* FACTOR: BE YOURSELF WITH PASSIONATE HUMILITY

William James, widely regarded as the father of social psychology, argued that one of the three main features of the self are the feelings and emotions that it arouses. Heart is the emotional component of authenticity. We develop self-feelings about who we are. Passion about who we are is a key element of authenticity. Thus, the first rule of authenticity is the heart factor – be yourself with passion.

A leader's ability to make their passion contagious is one of the vital characteristics to being an authentic leader. One of the things you will discover when talking to authentic leaders is that they embrace their personal story and are able to tell you what they have done in life and learned as a result. Their sense of self-awareness is unbiased, with a very balanced attention to their strengths and weaknesses in a variety of roles. This is important because a humble and balanced view earns the respect and trust of your followers. Leaders use their life stories to teach their values, beliefs and philosophy of management to their followers. This is how they motivate others through their passion and emotional appeal, developing an inspirational vision for others to follow.

I will introduce you to Rafael de la Rubia, whose passion in a multi-tracking life as an athlete, rock star and entrepreneur teaches us important lessons on how to stay true to multiple identities. You will next meet Hiroko Samejima to better appreciate the power of unsung heroes who motivate others through her unassuming contagious passion for creating ethical products in the Japanese fashion industry. And finally, Carlo Volpi will share his life story as part of this Italian winery to illustrate how to lead by biography and develop an inspirational vision.

You will learn lessons on passion, humility and the magic of storytelling. I offer practical guidance on how to apply these lessons and tell portions of your life story to develop greater authenticity: to achieve self-awareness, find and cultivate your passion, demonstrate vulnerability and develop an uplifting vision. You will also find self-assessment tools so that you can answer questions like: what's my heartfelt authenticity? And inauthenticity? How consistently do I behave across situations? How humble am I in a leadership role? What's my level of narcissism? And how do I see the story of my life? Remember, to become an authentic leader, you don't need to be a superhero. Instead, shift to the mindset of unsung heroes.

1

Heartfelt Authenticity: Take a Multi-dimensional View of Your True Self

There is no greater thing you can do with your life and your work than follow your passions – in a way that serves the world and you.

RICHARD BRANSON

Richard Branson is widely considered one of the most important entrepreneurs of the last half-century.[1] Not just because of the breadth and success of his entrepreneurial activities, which include Virgin Records, Virgin Airlines, Virgin Express, Virgin Mobile, Virgin Money, Virgin Hotels, Virgin Fuel, Virgin Cruises and Virgin Galactic among others; but because he is known as somebody who puts his heart into his business. He has shown 'it is possible to live a life filled with adventure, fulfilment, family, philanthropy, meaning ... and a tremendous amount of fun'.

But his idiosyncratic and successful leadership style remains a mystery. How did Richard Branson succeed where others have failed? The answer is that authenticity largely depends on emotional involvement. This is the essence of *Yours Truly*. This chapter is about the emotionally grounded aspect of authenticity; about how people discover and cultivate many passions in life to find their purpose.

Rafael de la Rubia: passion in a multi-tracking life (Spain)

He runs, he rides, he composes music, sings, and spends six months of the year sailing around the Balearic Islands making friends. Rafael de la Rubia has a passion for life and a youthful spirit that belie the Spaniard's fifty-seven years.

A regular guest speaker in my leadership classes, when asked about the meaning of success, Rafael explains why being true to himself over the years and across multiple tracks is fulfilling. 'I'm passionate about everything. My life is divided up into different areas. This way is like living three lives in one. I spend seven months running and playing music and five months sailing,' he says.

In his time as a professional athlete, he came second in the 4x200m World and European Championships and first in the Spanish Championships. He also came second in the Spanish Pentathlon Championship. 'I broke seven Spanish records in 100m, 200m and 400m. Athletics is more than a career, it is a school of life,' he says. 'It teaches you to work day after day towards medium and long-term goals.' To this day, he runs competitively, still chasing records.

His second career – sailing entrepreneur – started as pleasure but became a business when he founded Ibiza Vela Charters, a yacht tour company in the Balearic Islands.

Now, little by little, his career as a musician is coming to the fore. When his daughter introduces him to people as a businessman, he corrects her: 'I am a musician.' Running and music now take up most of his time.

Athlete, rock star and entrepreneur

'My life divides into two main chapters,' says Rafael. In the first chapter of his life he worked very hard for many years. In the second he came to realize that he has three loves: the sea, sport and music. 'When you come from a poor

PHOTO 1.1 *Rafael de la Rubia, athlete, sailing entrepreneur and musician (Spain).*

family you see your life from an economic perspective.' His early years were spent working for a car company as well as starting several businesses, but his goal was always to take control of his own life and to dedicate himself to music and sport.

His father worked in a factory and his mother was a housewife. He dropped out of high school and at the age of thirteen, began a flower business, buying from a nursery in the southern province of Almería and selling them to supermarkets. Rafael says he has always worked with hard-working people, but that when they retired, although they were very wealthy, and some still powerful, most of them had few friends and had fewer pleasures. Early on he realized this was not what he wanted for himself.

He liked sports and music from an early age, but was unable to pursue either, lacking the time and the resources. Once his obligations to his children were met and he was financially stable, he decided to make a radical change. At the age of forty-three, he made the most difficult decision of his life and broke with the past. He sold all his other businesses to the people who had created them with him, and was then able to devote himself exclusively to the business of sailing. When the time came to break with the past, 'all the demons were unleashed', he recalls. Finally, he had achieved his dream.

A decade later, Rafael dedicates half his year to Ibiza Vela Charter, saying he likes being around people who are taking a relaxed vacation: 'When you share a boat with people for a week they end up being almost like your friends.'

What is it that gives people like Rafael a passion for exploring different things in life? The answer goes to the fundamental aspect of authenticity – a positive feeling about yourself, being passionate about who you are. When we feel consistency with our values and goals, we experience a positive emotion – authenticity. In contrast, people experience inauthenticity as an unpleasant emotion when they believe their values and goals are not in harmony.[2]

Heartfelt authenticity and well-being: the empirical evidence

What makes someone authentic? The first – and most obvious – criterion is that authentic people feel good about themselves. They are the kinds of people who are self-determined, they live by their own standards, they seem to choose and create contexts that fit their personal strengths and project a sense of self-realization. Authenticity has been historically considered by humanistic and existential psychologists as the very essence of well-being.[3] However, empirical research on authenticity is patchy. Only recently have scholars developed validated measures to assess feelings of authenticity, and the lack of it: inauthenticity.

A group of researchers led by Alex Wood at the University of Manchester came up with a very good example of the way authentic people function. They conducted a series of studies to develop a measure of authenticity and test whether authenticity is related to well-being. In a nutshell, says Wood, authenticity involves 'being true to oneself in most situations and living in accordance with one's values and beliefs'. This is what they labelled as 'authentic living'. In addition, the authors developed another scale to measure *inauthenticity* or feelings of self-alienation which refer to the 'subjective experience of not knowing oneself, or feeling out of touch with the true self'.

In one study, Wood's team explored the relationship between feelings of authenticity and inauthenticity based on two indicators of subjective well-being: stress and happiness. They asked participants to indicate how often in the previous month they found their lives unpredictable ('upset about something that happened unexpectedly'), uncontrollable ('unable to control irritations in your life') and overwhelming ('felt that you were not on top of things'),[4] and asked them for their perception of happiness.[5] The results of this study showed an interesting pattern – authenticity was positively related to happiness and negatively related to stress. But the correlations of inauthenticity with less happiness and increased stress were particularly notable.

This principle also holds for other measures of subjective well-being such as self-esteem and gratitude. They found that people who subjectively felt authentic, reported higher levels of self-esteem and gratitude with significant correlations.

Perhaps more surprising is that subjective feelings of inauthenticity were more strongly correlated with reduced positive emotions towards both the self and others. People who subjectively felt inauthentic reported lower self-esteem and less gratitude. Gratitude for one's lot in life is clearly enhanced by authenticity. In general, feeling good, happy, interested, excited and enthusiastic is more widespread among people who feel authentic. Conversely, inauthenticity reduces all these positive feelings. These results illustrate the first principle of authenticity – the heart factor.

In a second study, the Manchester University team used the psychological well-being test developed by psychologist Carol Ryff[6] of the University of Wisconsin and an expert on aging to find an answer to the link between authenticity and happiness. In 1989, Ryff identified and measured the six elements of happiness: autonomy, environmental mastery, personal growth, positive relations with others, purpose in life, and self-acceptance. Wood's team found that feelings of authenticity are strongly related to the first element of psychological well-being – autonomy. This is what authentic people are like. They have a strong sense of being true to themselves; they are also independent, resist social pressures to act or think in conventional ways, and adjust their behaviour from within. These are examples of responses to Ryff's questions on autonomy which authentic people surpass:

- I am not afraid to voice my opinions, even when they are in opposition to the opinions of most people.

- Being happy with myself is more important to me than having others approve of me.

- People rarely talk me into doing things I don't want to do.

- I have confidence in my opinions, even if they are contrary to the general consensus.

- I am not the kind of person who gives in to social pressures to think or act in certain ways.

- I judge myself by what I think is important, not by the values of what others think is important.

In the case of Rafael de la Rubia, his authenticity is a reflection of his strong need for independence and making effective use of surrounding opportunities.

This sense of environmental mastery is the second element of psychological well-being that is significantly correlated to authenticity in Wood's study. This is surprising. The premise behind authenticity is that we *discover* our inner motivations, such as a desire for independence. But the point about authentic people is that by chasing every opportunity they also change and grow, as we will see in more detail in Part 2. These are examples of responses to Ryff's questions on environmental mastery in which authentic people excel:

- In general, I feel I am in charge of the situation in which I live.
- I am quite good at managing the many responsibilities of my daily life.
- If I were unhappy with my living situation, I would take effective steps to change it.
- I generally do a good job of taking care of my personal finances and affairs.
- I am good at juggling my time so that I can fit everything in that needs to get done.
- My daily life is busy, but I derive a sense of satisfaction from keeping up with everything.
- I have been able to build a home and a lifestyle for myself that is much to my liking.

What is our heartfelt authenticity – and inauthenticity?

You can take the quiz developed by Wood and his team. Indicate the degree to which these items describe you, ranging from 1, 'Does not describe me at all' to 7, 'Describes me very well':

1   I always stand by what I believe in.

2   I am true to myself in most situations.

3   I think it is better to be yourself than to be popular.

4   I live in accordance with my values and beliefs.[7]

Then, you can answer the following four items to evaluate the other side of the coin – your feelings of inauthenticity:

1   I feel as if I don't know myself very well.

2   I feel out of touch with the 'real me'.

3   I feel alienated from myself.

4   I don't know how I really feel inside.[8]

I have given this test to more than one hundred MBA students at IE Business School in Madrid as part of our *Authenticity and Well-being Longitudinal Study* with my doctoral student Sam Samoulidis. The participants are all in their twenties and about half of them are women. We replicate the results of Wood and his team's first study: the relationship between authenticity/ inauthenticity and stress and happiness using the same scales. As shown in Figure 1.1., we find a similar pattern: authenticity is associated with less stress at the beginning of the MBA programme and more satisfaction with life three months later; and the correlations of inauthenticity with less satisfaction with life and more stress are particularly significant, which carry on over a three-month period.

In another study, we explored how psychological well-being, a characteristic of authentic leaders, translates into their social well-being or social capital. Over ninety MBA students completed Ryff's measure of psychological well-being.[9] To measure students' social capital, we provided them with a roster of names of their classmates and asked them to check the names of people they go to for classwork. Using network analyses, we found that 'advice

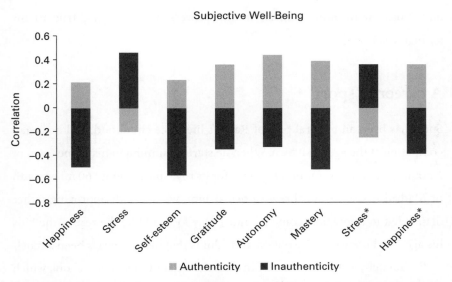

FIGURE 1.1 *Correlations of heartfelt authenticity and inauthenticity with subjective well-being.*

centrality' – how popular each individual as a source of advice is among their peers – is positively correlated to his/her psychological well-being in terms of environmental mastery, personal growth and purpose in life.[10]

Why is this? Because when it comes to building social capital, being valued by others as an influential source of knowledge is significantly increased when people feel authentic. Authentic people experience greater well-being – feelings of being in control of their environment, having a purpose in life and a sense of personal growth. These feelings of well-being make them socially attractive. Conversely, feelings of inauthenticity – having no clear purpose in life, little control over our environment and little interest in personal growth – increases our stress levels, making us less socially appealing and influential in the eyes of others.

This idea of the importance of feelings in authenticity for well-being has enormous implications for the way we organize our professional life. Let's see how Rafael de la Rubia developed his career in sport, entrepreneurship and music, reinventing himself in the process, while staying true to his authentic self.

A career in sport

Sport has been an integral part of Rafael's life since childhood, and he began competing at the age of sixteen. When he started running in his home town of Aranjuez – a small community famous for its royal palace about 60 miles south of Madrid – some boys threw stones at him, while his disapproving father demanded to know how come he didn't play football like the rest of the kids his age. But he wasn't to be put off and admits that he has always been a rebel.

Fortunately, just as his interest in athletics began to fade, his school, which had a strong sports focus, helped him stay the course. The school closed its classrooms for one week a year to organize its own mini-Olympics. And, over the years, it has produced several world-class athletes, and half a century later still organizes its own mini-Olympiad. Participating in these games, Rafael realized he was running faster than the others and that he had a talent for athletics.

In 1978, after completing high school at the age of eighteen, he decided to enter the Spanish Air Force Academy. His athletic abilities did not go unnoticed and he was invited to compete in Spain's university championships, becoming university champion of the military academy in the 100 and 200 metres without any formal training, reinforcing his belief that he had the makings of a professional athlete. A year later, he left the academy, rejecting the hierarchical nature of the military, and returned to Aranjuez and joined the athletic club of which he is now president. In the club, he began to train, compete systematically and win competitions.

Rafael moved from athletics to the pentathlon thanks to an opportunity when he was aged just nine. The Paviá cavalry regiment decided to invite local young people who wanted to learn to ride free of charge.

By the age of 16, he was already making money from his riding skills. Wealthy residents with large estates in the area would often have two or three horses that needed exercising: Rafael rode up to twelve horses on weekends on several estates, allowing him to become an expert rider: 'If you always ride the same horse, you will never learn all the ways a horse can react.'

At the age of 30, a new sporting opportunity presented itself when he was invited to enter a show jumping competition, which he won. Among those watching the event were representatives of Spain's pentathlon federation. This sport involves athletics, swimming, fencing, pistol target shooting and riding. The federation's approach was to register athletes and swimmers who could easily learn fencing and shooting. However, riding remained a problem. Most athletes learned from riding a single horse. But participants in the pentathlon trials cannot ride their own horse. The horse is assigned by lot and all they are given is a 10-minute warm-up.

Few athletes ticked all the boxes, so the pentathlon federation decided to change its strategy and recruit horse riders who could be trained in the event's other disciplines. The officials who saw Rafael ride were impressed when they learned he was a fine athlete and strong swimmer. They signed him up and sent him to a high-performance training centre in Madrid. There he was given training in his two weakest disciplines: fencing and shooting, in which he underwent three daily workouts. From 6am to 8am he trained on the athletics track. During his two-hour lunch break, he swam lengths, and from 9pm until 10.30pm, he alternated fencing and shooting. On weekends, he continued riding.

Entrepreneur

But Rafael knew he was never going to make any money from athletics and so began looking for work, starting in a machinery company where he worked without pay for several months as he learned the trade in different departments.

During this time, he learned about business administration and quickly realized that he was passionate about sales.

In 1985, at the age of twenty-five, he learned that SEAT, the Spanish car company, was opening a dealership in Aranjuez owned by a well-known local figure. One day, out for a stroll in the town, he saw the newly appointed director of SEAT in a hairdresser's. Without further ado, he went inside and introduced himself. The man was so surprised by this bold approach that he interviewed him on the spot while having his hair cut.

Rafael was invited to a meeting that night where he was offered a job. He spent three months on a training course with SEAT and started working at the newly opened dealership. Six months later he was appointed head of sales, and two years later became managing director for SEAT, Audi and VW in Spain. This was the world he worked in over the next thirteen years, in charge of about twenty-five people and with a free hand to manage the business. 'Even when I worked for others I felt I was working for myself because I had a lot of freedom.'

At the same time, Rafael began to think about the long hours he was working: some days he didn't leave meetings until midnight. The business was a success, but the real profits were going to the owners. He wondered what areas would offer him more opportunities, given that his only experience was in the automotive sector. At thirty-eight, he took the second most important decision of his life and left SEAT to set up his own used car showrooms. He had always wanted to run his own business and felt a phase in his life had come to an end.

It was a difficult decision, but he had every confidence in himself and his abilities. Athletics taught Rafael the need to believe in himself. It also taught him that while talent is essential, it is nothing without discipline and perseverance. 'Things go wrong when competing because your approach is wrong, because of injury, or because of other circumstances. In a competition, the stopwatch makes the decision for you, and often it is below your expectations,' he says. Rafael's philosophy is that there are only two options in the face of failure: walk away or return to the track to see where you have failed and continue working to improve. When this happens several times over the course of a season, 'you learn to continue and to believe that things will end well'.

The used car business did well and Rafael was able to repay his eight-year loans in just three years. Rather than spending his profits, he invested in the company. 'The company was always well endowed with resources,' he says, explaining that his budget was so tight that he refused to buy a new television, preferring to wait a year.

He says he learned the idea of reinvesting in the company from his first boss, the director of SEAT. He would talk with his boss not just about work but about life. His business's success lay in having a large stock of used cars that he could distribute to his partners from other dealerships. This network of partners kept his overheads down and sales high, with good profit margins. Over the next seven years the company grew and consolidated.

Eventually, Rafael decided to sell up and dedicate time to himself. At the age of 43, he was no longer scared about launching a new venture. Financially secure, he spent some time thinking about what he really wanted to do and how much it would cost. 'I need a project that I will enjoy and that won't take up too much of my time,' he concluded. Sailing in Ibiza ticked both boxes. He decided to work four or five months a year at something that he really enjoyed and to spend the rest of the year on his other passions.

He sold his stock of vehicles to his partners who had helped him, renting out his premises to them. The rental of these properties still provides a regular income that buys him invaluable time. His personal life also underwent a change, separating from his wife by agreement. She saw her life going in a different direction, he says, adding that the passion had disappeared over the years through daily routine. Equally, Rafael accepts that it is not easy being in a relationship with somebody who when he is not at sea for five months of the year, is training and working on his music.

Musical career

Rafael says that launching a career in music gave him the feeling of finding his true self. He taught himself to play the guitar, learning songs like Led Zeppelin's 'Stairway to Heaven' by going to the cinema several times to see *The Song Remains the Same.*

He has been composing songs for several years now, and has filled a trunk with his material. He contacted a relative with a small recording studio in Madrid and timidly showed him the contents. From there the pair put together some arrangements and started recording. His first songs were recorded by a young woman still an amateur. As he recorded more songs, Rafael began taking the music more seriously, deciding to sing his material himself. Using the stage name *Perro Gris* (Grey Dog), Rafael accepts that he's not a particularly good singer, but feels he best expresses his songs. So far, he has recorded five albums.

What he most loves about music is the creative phase, the process of building something he is passionate about: 'Working on the arrangements, seeing what works and what doesn't, and whether I can convey the idea I want . . . Exploring how things sound when you combine your voice with all those hours of rehearsal.' He now has a small studio at home and from time to time invites a friend over to play his latest compositions.

Rafael says he spends no money on marketing and that his greatest pleasure comes from those days, weeks and months spent rehearsing and recording. 'The day I'm going to record, I'm so excited, I don't care about anything else, I hardly care if the album's a success.'

There is an authenticity to his songs: 'When you write the words to a song, you feel them as your own.' Even when talking about the experiences of other people, he makes them his own, singing in the first person and feeling empathy with his subjects. 'I try to relate experiences that can make people see what is inside them.' When he writes a song, he says he wants the listener to identify with his personal experience. The recurring theme in his songs, most of which are written on the beach, is falling in and falling out of love. He leaves for Ibiza before the sailing season begins, looking for somewhere with minimal Wi-Fi, and then spends days and nights writing songs, most of which he has already been going over in his mind for the preceding months in Madrid. What he's looking for is the peace and quiet to be able to write.

Sometimes Rafael's clients open up while sailing with him and he becomes not just a skipper but a life coach as well. 'It's a good place to talk, people are on vacation, they are relaxed and think they will never see you again,' he says.

Other songs are inspired by things that have happened to close friends, such as his crewmate Marc. One night in Ibiza Marc called him up, desperate after breaking up with his girlfriend. Now in his late thirties, Marc loves his freedom and lack of commitment. He met a woman with a career and expectations of stability, but the idea frightened him and so he broke off the relationship. Two months later he decided to try to get back with her, but she had moved on. He called Rafael, in tears, asking him what he could tell the girl to convince her. So that night Rafael wrote a song called 'My Soul is for You', which features on his third album.

Rafael recorded the song that night, accompanying himself on guitar. He then sang it to his friend over his cell phone, telling him, 'This is what you have to tell her.' Marc confessed to his girlfriend that this was the best way he could express his feelings for her. They are now getting married. Of course, Rafael has been invited to the wedding.

Multiple selves: changing the authenticity script

One self or multiple selves? The tension between the true self and multiple selves is important. As we have seen, Rafael has multiple selves that he activates depending on the situation. We all have different masks that we wear across the roles we play in our everyday life. Authenticity is not a straightforward mode of simply being one's true self. It involves resolving paradoxes such as having multiple selves and the choice of enacting one's true self in different situations and across the life span. Can we be authentic given the need to create multiple selves?

Susan Harter, Professor Emerita in Psychology at the University of Denver and a pioneer in self-concept research, has developed an exercise called the Multiple Selves Procedure. Think of five or six relational contexts. For example, your role as parent, employee, co-worker, friend, spouse, partner or lover, and member of a sports club. Next, generate attributes that describe you in these different relational contexts: caring, outgoing, introverted, happy, nervous, talkative, and so on. Then identify whether any pairs of attributes reflect 'opposites' (e.g. outgoing with friends, but introvert with bosses). Some inconsistency across situations is normal but too much conflict may create feelings of anxiety. This is one example of an adolescent reported by Harter: 'I really think of myself as friendly and open to people, but the way the other girls act, they force me to become an introvert, even though I know that's not my true self.' The idea behind the game is to try to link feelings of authenticity across different contexts.

Nowadays, society encourages us to create *multiple selves* associated with different roles or contexts. Not only that, but many of us may have different experiences across different contexts. For instance, 'one may be depressed with parents, cheerful with a group of friends, shy with a romantic other, open with a close friend, hardworking in school, responsible on a job, rowdy and less responsible with peers, and so forth', explains Harter. Given this complexity, people use authenticity as a relevant personal attribute in their everyday conversations to describe true-self behaviour with expressions such as 'the real me inside', 'saying what you really think or believe', 'expressing your honest opinion' and 'telling someone how you really feel'. But also, inauthenticity language is used to describe 'false-self' behaviour, such as 'being phony', 'hiding your true thoughts and feelings' and 'saying what you think *others* want to hear, not what you really think'. How do people then react to the possibility of multiple selves?

On the one hand, 'the creation of multiple selves to conform to the demands of a relationship may compromise the sense that one has an immovable core self that is authentic, thereby casting doubt on one's true identity', Harter says. However, an alternative situation is that 'multiplicity may provide people with a sense of optimism and possibility as they navigate their interpersonal waters'. They key question becomes what it means to be true to oneself.

A group of psychologists at the University of Rochester, led by Kennon Sheldon,[11] contrasted two alternative answers to this question: the trait view and the contextual view. They write:

> In the trait view, people are assumed to have trans-contextual personality dispositions that are highly stable over time, situations, and social roles. Not only do our traits characterize us, indeed, they may be 'our very selves.' In the contextual, people do not always act in accord with their self; instead, they vary from situation to situation in the degree to which they contact and enact their true feelings and values. To be true to oneself within a role is to be able to behave in ways that feel personally expressive.

To test these two views, Sheldon and his team conducted two studies. First, they measured participants' authenticity and their personality in terms of the 'big five'[12] roles: student, employee, child (son/daughter), friend and romantic partner. In their second study, participants also evaluated the amount of conflict they experienced between each role (e.g. 'to what extent does each role conflict with, or feel discordant with, each other role?').

The results of their two studies offered support for both views: the contextual and the trait view of authenticity. On the one hand, people showed some inconsistency across roles. People varied their expression of themselves depending on their role and still felt authentic. For example, participants reported 'being relatively most extroverted in the friend role, most neurotic in the student role, most conscientious in the employee role, most open to experience in the romantic partner role, and least agreeable in student and child roles'.

Having said that, people showed strong cross-role consistency in all big five measures of personality. For example, extroverted individuals tended to be above average across roles; but they expressed their extroversion to a higher degree when playing the friend role and the least when they were in the student role. Highly conscientious individuals are always reliable, especially in the employee role, but they relax more when they are with friends. Furthermore, it was not surprising when participants felt more conflict between these five roles: the less authentic they felt, the less well-being they experienced in their lives.

What is interesting about these two views of authenticity is that they are not exclusive: they are compatible. When we say that a person is authentic, we may be thinking of someone with multiple roles and passions who adapts their behaviour to the immediate situational cues with no role conflict. In 1974, Mark Snyder, a psychologist at the University of Minnesota, developed the now popular concept of self-monitoring, which indicates the extent to which people are consistent in their behaviours across situations.[13] High self-monitors tailor their actions in accordance with the immediate demands of the situation; in contrast, low self-monitors are less able or willing to modify their behaviour.

Here, then, is the explanation as to why Rafael de la Rubia has multiple selves and still feels authentic about his values and goals. He values, for example, freedom above financial success, and this is consistent across his multiple professional roles. When he competes in sports, runs his businesses and plays music, he adapts his expressive behaviour to the situation at hand, but the underlying value of independence is present across all roles.

Are you a high or low self-monitor?[14]

Take this quiz to find out how much you change your personality in different contexts. Your task is to indicate the strength of your agreement with each statement, using a scale from 1, 'Strongly disagree', to 5, 'Strongly agree':

1 In social situations, I have the ability to alter my behaviour if I feel that something else is called for.

2 I have the ability to control the way I come across to people, depending on the impression I wish to give them.

3 When I feel that the image I am portraying isn't working, I can readily change it to something that does.

4 I have trouble changing my behaviour to suit different people and different situations.

5 Even when it might be to my advantage, I have difficulty putting up a good front.

6 I have found that I can adjust my behaviour to meet the requirements of any situation in which I find myself.

7 Once I know what a situation calls for, it's easy for me to regulate my actions accordingly.[15]

Sailing in the waters of authenticity

Rafael de la Rubia uses the analogy of a ship's captain to visualize authentic leadership. 'Some leaders are trained to manage and command a group based on their technical ability, but an authentic leader has a special charisma that makes people trust them,' he says. 'An authentic leader is able to say we are going to go through a rocky patch, but people follow him because he inspires confidence that they will make it. An authentic leader gives that peace of mind that everything will work out, that you will get to a safe place.'

Over the course of his multi-tracking life, Rafael's idols have been few, but authentic. In sport, his hero is Carl Lewis, an athlete who excelled in different disciplines. In addition, he showed that when beaten, he worked all the harder to win. The tennis player Rafa Nadal, and particularly his humility, has also proved an inspiration: 'It's an admirable quality in somebody who is the best in the world at what he does.' Rafael's musical idol is John Lennon – not only for his songs, but for leading such talented people. Paul McCartney is an example of a musician whose success has been sustained.

Rafael sees business in two ways: one through people like Steve Jobs, a man who made something out of nothing and who came to dominate the world; the other characterized by the sacrifice, dedication and generosity of small-scale entrepreneurs, whom he really admires: 'The unknowns, the people who get up every day and work long hours to provide for their families.'

Success is the way forward, and there is no looking back. He recently punctured a tyre. When he looked for the spare in his boot, he found the medal he won for his second place in the 200 metres. The trophies he has won throughout his sports career are stored in boxes, not displayed. Spring cleaning, he found a drawer packed with cups and medals. When Rafael wins a medal, he wears it for the few seconds he is on the podium. When he steps down, he takes it off and stores it away, already thinking about the next competition. There was a time when it was important to win trophies. But over time he says he has become aware that if you pay attention to what people think, the good they can do you on your way up can be matched by the hurt they can cause when you're down.

Looking to the future, he says he wants to continue with what he's doing. The present is the future for Rafael and he's not worried about what other people think: if he did, it would simply make him a slave to success. Instead he prefers to be a journeyman. As the Spanish poet Antonio Machado wrote, 'Walker there is no road, the road is made by walking.'

10 ways to stay authentic nurturing your multiple passions

1   *Where does your heart lie?* We can discover our multiple passions by
    writing our life story and thinking about past decisions. In the second

chapter of his life, Rafael de la Rubia came to realize that he has three loves: the sea, sport and music. However, passion alone is not enough. We need to cultivate our passions with perseverance, patience, sacrifice and discipline. In a paper with my colleagues Maria Kakarika of NEOMA Business School in Paris and Marina Biniari of Aalto University in Helsinki,[16] we discuss how to manage role transitions and keep the entrepreneurial passion. When failure strikes, Rafael's passion for what he does gives him the inner motivation to 're-arm and renew' himself.

2 *Embrace contradiction.* Change the authenticity script to manage multiple identities across situations and time. We can find multiple identities that complement each other. For instance, Rafael finds complementarity between his athletic and musician selves. 'Running feeds the body while music feeds the soul,' he says.

3 *Be aware of the importance of our multiple selves.* The extent to which a social role such as musician, entrepreneur or father is self-defining – used for defining yourself across different situations. Being true to one's self requires self-awareness.

4 *Picture your self-concept.* Reflect on the social role that best defines yourself – the one most salient in your mind – and place it at the top of a hierarchical structure. For example, Rafael places the musician role at the top of his self-concept at this stage in his professional life.

5 *Engage in active identity negotiation.* Tell others the way you see yourself to avoid cognitive dissonance arising from discrepancies between your identity and how others define you. For example, when Rafael's daughter introduces him to people as a businessman, he corrects her: 'I am a musician.'

6 *Manage identity confirmation.* Seek support for your identity from others by engaging in activities that match the way you see yourself.

This might make you a rebel. When Rafael started running, boys threw stones at him and his disapproving father wanted him to play football like the rest of the kids at that time.

7   *Seek healthy environments.* Finding a context that is self-affirming gives us the confidence and vitality to experiment with possible selves and pursue our passions. Rafael did not give up his favourite sport; rather, he moved from athletics to the pentathlon, seeking every opportunity. In his entrepreneur role, he was passionate about sales and restlessly went after the job at SEAT.

8   *Manage professional and life role transitions.* Be clear about your goals and create a long-term plan to achieve them. For example, Rafael rates freedom above success, and his passion for what he does gives him the inner motivation. When the time came to break with the past, he had a plan and sold his other businesses to the people who had created them with him.

9   *Find enrichment across your multiple roles.* The skills and values that you learn in one role can spill over to other roles. For example, Rafael says how his values are forged on the track and field and then he applies them to a new business adventure. This builds self-confidence and the ability to reinvent yourself.

10 *Face the dilemma of being yourself in multiple roles.* Self-monitor to find the piece of yourself that best fits the environment. Political savvy does not make you less authentic.

In his autobiographical book *Losing my Virginity*, Richard Branson explains how to survive, have fun and make a fortune doing business in his genuine and authentic way. This might be a way that is hard to imitate, but if Branson and De la Rubia have one thing in common it is that they are equally passionate about what they do. That's something we can try to imitate.

2

Confident Humility: The Power of Unsung Heroes

Beauty begins the moment you decide to be yourself.

The most courageous act is still to think for yourself. Aloud.

Hard times arouse an instinctive desire for authenticity.

COCO CHANEL

Coco Chanel is the only fashion designer on *TIME* magazine's list of the 100 most influential people of the twentieth century. She is admired for her revolutionary ideas, her personality, determination and vitality. But few people know about her humble beginnings. The daughter of a farmer and a street vendor, after her mother died, the 12-year-old was placed in an orphanage run by a convent until she was 18. The austerity of the convent inspired her taste for black and white, her philosophy of beauty as simplicity and her work ethics. The secret behind Chanel's luxury was 'labor intensive beyond belief' according to Karen Karbo in her book *The Gospel According to Coco Chanel: Life Lessons from the World's Most Elegant Woman*. Chanel reinvented herself and developed a natural skill for networking.

She is an example of the power of simple yet revolutionary ideas. The thinking behind the Little Black Dress in the 1920s was to provide women with affordable elegance.

Hiroko Samejima: contagious passion for ethical ideas (Japan–Ethiopia)

Like Coco Chanel, Hiroko Samejima has a revolutionary and contagious passion for fashion. Hiroko is the founder, CEO and chief designer of andu amet, a brand of leather bags made from exquisite Ethiopian sheep's leather. 'Andu amet' means 'one year' in Ethiopia, a name that reflects Hiroko's passion for ethics. I was introduced to Hiroko through Hidemi Takano, a volunteer in her company and former student of mine. Hidemi worked pro bono for Hiroko in the early stages of her start-up to gain experience and fulfil her passion for ethical fashion. After graduating with an MBA, Hidemi now works at Amazon.

When I asked Hidemi why she gave her time and talent to the new venture, she answered, 'Hiroko is one of the most outstanding Japanese female entrepreneurs and attracts a lot of attention in the country nowadays. Japanese society is flooded with cosmetics and consumers have more than ten or twenty such products at home, and they certainly don't use them all.'

She admires Hiroko's philosophy and motivation. 'Hiroko sometimes felt that she produced "beautiful trash" although she made an incredible effort to create these products. She felt that people were losing their passion and that they didn't appreciate her products.' Furthermore, she respects Hiroko's decision to do something about the problem: 'Hiroko believed that Japanese consumers craved new concepts and values that set themselves apart from mass-production and mass-consumption.' When Hiroko decided to create andu amet, Hidemi had not doubt she wanted to be part of this exciting project.

Authentic leadership is about more than creating a positive working environment. Authentic leaders are passionate about what they do, and passion for what they do is their true motivation: what they do is what makes them who they are. Their passion is contagious and is picked up by their followers or employees. The passion and enthusiasm of authentic leaders spark creativity in others.

Experiential exercise: passion is contagious

Hiroko's passion for what she does and her belief in ethical luxury is infectious. Which is not that surprising, because happiness can be contagious, as shown by James Fowler of the University of California, San Diego, and Nicholas Christakis of Harvard Medical School in the book *Connected*.[1] They have tracked individuals over two decades (1983–2003) asking them about various emotions, including happiness, and have found clusters of happy and unhappy individuals. The network from 2000 is depicted in Figure 2.1. It shows white as happy, black as sad, and grey as in between. Like tends to attract like, but they also found that happy people could make others happier people. In psychology, this is known as emotional contagion.

Our happiness is influenced by the people we are directly connected to. Happiness is an 'emotional stampede' among humans, says Christakis.

It is easy to explore our network of friends to find out how much we share positive feelings with them. As you can see in Figure 2.2, emotions can be

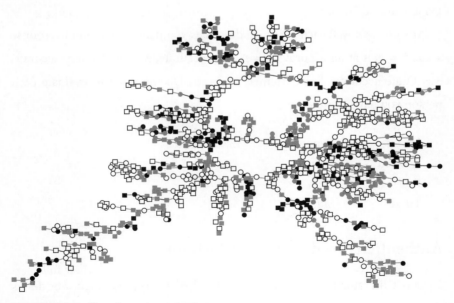

FIGURE 2.1 *Happiness is contagious.*

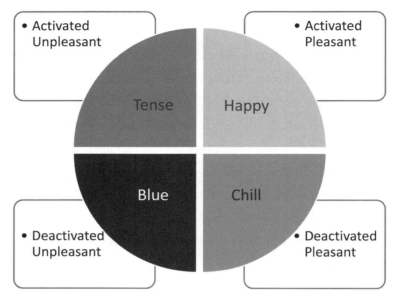

FIGURE 2.2 *The circle of emotions.*

described in two dimensions: hedonic tone (its positive or negative nature) and intensity (its level of activation), known as the circumplex by Randy Larsen and Ed Diener.[2]

Answer how well each adjective describes you using a five-point response scale: 0 = Not at all accurate, 1 = A little accurate, 2 = Moderately accurate, 3 = Quite accurate, 4 = Extremely accurate. Do the same to evaluate each person you have chosen.

Lively	Peppy	Enthusiastic
Relaxed	Calm	At ease
Fearful	Nervous	Anxious
Tired	Sluggish	Bored[3]

Authenticity by design: slow fashion

Hiroko talks quietly and slowly, thinking her answers through. She looks exactly like the picture on the company website: happy, mindful and attractive.

She holds the leather handbag that she designed like a mother would hold her baby.

On 1 February 2012, Hiroko launched andu amet in Japan. She then appeared before the World Bank on 10 July 2014 as 'founder, CEO and chief designer of *andu amet* Ltd'. Her idea and enthusiasm about slow fashion rippled through her social network.

andu amet is a leather brand whose products are made from exquisite Ethiopian sheep's leather, known as the world's best for its silky smoothness and durability. She has won several awards for her entrepreneurial endeavours, including Nikkei Woman Magazine's Woman of the Year in 2013 and Young Female Innovator of APEC (Asia-Pacific Economic Cooperation). In 2014, she accompanied Prime Minister Shinzo Abe on his state visit to Ethiopia.

The making of authentic products

Recognized in Japan for the success of andu amet, Hiroko is nevertheless humble. When asked about the key to her success, she immediately replies, 'our company is very small and cannot be considered a success'. andu amet has only fifteen employees in Ethiopia and two full-time employees in Japan, plus fifteen volunteers.

However, talking to her, it becomes clear that the key to her success lies with her commitment to delivering the 'most authentic product'. With a can-do mentality, Hiroko displays confidence in her ideas, plans and principles, seeing opportunities to be harnessed. The company's manufacturing process is 'ethical' and 'beautiful'. There is a global principle of beauty in authentic products: 'beautiful material, design and process'.

The first principle is material. Ethiopian sheepskin is used by leading companies like Mercedes-Benz to produce car seat covers. 'We are using the best leather in the world.' Hiroko explains that because of the negative associations Ethiopia still has in many people's minds, the country does not promote its leather: it is often exported to countries like Italy and is then sold as an Italian product.

Second, andu amet's authenticity lies in its designs: Hiroko began her career twenty years ago at Chanel. She has also been inspired by other leading global fashion brands like Dior, as well as ethical firms from Japan like HASUNA and People Tree – the fair-trade fashion pioneer. Her dream was to create her own designs by combining the elegance of top brands, African colour schemes and the techniques of Japanese traditional arts and crafts.

Third, andu amet's manufacturing process follows the ethical Kaizen principles of Japanese management culture. When Hiroko accompanied Prime Minister Abe to Ethiopia on 14 January 2014, she represented many of his ideas. In a speech to the African Union in Addis Ababa, Mr Abe explained the principle of Kaizen, which starts with 'organizing' – getting rid of wasteful materials – and 'arranging' – setting out the tools to make them easy to access. He continued, 'Through organizing and arranging the line, it becomes exemplary in

PHOTO 2.1 *Hiroko Samejima, founder and CEO of andu amet (Japan).*

appearance and performance. People everywhere recognize the beauty of the line and enjoy a sense of accomplishment, regardless of national boundaries or cultural differences.' As a result, Kaizen is also an approach that 'fosters self-esteem' Hiroko said. 'In this way, *kaizen* is applicable to any country or culture as a type of managerial know-how. But that is not all. As people come to be engaged in the *kaizen* process, a culture that values the creativity and ingenuity of everyone begins to permeate the workplace, which shows the profound nature of *kaizen*.' Ethiopia has the only Kaizen Institute in the world outside Japan.

The beginnings: turning passion into action

andu amet's beginnings were difficult. 'I started as a very small company, it was just myself. I did not have a company for the first two years in Ethiopia. I was working as a buyer. I bought a small number of bags from Ethiopia and sold them in Japan,' explains Hiroko. During those first two years Hiroko learned about how to produce the best product, making samples and learning about how to do business in Ethiopia. Her passion persuaded others to join her.

Hiroko's passion for ethical fashion was rooted in her time at Chanel. 'People are very attracted by Chanel – its products, its story, and so on,' she says, adding that she wanted to create a brand like Chanel: 'It was really hard, but we tried to make the best quality with the most authentic products.' For her, this is one of the factors of success.

When she joined Chanel, Hiroko had already decided to start her own business. She developed the idea while working in Ethiopia as a volunteer for three years with the Japan International Cooperation Agency.

When I asked Hiroko how she stayed motivated during those early difficult days, she was surprised, answering confidently, 'I just knew I could do it.' She says she knew the leather she had found was the best and that she trusted herself as a designer as well as her craftsmen's skills. Eventually, the awards and the recognition came.

A turning point: becoming a national celebrity

On 9 January 2014, Hiroko appeared on a popular television programme in Japan, becoming a national celebrity overnight. As a result, there was such demand for andu amet products that all its goods in boutiques and department stores were soon sold out and even the webpage was so overwhelmed it was closed for a time. 'There was a lot of interest,' Hiroko recalls with typical understatement.

'There was a good side and a bad side to this,' she continues: the company attracted huge numbers of customers, yet she had just terminated a contract with her business partner in Ethiopia. andu amet was inundated with orders in Japan at exactly the time the manufacturing process had stopped in Ethiopia.

When I asked her about the reasons for terminating the relationship with her Ethiopian business partner, she explains that she was no longer able to meet her ethical standards.

The Ethiopian team leader was motivated and a hard worker. But Hiroko began to experience problems concerning a range of key issues, among them planning and the manufacturing process. Hiroko had planned to extend the production facility, but her business partner disagreed and moved to another location without consulting Hiroko. She was sending just one or two emails a year, making it very difficult for Hiroko to monitor progress and production levels in Ethiopia.

After ending the contract with her, Hiroko started a new manufacturing operation, setting up her own company in Ethiopia in 2014. Non-Ethiopians must invest at least $20,000 to establish a business, a huge investment for Hiroko. But she says she feels no resentment towards her former business partner, and in fact is grateful, saying she learned so much from her.

A new start: the rebirth of andu amet

Now Hiroko had to hire her own Ethiopian craftsmen, which turned out to be very time consuming. Following her appearance on Japanese television, she had to stop all new orders for two years in shops and for one year on her website.

Her approach was to hire apprentices alongside more seasoned workers from other Ethiopian companies, who were given some training from a Japanese craftsman Hiroko hired. The Ethiopian factory now has fifteen new full-time employees.

andu amet began manufacturing again in December 2015, first supplying its online store and since March 2016 shops as well. The rebirth of andu amet is remarkable. Every time I visit its website, I am impressed not only with the beauty and sophistication of its products, but also by their variety. Behind this renaissance lies much work and commitment. Over the course of two years, Hiroko spent eleven months a year in Ethiopia and one month in Japan – fifteen days in July and fifteen days in December.

I wonder how Japanese customers reacted when her business stopped for two years. Did they forget about andu amet products? Or were they even more eager to buy them? 'Many customers kindly waited, but some cancelled,' Hiroko says. But even that small number of cancellations created problems. Before 2014, there was a waiting time of around six months for andu amet's products. These customers had pre-paid for their goods at department stores. When they cancelled their order, andu amet still had to pay service charges to the department stores, in some cases more than 30 per cent of the value of the products, a significant expense for the company.

andu amet's management philosophy: from passion to compassion

Hiroko overcame these difficulties with a clear management philosophy, the first principle of which is to make only authentic products. As mentioned earlier, this core value applies not only to design but also to materials and the manufacturing process. The second principle, explains Hiroko, is not only making bags and leather goods, 'but also to produce a smile and happiness for our stakeholders: our customers, designers, manufacturers, craftsmen and shop staff'.

For her employees in Ethiopia, most of whom have only an elementary education, happiness means training, a good salary and a stable life. In Japan, her team is made up of two full-time workers, one part-timer and fifteen volunteers. 'They are very motivated because of our mission and products,' says Hiroko, who only hires highly committed volunteers able to work for at least one year. One pro bono team member explains her reasons: 'This is not a matter of money, I really love the concept of *andu amet*. In the future, I would like to start my own company.'

Hiroko believes that other people have joined her project because of an interest in Africa. For most Japanese, Africa is still largely an unknown place and working at andu amet is an opportunity to get to know a fascinating continent: some of her pro bono employees have visited the factory in Ethiopia. Equally important is the opportunity to learn. Some of the pro bono workers want to start similar businesses to andu amet in the ethical fashion industry. Rather than a threat, Hiroko sees them as future business partners, pointing out that she worked pro bono for the ethical jewellery brand HASUNA before launching andu amet.

Such collaboration is a win–win relationship, she says: 'If because of my brand, the ethical fashion market in Japan is expanding, this is great news and we can give advice to each other.' Hiroko told me that ethical fashion is more than just fair trade or using organic materials. When she worked in the traditional fashion industry, she was faced with the challenge of creating a new product each season. As a result, people tend to discard their clothes and accessories every three to six months. 'This means pointless work for designers whose products will be discarded so quickly; customers have to overspend to keep up with fashion and we waste natural resources.'

For slow fashion like Hiroko's to be a success means changing consumers' habits and mindset. In Japan, the March 2011 earthquake impacted on Japanese consumers' way of thinking, prompting increased interest in ethical and fair trade goods. At the same time, growing numbers of people became more interested in the andu amet back story. It's a positive and interesting trend, says Hiroko, but she's not sure how long it will last.

In the meantime, Hiroko continues telling the story of her company to her customers via a well-developed marketing strategy. After product design, marketing is her second area of expertise, having worked in that area for Chanel. She maintains an active presence on the social networks through andu amet blogs on Facebook, Twitter and Instagram. The company also has a magazine for subscribers. Hiroko is also a frequent speaker on ethical fashion at Japanese universities and companies. Her own company also organizes events to promote its products, story and brand.

Why humble people make better leaders

The research is clear: when we choose humble, unassuming people as our leaders, the world around us becomes a better place.

Humble leaders improve the performance of a company in the long run because they create more collaborative environments. They have a balanced view of themselves – both their virtues and shortcomings – and a strong appreciation of others' strengths and contributions, while being open to new ideas and feedback. These unsung heroes help those around them build their self-esteem, exceed their expectations, and create a community that channels individual efforts into an organized group working for the good of the collective.

A 2015 study by Amy Y. Ou, David A. Waldman and Suzanne J. Peterson[4] examined 105 small-to-medium-sized companies in the US computer software and hardware industry. Their findings revealed that when a humble CEO is at the helm of a firm, its top management team was more likely to collaborate and share information, making the most of the firm's talent.

Another study,[5] conducted by Bradley Owens, Michael Johnson and Terry Mitchell, talked to more than 700 employees in a large US health services organization. Participants rated the humility of their leaders and their level of engagement at work (e.g. how much they invest their 'entire selves' at work, showing dedication and vitality). When leaders show humility by recognizing the strengths and contributions of others, rather than taking all the credit for success themselves, their employees reported higher engagement. In line with the brilliant book by Susan Cain, *The Quiet Revolution*, the authors listed a '"quieter" leadership approach based on listening, transparency about limitations and appreciating workforce's strengths and contributions as effective ways to engage employees'.

Here is another example of the nuances of humility. Bradley Owens and David Hekman[6] showed that a leader's humility can be contagious: when leaders behave humbly, followers emulate their modest attitude and behaviour. A study of 161 teams found that employees following humble leaders are themselves more likely to admit their mistakes and limitations, share the spotlight by deflecting praise to others, and be open to new ideas, advice and feedback.

In a clever experiment, the authors manipulated leaders' humility to try to understand how followers emulated their humble behaviour, creating a shared climate of group humility. They hired and trained four research confederates to play the roles of the team leader and one of the team members. The scripts for the humble/non-humble leaders included statements for the confederate leader and the confederate follower. In the leader humility condition, the leader is open to the ideas of others and acknowledge their contribution. Here is the segment in full:

Humble Leader Confederate: *Let's start. What do you guys think about how to do the ranking task? I'm not sure I'm an HR expert, but I've a suggestion – How about doing the ranking in an ascending order? That is, rank the items from 1 to 20, from the most valuable practices to the least valuable ones.*

Follower Confederate: *I've another idea. How about we start by putting a plus next to the best ones and a minus next to the ones we think are bad? So we do a first cut at the items, and then after that we go through and rank them individually?*

Humble Leader Confederate: *Yes, great idea! What do the rest of you think? Although I'm the leader, I may not be the smartest in HR practices and I welcome your suggestions.*

(Wait for others to respond, listen and nod.)

Follower Confederate: *Having a first cut at the items makes things easier.*

Humble Leader Confederate: *I really appreciate all these great ideas. Let's do what Sarah has suggested.*

Follower Confederate: *Yes!*

Humble Leader Confederate: *Good! Let's start!*

In contrast, in the non-leader humility condition, the leader takes a unilateral position. Here is the segment in full:

Non-Humble Leader Confederate: *Let's start. As I'm the leader, I hope you guys can follow my suggestion. Can you guys start by ranking in an ascending order? That is, rank the items from 1 to 20, from the most valuable practices to the least valuable ones.*

Follower Confederate: *I've another idea. How about putting a plus next to the best ones and a minus next to the ones we think are bad? So we do a first cut at the items, and then after that we go through and rank them individually?*

Non-Humble Leader Confederate: *No, let's follow my suggestion. I like my way more. I am so glad I was chosen to be the leader. The role really fits my personality.*

Follower Confederate: *But I think my way is also good.*

Non-Humble Leader Confederate: *No, just follow my way. Let's start.*

Now here is where the study gets interesting. The critical thing about authentic leaders is that they are humble and influence followers through the contagion of their behaviour. As shown in Figure 2.3, what differentiates them is that they create collaborative environments where everyone's contribution is considered. 'Leaders who express humility may help their teams to transcend the comparative–competitive social lens that often leads to over-estimating oneself and underestimating others, which is arguably a poor foundation for effective teamwork.' These results suggest that humility is 'far from being a sign of [the] weak-willed . . . humility keeps individuals in a state of continual adaptation'. Further, their study underscores the importance of leading by example and why employees view leaders' humility as a motivation to keep them focused on achieving success. Employees are closely attuned to leaders who are aligned with their 'authentic, true self'. Thus, leaders must act virtuously if they want virtue to spread among their followers.

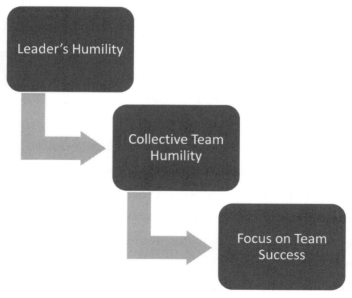

FIGURE 2.3 *The social contagion of a leader's humility.*

The bright side: how humble are you in a leadership role?

Indicate the degree to which you agree with the following statements based on the system developed by Bradley Owens using a scale from 1, 'Strongly disagree', to 5, 'Strongly agree'. Alternatively, you can give this survey to a significant other and have him/her complete it for you:

1 I actively seek feedback, even if it is critical.

2 I admit it when I don't know how to do something.

3 I acknowledge when others have more knowledge and skills than me.

4 I take notice of others' strengths.

5 I often compliment others on their strengths.

6 I show appreciation for the unique contributions of others.

7 I am willing to learn from others.

8 I am open to the ideas of others

9 I am open to the advice of others.[7]

The dark side: what is your level of narcissism?

In contrast to the above, you can now rate your level of non-clinical narcissism using this 9-item scale of narcissism developed by Daniel Jones and Delroy Paulhus of the University of British Columbia in Canada, experts on the Dark Triad of personality.[8] Indicate your level of agreement with the following statements using a 1, 'Strongly disagree', to 5, 'Strongly agree'.

1 People see me as a natural leader.

2 I love being the centre of attention.

3 Many group activities tend to be dull without me.

4 I know that I am special because everyone keeps telling me so.

5   I like to get acquainted with important people.

6   I do not feel embarrassed if someone compliments me.

7   I have been compared to famous people.

8   I am not an average person.

9   I insist on getting the respect I deserve.[9]

If humble people make better leaders, why do we fall for charismatic narcissists?[10]

The Greek word *Kharisma* means 'divine gift', and charisma is the quality of extraordinary charm, magnetism and presence that makes a person capable of inspiring others. The German sociologist Max Weber defined charisma 'as of divine origin or as exemplary, and based on it, the individual concerned is treated as a leader'. Research evidence on charismatic leadership reveals that charismatic people are more likely to be endorsed as leaders because of their energy levels and unconventional behaviour.

While charisma is conducive to orchestrating positive large-scale transformations, there can be a dark side to charismatic leadership, as Jay Conger and Rabindra Kanungo's seminal *Charismatic Leadership in Organizations*[11] explains: 'Charismatic leaders can be prone to extreme narcissism that leads them to promote highly self-serving and grandiose aims.' Clinical studies show that when charisma overlaps with narcissism, leaders tend to abuse their power and take advantage of their followers. Another study led by Benjamin Galvin[12] at the University of Washington indicates that narcissistic leaders tend to present a bold vision of the future, which makes them more charismatic in the eyes of others.

Why are such leaders more likely to rise to the top? Some research suggests that despite being perceived as arrogant, narcissistic individuals radiate 'an image of a prototypically effective leader'. Narcissistic leaders know how to draw attention towards themselves. They enjoy the visibility. It takes time for people to see that these early signals of competence are not fulfilled, and that a leader's narcissism reduces the exchange of information among team members and often negatively affects group performance.

It's not that charismatic and narcissistic people can't ever make good leaders. In some circumstances, they can. For example, the study by Galvin's team found that narcissistic CEOs 'favour bold actions that attract attention, resulting in big wins or big losses'. A narcissistic leader thus can represent a high-risk, high-reward proposition.

Equally, humble leaders can be charismatic. Researchers agree that we could classify charismatic leaders as 'negative' or 'positive' by their orientation towards pursuing their self-interested goals versus those of their groups. These two sides of charismatic leadership have also been called *personalized* and *socialized* charisma. Although the *socialized* charismatic leader has the aura of a hero, it is counteracted by low authoritarianism and a genuine interest in the collective welfare. In contrast, the *personalized* charismatic leader's perceived heroism is coupled with high authoritarianism and high narcissism. It is when followers are confused and disoriented that they are more likely to form personalized relationships with a charismatic leader; whereas socialized relationships are established by followers with a clear set of values who view the charismatic leader as a means to achieve collective action.

Negative charismatic leaders have a grandiose view of themselves, low empathy, are dominant towards others, and have a strong sense of entitlement and tend to transform their environments into a competition in which their followers also become more self-centred, giving rise to organizational narcissism.

The romance of leadership hypothesis, put forward by the late social psychologist James Meindl of the State University of New York (SUNY), Buffalo, suggests that we generally have a biased tendency to understand social events in terms of leadership, and people tend to romanticize the figure of the leader.

My own research[13] shows that our psychological states can also bias our perceptions of charismatic leaders. Emotion can make us hungry for charisma. As a result, stressful or exciting contexts increase not only the search for charismatic leaders, but also our tendency to *perceive* charisma in our leaders. At SUNY, Buffalo, we tested this idea with an unusual experiment. We manipulated the intensity of emotions by having participants ride a stationary bike at low speed or high speed while watching a video of a business leader with some charismatic appeal. The results were fascinating. Highly emotional individuals, those riding the bike at high speed, reported significantly higher ratings of charisma for the business leader than did less emotional individuals.

Economic and social crises thus become a unique testing ground for charismatic leaders. They create conditions of arousal and uncertainty that would appear to be ideal for the ascent of charismatic figures. Yet at the same time, they also make us more vulnerable to choosing the wrong leader. Crises and other emotionally laden events increase our propensity to romanticize the grandiose view of narcissistic leaders. The paradox is that we may then choose to support the very leaders who are less likely to bring us success. Leader humility is often thought to be more beneficial during everyday challenges, in times of low to moderate amounts of stress, pressure or threat. In a time of crisis, it's easier to be seduced by superheroes who could come and rescue us, but who could possibly then plunge us into greater peril.

While this may sound hopeless, there is another way of looking at it. Essentially, we get the leaders we deserve and we become the leaders we want to be. Collectively, we select and construct our leaders to satisfy our *own* needs and desires. Thus, we have the power to make choices about whether to follow unsung heroes or superheroes. Individually, we have the choice of becoming passionate humble leaders or charismatic narcissists.

The power of unsung heroes: sticking to ethical values

I tell Hiroko her story is a wonderful example of an authentic leader – humble and passionate about what she does – and then I ask, 'What does leadership mean to you?' She takes time to think and replies modestly: 'I was just a designer before I started this business.' But after setting up her company, her viewpoint about leadership changed dramatically. Up until then she concentrated on designing the product itself. But now she must see the big picture. Of course, she still must focus on the product, but at the same time she needs to think about broader issues like the political situation in Ethiopia, her employees' motivation, the pro bono volunteers in Japan, the sales figures and remaining true to her ethical principles. Everything is important to her and it is difficult to make any single thing a priority. In the final analysis, she thinks that as a leader 'I must judge the situation and make decisions,' adding, 'if I doubt, nobody will follow me,' and finally: 'I am not the typical kind of leader.'

The most important leadership lesson she says she has learned over her five years of experience as an entrepreneur is about trust: 'If I trust myself and my skills to do good things, people will trust me and they will follow me.' This self-confidence has been the key to overcoming many of the difficulties Hiroko has faced along the way.

'When I terminated with my Ehtiopian business partner I did not know what I should do.' She recalls her dilemma: she knew there were customers waiting for her products and the danger of deleting their orders. But at the same time if she did not make the break she could not apply her ethical policies. The conclusion was clear: 'I had to remain loyal to my principles.'

To meet those principles in the manufacturing process, the company has to comply with four criteria. First, planning and designing should follow the Kaizen approach of using traditional techniques. Second, procurement of the leather must come as a by-product of meat processing. Third, processing the leather involves chemicals (like chrome), so a water-treatment system is essential. By law, these systems must be in place in all leather factories, but they require close monitoring. Hiroko regularly checks to see if the system is working properly and that she is using only environmentally-friendly leather. Finally, sales and marketing follow ethical principles. Although her products are high-end – the average price of a leather bag is about €1,000 – andu amet does not want to sell only to wealthy customers who may discard the product quickly. Instead, her target customers are expected to use the product all year round, doing justice to its name, andu amet.

We laugh over the high price of her leather bags. Who can afford her products? I tell her that the most expensive handbag I ever bought was a €400 Burberry, which I think is an extravagance. But it is true that I use it all year round. This is the mentality of slow fashion, as opposed to buy-and-go until the next season. But just who are her customers? After her 2014 television appearance, her customer base expanded to include a wider demographic. At present, they are typically women in their thirties and forties, and the company has just started a beautiful collection of bags for men. Hiroko says the average annual salary of her customers is something like €42,000. 'I do not want to sell to rich people and become trapped in fast fashion,' she says. Hiroko is conscious of the many challenges she faces to produce just one bag: 'These are really like my children, part of my soul.'

Since she does not yet own a store, she uses a gallery to show potential customers her products, encouraging them to place their orders online. Much like an art gallery, twice a month she invites loyal customers to get to know her new products. Given their high price, customers want to be certain they like what they are buying before ordering online.

What makes an authentic leader?

Hiroko was born in Tokyo in 1973 and studied fine arts at Asagaya College of Art and Design. Her mother was a housewife who supported her daughter's early interest in the arts: she loved painting, drawing and playing music, to the extent that her mother sometimes told her to stop drawing and go out to play with her friends. She lived in Iran for two years during the Iran–Iraq War, when her father was posted there by his company, and remembers the poverty and deprivation, saying the experience changed the way she looked at the world, opening her eyes to how lucky she was. She also came to appreciate what she had, remembering her shock at an Iranian lady who was very kind to her while very hostile to her political enemies. 'Poverty does not mean just hunger, poverty changes people inside and make[s] the world unstable and fragile,' Hiroko reflects.

She says her parents are proud of her accomplishments, even though during the two years of preparation before setting up the company, they were unhappy. 'Chanel is a big company and they wanted me to stay there,' Hiroko remembers. I tell her that her career decision seems to me have been brave and risky. She quickly corrects me: 'I did not feel this was risky. I was very confident that I would succeed.' Again, she points to the winning combination: excellent raw materials, she could teach the craftsmen and there were customers waiting for her products. Equally importantly, she was tired of mass production. She did not want to buy a product, even though it was cheap, if everyone else had the same, and then after six months replace it. Instead, she wanted to buy something very special, but she could not find it. So, she created her own company.

When I ask Hiroko about her future and that of her company, she responds, 'Some people think that *andu amet* is the best ethical fashion brand in Japan.' Taking this a step further, she wants to apply 'ethical' principles to other products and services. For example, in 2017 she started making jackets and dresses. Hiroko also has a longer-term plan: maybe ten years down the road, she wants to build a hotel and a restaurant using Ethiopian leather to decorate the interiors. 'This is my dream,' she says, explaining that it would provide an opportunity to apply her ethical principles and Ethiopian designs and craft beyond simply fashion.

Hiroko's life, and her soul, is now divided between Japan and Ethiopia. She has spent most of 2015 and 2016 in Ethiopia, but plans to return to Japan now that the factory there is working well and she needs to focus more on selling and marketing in Japan – and not only in Japan, for she also wants to sell to other countries in Europe and Asia. She has not yet worked out the details, but a vague plan of internationalization is already in his mind. I hope she comes to Spain. She loved the country when she visited the Balearic Islands as a child. Perhaps one day, Hiroko will take a sailing holiday on one of Rafael de la Rubia's yachts.

When I ask Hiroko how she balances her professional and personal lives, she laughs and says, 'I do not have enough private time.' For example, during her brief stays in Japan, her parents visit her for just one hour. She says this is all the time she has available as she must focus on business 100 per cent, otherwise she fears the company will go bankrupt. But as her parents are getting older she also worries about them. In 2016, her father had a serious accident, which made her more aware of the passage of time and that she has been unable to spend much time with her parents over the last five years: 'I want my business to be stable as soon as possible so I can spend more time with my parents.'

For the moment, her mission is to create a bridge between Japan and Ethiopia based on ethical products.

Some of the problems that Ethiopia and Japan have can be solved by connecting these two countries. There are so many people who are more experienced than me in my fields such as design, creation and branding and networking in Ethiopia. However, no single person covers every aspect. In that sense, I am the only one who can connect these two countries and create new value for both of us.

Hiroko is on her way to carrying out Shinzo Abe's belief that '"Abenomics" will not succeed without "womenomics." For Japan, making the best use of women's potential is not a luxury or anything of the sort; it is a necessity.'

Echoes of our upbringing

The whole question about humility versus narcissism may carry echoes of our upbringing.[14] A study by Sean Martin of Boston College, Stéphane Côté at the University of Toronto and Todd Woodruff at the West Point Military Academy involving soldiers shows that, all else being equal, higher parental income during an individual's upbringing is associated with higher levels of narcissism in adulthood. Furthermore, narcissistic individuals are less effective leaders. Narcissistic leaders are reported to be less friendly and approachable, to insist on the use of uniform rules and procedures and to be less open to new ideas. The results of this study show that our early experiences with income influence our level of narcissism and our behaviour in leadership roles. How does narcissism manifest itself?

Growing up in wealthy families creates a self-sufficient mentality and distance from others. By contrast, lower-income individuals struggle to meet their needs on their own and appreciate closeness to others. This income inequity supports the self-sufficient hypothesis that suggests a higher-income upbringing is likely to increase a person's narcissism because of its tendency to prioritize the self over others. In contrast, they write:

> Lower-income parents have smaller houses in more dangerous neighbourhoods and rely more on time-consuming and unreliable public transportation. These conditions cause lower-income parents to perceive that they struggle to meet their needs for access to resources (e.g., transportation, childcare) to meet their basic needs. This dependence, in turn, increases closeness to others among lower-income individuals.

This is not to say that leaders with higher parental income turn into ineffective leaders. Parental income can exert positive effects on leadership outcomes through different leadership skills (e.g. networking). The results should, however, call our attention to the entitlement shown by some leaders from wealthy backgrounds and point out to compensatory mechanisms such as eliciting compassion.

10 ways to stay authentic with passionate humility

1 *Infect others with the passion virus.* Express your passion and enthusiasm through your verbal and non-verbal behaviour. For example, smiles and micro-movements in our face communicate our positive emotions. Use your passion to develop your authenticity, bonding emotionally with others and spreading contagious passion. Even the way Hiroko holds her leather bags transmits a positive feeling about her company.

2 *Practice confident humility.* Humility should not be interpreted as a sign of weakness; humble people show their strengths and their limitations and are open to learning from others. For example, Hiroko's can-do mentality manifests itself through her ideas, plans and principles. She trusts herself as a designer and her craftsmen's skills. When we practise confident humility, others will follow.

3 *Express your humility to others.* Admit when you do not know how to do something and show appreciation for the unique contribution of others. When we show gratitude, we are more likely to compliment others. For example, when Hiroko finished her professional relationship with her Ethiopian business partner, she didn't feel resentment towards her, and indeed she was grateful, saying she learned so much from her.

4 *Show your difference.* Your contagious passion is the glue that enables the team to take collective action following ethical principles and standards. For example, the manufacturing process of andu amet follows the ethical Kaizen principles of Japanese management culture.

The leaders' passion translates into employees who are vital, energetic, feeling alive and fully functioning, promoting creative behaviour at work.

5   *Capitalize on shared passion.* Passionate individuals defer to the authentic leader and merge their self-concept with the mission of the leaders, promoting citizenship and helping behaviour. Such collaboration is a win–win relationship. For example, Hiroko is proud that the ethical fashion market is expanding because of the influence of her brand.

6   *Who is the first follower to succumb to the passion virus?* Like 'catching a cold', some individuals are likely candidates to follow authentic leaders because of their need for meaning and action. Hiroko was equally infected by the passion of others. She was inspired by leading global fashion brands like Chanel and Dior, as well as ethical firms from Japan like HASUNA.

7   *Provide passion with meaning.* Leaders are issue interpreters that give meaning and purpose to peoples' life and organizational events. Motivate others with new ideas that are significant and inspirational so they can identify with your vision. For example, Hidemi strongly believes in slow fashion. This is the reason why she and other pro bono volunteers help Hiroko in andu amet. We want to be part of projects that can make the world a better place.

8   *Avoid narcissistic charisma.* Do not behave in secretive ways to serve only your own self-interests. Instead, share information with your collaborators and have a balanced perspective. For example, when Hiroko appeared on national television and became a national celebrity, she kept a balanced view of the situation – there was a good and bad side to it, she recalls.

9   *Cultivate compassion.* Passion is a social emotion transmitted from person to person and is the basis for empathy. For example, when

Hiroko lived in Iran for two years, she saw poverty and privation. That experience changed the way she looked at the world, opening her eyes to how lucky she was. When we are exposed to others' experiences, we are more likely to feel empathy and act in altruistic ways.

10   *'Shift gears' on your entrepreneurial passion.* Entrepreneurial passion takes different forms throughout the business life cycle; being overly passionate about a given role may block the opportunity to change. As designer, founder and developer, Hiroko showed a harmonious passion that was flexible and adaptive. She was able to 'wear different hats', among them design, founding and development.

Coco Chanel's story is a good example of a passionate leadership narrative, rising from humble origins. The way she made progress was to be courageous, speak for herself and embrace new ideas. Hiroko Samejima is following her footsteps.

3

Authentic Storytelling: Embrace Your Life Story

Have the courage to follow your heart and intuition. They somehow know what you truly want to become.

STEVE JOBS

Steve Jobs revolutionized the world we live in today. Recounting his fascinating life story in less than twenty minutes in his famous speech at Stanford University in 2005, Jobs revealed his life's ups and downs in just three chapters: connecting the dots, love and loss, and death. Let's focus on chapter 1:

I dropped out of Reed College after the first six months, but then stayed around as a drop-in for another eighteen months or so before I really quit. So why did I drop out?

It started before I was born. My biological mother was a young, unwed college graduate student, and she decided to put me for adoption . . .

If I had never dropped out, I would have never dropped in on this calligraphy class, and personal computers might not have the wonderful typography that they do . . . Of course, it was impossible to connect the dots looking forward when I was in college. But it was very, very clear looking backward ten years later.

Again, you can't connect the dots looking forward; you can only connect them looking backward. So you have to trust that the dots will somehow connect in your future.

Reviewing, writing and rewriting your life story means looking back and connecting the dots like Steve Jobs did.

Carlo Volpi: leading passionately by biography (Italy)

We all have a life story. In our stories, we reconstruct the past and anticipate the future. Every company has a story. Some are worth hearing more than others, some are the guiding light behind a company's evolution and its values, stories forged through adversity. Carlo tells his own story to new employees: 'We are a blend of history, a name and wine. It all started with a small tavern run by two or three people. We don't just sell wine, we sell wine and a name. The wine is the name of the family and Volpi is on the labels. This is important because the story behind the name gives confidence to our customers.'

Cantine Volpi was founded in 1914 in the Piedmont region of northern Italy as a small tavern and winery. Carlo Volpi, the current president, has lived through tragedy, losing his father when he was fifteen. When his older brother died seven years later, he took charge of the company. He went on to rescue not just a family business, but his family's identity. Volpi's wines are now sold in forty countries around the world and have won numerous prizes. Carlo Volpi's philosophy is based on the belief that 'the marriage between experience and technology produces the best quality wine'.

Developing a vision for the future is not enough, says Carlo Volpi: authentic leaders create a truly inspiring story, a thread that ties together the meaning of what their company does, and then they plan for the future. Authentic stories are forged out of adversity and honed by passion.

A life-story approach to authentic leadership

The pioneer in applying life story analysis to leadership is the late Boas Shamir, Professor of Sociology at the Hebrew University of Jerusalem. In 2007, I invited Shamir to give a talk at IE Business School. His presentation was based on two articles he had published with his colleagues in 2005.[1] His talk was one of the most inspirational I have ever heard. His message was clear: 'Leaders may lead by their biographies no less, sometimes even more, than by their observed behaviours or leadership style.'

Why do leaders tell stories from their lives? Shamir identified four reasons: to justify their leadership; to convey selective information about their traits, values and achievement; to present themselves as role models; and to create followership. For example, leaders tell stories that highlight the similarities between themselves and their group in terms of background, values and preferences. This identification sets the stage for acceptance of the leader's messages. How do leaders then account for their leadership in their life stories?

Shamir asked the fundamental question: 'How have I become a leader?' To answer it he and his colleagues carried out an analysis of eleven autobiographies of world-class leaders and sixteen in-depth interviews with male, middle managers in their thirties working for Israeli high-tech companies.

Their analysis identified four prototypes of leaders' life stories: first, as a natural process – a story of a born leader or a story of a late bloomer such as Bill Clinton; second, out of struggle – a story about overcoming many difficulties such as Steve Jobs; third, through a cause – a story that combines a personal narrative with that of a people, such as Nelson Mandela's; and fourth, as learning from experience – a story of learning from failures or from role models, such as Oprah Winfrey.

Shamir's presentation ended with two recommendations for leaders: 'Who you are may be more important that what you do – come on, get a life'; and 'Leader development should focus less on the acquisition of skills or

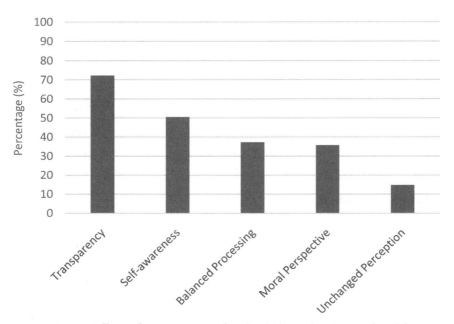

FIGURE 3.1 *Followers' perceptions of a leader's authenticity after life-story sharing.*

"style" and more on aiding leaders to acquire self-knowledge and clarity through developing their life stories.' Would these recommendations work? In 2012, a Master's thesis conducted by Courtney Calinog at Northwestern University[2] tested this idea. As you can see in Figure 3.1, the results show a strong positive correlation between followers' awareness of their leader's life stories and their perceptions of the leader's authenticity – being open and forthcoming and aware of their strengths and limitations. Another interesting finding is that the type of story that had the greatest impact in revealing the supervisor's true self is 'challenges' stories, representing tales of personal hardship.

So how did Carlo Volpi develop and share an authentic narrative of his life?

The story behind the name

When I met Carlo Volpi, he had prepared answers to every single question I had sent him in advance of our interview. His appearance is casual, friendly yet assertive. His confidence in himself and his business is unshakable. Sitting next to his son Marco, Carlo was passionate not only about his wine but also about his family.

We started with the founding story his son Marco has heard over the years from his father and that he had already shared with me:

Cantine Volpi is a family business founded in 1914 by my great-grandparents in Tortona, in the region of Piedmont, from the river Po and the Appennini Liguir. This land is famous all over the world for quality wines like Barbera, Timorasso and Cortese. From the grape varieties found here, the small winery began producing a small quantity of bottles a year solely for the family's other business, a small tavern. The demand for Volpi wine increased during World War I because the Volpi family's restaurant was very popular among the soldiers stationed at the nearby barracks in Tortona. They appreciated the wine in addition to the food. Gradually, as the wines' popularity increased, the focus of the family business shifted from the tavern to the wine industry.

Despite the vagaries of each vintage, Volpi's history reassures customers that they are buying a top-level wine. 'Customers have confidence in our wine,' Carlo says, referring to Volpi's website:

With the flowing of the generations, the Company was able to build, step by step, a distinctive role in its territory and an image of high quality for its wines, both on the domestic and international markets. Cortese, Barbera and Dolcetto are then produced with a careful and proper vinification in the winery at Viguzzolo, [the] centre of collection and pressing of the grapes for some fifty years ... Today, the marriage between experience and technology goes on to give continuity to the proposal of the complete expression of the best wine quality.

Volpi plays with tradition to build its future. Its mission bridges the past and gives continuity for future generations.

PHOTO 3.1 *Carlo Volpi, CEO of Cantine Volpi (Italy)*.

The neuroscience behind storytelling

Storytelling is a powerful tool that over thousands of years has helped people learn, remember and change. 'The struggles, losses, joys, and the journeys we take in our own lives are reflected back to us in the imaginary world of storytelling,' says Jenny Nabben in her book *Influence*, where she explores how our brain processes information compared to stories. When we are presented with basic facts, such as data and graphs, we process this information mainly within two parts of our brain – Broca and Wernicke's areas, where words are decoded into meaning.

In contrast, when we listen to stories, many different areas of the brain are activated because stories provoke emotions and empathy. Neuroscientists have examined the different areas of the brain that are lit up when listening to a story with vivid language. For example, Keith Oatly, a cognitive psychologist at the University of Toronto, suggests that stories function like a simulation of reality that 'runs on the minds of the readers just as computer simulations run on computers'. And Jennifer Aaker, a marketing professor at Stanford Business School, has studied how our brains are wired to understand stories and concludes that 'storytelling lights up the sensory cortex in the brain, which can make you feel, hear, taste, and smell the story'.

Notice what happens when you read the passage about the story of Cantine Volpi. Multiple brain regions 'light up' when presented with different information:

> Cantine Volpi is a family business founded in 1914 by my great-grandparents in Tortona, in the region of Piemonte, from the River Po and the Apennine Liguir. . . The demand for Volpi wine increased during World War I because the Volpi family's restaurant was very popular among the soldiers stationed at the nearby barracks in Tortona. They appreciated the wine in addition to the food.

- The amygdala, which is associated with emotions, is activated when you read 'a family business', evoking memories of your own family.
- The visual and auditory cortex is stimulated when visualizing the landscape of the Po and the Apennine mountains, evoking familiar colours, shapes and sounds.
- The motor cortex is triggered when imagining the soldiers walking from their barracks to the Cantine.
- The olfactory cortex lights up at the memories of the aromas of wine and food.

Empathy through storytelling can also lead to persuasion and action. Paul Zak[3] has researched a neurochemical called oxytocin that motivates cooperation with others. He found that character-driven stories shown on a video caused the brain to release more oxytocin, which predicted people's motivation to cooperate, such as donating money to a charity associated with the story they were listening to. The implication of these studies is clear: embrace your life story.

Embrace your life story

Volpi's story is closely tied to Carlo's life. He lived through two tragedies at a very young age, losing his father, Giovanni, in 1972 when he was just fifteen years old. Seven years later, his older brother Giuseppe, who had taken over the company after the premature death of their father, suddenly died. The 22-year-old Carlo and his mother Elsa were left in charge of 50 per cent of the company. The other 50 per cent was owned by Carlo's cousin Bruno Volpi, eighteen years his senior.

Even at that young age, Carlo was very much aware of the history of the name and had a sense of ownership. 'The winery was mine. This was one of the things that gave me the strength to go on.' He recalls how he used to accompany his father to the wine fair in Milan. He grew up around grapes and wine and there was always wine on the dinner table. When his older brother was running the company, Carlo saw his father in him. After the tragedy, he says he thought, 'Now it is my time.' He had been studying economics at Bocconi University in Milan for less than a year when he had to quit his studies and return to Tortona to help run the company. 'When I quit Bocconi, I knew nothing about economics or wine,' Carlo recollects.

Carlo started working at the winery in 1976, six days a week, 'at the lower levels', three years before his brother's death. Bruno had already been working for the company for fifteen years under their father's leadership. With that experience, it was natural that he took over as manager and decision-maker. Meanwhile, Carlo continued learning the secrets of wine making.

'I was very curious and I wanted to understand the winery inside out by working with the most experienced employees,' Carlo recalls, an approach that gave him a solid grounding in all aspects of the business. He also dealt with banks and suppliers, a period that lasted for four years and during which time he kept up his studies. His daily routine meant working from 8am to 4pm and then studying viticulture, accounting, marketing and English in the evenings.

After seven years, he began accompanying sales representatives to present new products and meet new customers throughout northern Italy. He says the most important lesson he learned during these years was humility, particularly with the winery's employees: 'Remember, they are your colleagues.'

These early experiences in the company have forged his leadership style, Carlo says. Instead of telling people what to do, he prefers to ask: 'What would you think if we did this?' Carlo's democratic leadership style increasingly set him apart from Bruno's more directive approach.

Over the course of a decade Carlo worked in every area of the business: the production line, sales and marketing, administration and tasting. This all gave him the opportunity to learn the business inside out, to develop a strategic vision and to consolidate his authentic approach to leading the company.

By the early 1990s, Cantine Volpi was one of the leading producers of Italian sparkling wines. It had twenty-eight employees and thirty sales people, with a solid market in northern Italy and annual profits of around €3.1 million. By now Carlo was beginning to develop a systemic view of the company and the industry. He now had the big picture of the winery: from the vineyard to the market. What's more, he was worried about a possible decline in the Italian market and therefore the need for internationalization.

Experiential exercise: write your life story

To develop your authenticity, take a leaf out of Carlo's book and try writing your own life story. Focus on 'trigger events', because they represent transitions in your life. It can be as simple as drawing a time line, identifying major events and turning points, and reflecting on them. These major events or 'crucibles' are circumstances that present you with a dilemma or difficult choices.

Think of your life as if it were a book. Most books are divided into chapters. Divide your own life into chapters in any way you see fit. Each chapter tells a small story; that is, it has a plot. Try to think about the major events in your life as 'turning points' or 'nuclear episodes' leading from one chapter to the next, and give each chapter a name. Use your life narrative to develop your authenticity following several steps:

1   *Peak experiences.* Describe moments in your life in which you feel a sense of transcendence and inner joy.

2   *Nadir experiences.* Describe moments in your life in which you feel a sense of disillusionment or despair.

3   *The people who had the greatest influence.* Identify four or five people who have had the biggest impact on your life story.

4   *Your early memories.* Describe both positive and negative experiences from your childhood.

Carlo faced a crucible event when his vision for the company conflicted with his cousin Bruno. This situation presented Carlo with some difficult choices.

Two visions in conflict

The advantages of international growth were clear in Carlo's mind: prevent future problems when the local market declined by developing new products and services and explore the 'made in Italy' brand internationally. But Bruno could see the challenges such an approach involved: lack of capacity – they could barely meet demand in Italy; and they had failed in their attempt to enter the Canadian market, where they didn't adapt to local needs. At the same time, Volpi's sparkling white wines were facing increasing competition. Finally, Bruno was not confident negotiating with international partners in English.

These two conflicting visions for the company were starting to harm the bottom line of the business. Profits declined from 1991 to 1996 because it was impossible to agree on investments, while at the same time, exports were neglected.

Carlo had developed a strategic vision for the company and was ready to transition to a management role. The first signs that the Italian market was in decline did not go unnoticed by him and he was determined to make Volpi a great international winery. In short, he wanted to export 80 per cent of output by 2000. But this was not a decision he could make on his own. Such a transition required negotiating with his cousin and business partner Bruno. Carlo and Bruno now entered a period of reinventing themselves and their company.

Carlo says he could see 'what others couldn't'. Cantine Volpi was a leading sparkling wine in the domestic market, but these types of wines were not popular abroad. This is one of the reasons why exports made up barely 10 per cent of sales, most of which went to Germany. In the international market, Italian wines are associated with full-bodied reds.

Carlo says Bruno's management style contributed to a lack of expansion in the international market. Far from fluent in English, Bruno would say, 'I don't understand why my customers do not speak Italian.' What's more, Bruno had grown used to running the company without consultation and didn't like delegating.

At a crossroads, the company was increasingly paralysed because of Bruno and Carlo's failure to agree on important strategic questions. By 1996, there were three options on the table for Bruno and Carlo: sell the winery; Carlo to buy out Bruno; or hire a third party to run the company. Finally, Carlo made the decision to go it alone.

It was a tough decision: Carlo looked back not just to the accomplishments of previous generations but also forward to the future of his young family. To achieve the buy-out he had to sell several properties, but his desire to invest in the winery with a new facility, new products and new employees drove him on.

International growth

In September 1996, Carlo bought out Bruno. His vision now was to lead a great company, just as he had seen his father do when he was a small boy. As he had predicted, demand in Italy began to slow down and Cantine Volpi began losing customers. But Carlo had readied himself for the international market by attending international wine fairs, particularly in London and Bordeaux. 'I understood the different mentality of the international market,' he says.

As Carlo explains, the traditional approach of Italian winemakers is this: 'I have these wines. Do you like them? If you do, OK, if not, thank you and goodbye.' The new, customer-oriented mentality Carlo adopted was this: 'We can do something for you, we offer wines from my region, with different labels and bottles. If you do not like this, we can create something new for you.' This shift has meant that Cantine Volpi can offer its customers the best wines and will also work with them to find the right product.

In 1999, Carlo coupled his international strategy with the decision to start making organic wine. He met one of the most important agents in London, Bottle Green, and started working with them on a few organic wines. Bottle Green was looking for a winery in Italy with official certification to produce organic wines to export to the United Kingdom. This was key for Cantine Volpi's long-term success. It was one of the first players in the Italian organic wine market, giving it an advantage.

Carlo applied his leadership mantra: 'If you want to be a leader in the market, you must see what other people are unable to see.' Organic wines were becoming more popular, but there were just three such wineries out of more than 30,000 in Italy. Carlo was a visionary. Many traditional players thought organic wines were a fad that would soon disappear. Today, most Italian wineries have organic lines, which make up almost 20 per cent of the market. For Cantine Volpi, organics are now 60 per cent of its total output.

Bottle Green and Cantine Volpi then looked for reputable suppliers for organic wines in Italy while producing, labelling and storing the wine in Tortona. Cantine Volpi met the strict rules for organic status and was given certification to sell in the United Kingdom. In that first year of production, Carlo bought a lot of organic grapes from around Italy but acquired no customers.

Believing in his business relationship with Bottle Green, the strongest player in the UK market at the time, he was determined to succeed. Eventually, he realized the 'you must buy my wines because they are organic' approach wasn't going to work and that he needed to be able to say to customers, 'You must buy my wines because they are good and they are *also* organic.' He and Bottle Green started to sell in the United Kingdom.

A year later, they went to one of the most important organic wine trade fairs in France, finding new customers from Switzerland, Japan, Germany, the Netherlands, Denmark and Belgium. By offering organic wines, Volpi was able to enter many new markets. To produce those wines, the company had to go through a process of reconversion that can take up to three years. Carlo had prepared his organic ground well, and it took him just one year to get official certification.

Today, this family-run Italian winery has thirty employees, not a huge number, but it should be remembered that a prestigious brand like Spain's Protos has only fifty employees. Carlo is personally in charge of tasting and choosing wines together with his winemaker Federico Ridolofo. He also employs a biologist who assists in the winemaking. An accountant and production manager report directly to Carlo. There are an additional four export agents covering the United States, Japan, Canada and Germany who also report to Carlo: the other agent is free to sell special and customized products all over the world, an approach that follows the philosophy of investing in both innovation and tradition by exploring the particularities of the vines while retaining a passion for tradition.

Carlo is passionate about Volpi's two very different product lines. The first is a range of traditional regional wines with deep roots from his family's lands, the labelling of which has remained unchanged for decades. The second is a range of organic and non-organic wines from other regions in Italy. These may have many different labels, bottles, presentations and even advertising. A new product can be designed in conjunction with customers to meet their needs and tastes.

In total, Volpi wines sell in forty countries and are reviewed in the world's most prestigious wine magazines. Whereas in 1996 exports represented 8 per cent of the output, two decades' later overseas sales make up 80 per cent of the business.

The components of authentic stories

Psychologist Dan McAdams of Northwestern University and his team[4] studied personal narratives similar to Carlo's and concluded that people 'seek to construct more-or-less integrative narratives of the self to provide their life with a semblance of unity and purpose'. The critical thing about authentic leaders is that they are not self-centred. What sets them apart is that once they figure out their personal goals, they want to create a positive legacy that will outlive themselves. This is what McAdams calls 'generativity'. His team compared the life stories of a sample of highly generative schoolteachers and community volunteers with a sample of less generative adults who were like the generative group with respect to demographic attributes. The most interesting result of this study is that it reveals a prototypical life story of authenticity with five elements: family blessing, the suffering of others, moral steadfastness, redemption sequences, and pro-social goals for the future. As they describe it:

The protagonist comes to believe early on that he or she has a special advantage (family blessing) that contrasts markedly to the pain and misfortune suffered by many others (suffering of others). Experiencing the world as a place where people need to care for others, the protagonist commits the self to living in accord with a set of clear and enduring values and personal beliefs that continue to guide behaviour through the life span (moral steadfastness). Moving ahead with the confidence of early blessing and steadfast belief, the protagonist encounters an expectable share of personal misfortune, disappointment, and even tragedy in life, but these bad events often become transformed, or redeemed, into good outcomes (redemption sequences), sometimes because of the protagonist's own efforts and sometimes by chance or external design. Thus, bad things happen, but they often turn into good, whereas when good things happen, they rarely turn bad. Looking to the future with an expanded radius of care, the protagonist sets goals that aim to benefit others (prosocial goals for the future), especially those of the next generation, and to contribute to the progressive development of society as a whole and to its worthier institutions.

You can now analyse the life story you wrote before. Consider these elements by looking at the nuclear episodes, plot structure and emotional tone of your narrative. Nuclear episodes are 'particular scenes that stand out in bold print in the life story'. Plot structure refers to the sequence of events or experiences, and it can take several forms – redemption sequence is when the plot moves from negative to positive life events; that is, there is recovery after failure. Finally, you can evaluate the overall emotional tone of your life story from negative (–10) to positive (+10). Consider the following examples of Steve Jobs' life story and Carlo Volpi's life story, depicted in Figure 3.2.a and Figure 3.2.b, respectively.

Following McAdams research, I asked a group of MBA students about their peak experiences – episodes in which they felt a sense of transcendence, being uplifted and inner joy. These experiences have been characterized as wholeness, perfection, aliveness, richness, beauty, uniqueness or insight. Then, I asked

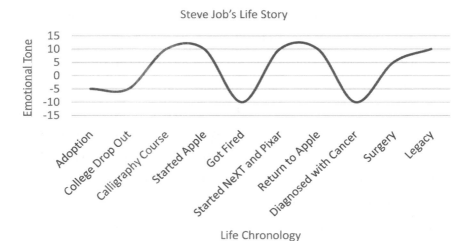

FIGURE 3.2.A *Emotional tone of Steve Job's life story.*

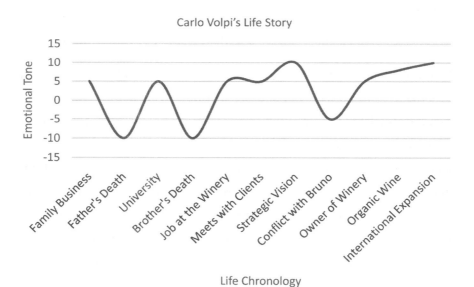

FIGURE 3.2.B *Emotional tone of Carlo Volpi's life story.*

them about nadir experiences – moments in which they felt a sense of disillusionment or despair. At the end, the participants were asked to picture what they planned to accomplish in the next five years.

In this study of life stories[5] I collaborated with Ronit Kark at Bar Ilan University in Israel. In 2013, I took a trip to Tel Aviv to give a research talk in the Department of Psychology. Working in coffee shops from Jerusalem to Caesarea, we examined the structure, content and emotional tone of the life stories of leaders-to-be to find a pattern. We wanted to understand how highly authentic leaders-to-be differ from their less authentic peers in the ways in which they narrate their lives to make sense of 'who they are, who they have been, and who they may be in the future'.

We found differences in how they reconstruct the past and anticipate the future. Those that set future goals to benefit society (pro-social goals) were more likely to reconstruct the past based on an authenticity story in which the protagonist experiences a crucible event with a clear point of discontinuity. In other words, they made sense of their own lives and their future goals by tracing them back to a formative event that changed them. For example, one participant, whose vision for the future was 'to put my effort into an entity that will carry my name and will serve others', reconstructed his past as 'The awakening: I wake up feeling very down and low ... I went through a phase where I reorganized my life. I become more spiritual, self-aware, sensitive to others.'

I conducted a similar life story exercise as part of an executive education programme of authentic leadership development in a multinational industrial company. This involved women executives with more pro-social goals such as leaving a legacy. 'I want others to remember me as a person who made changes in this company,' said one female executive.

How does the life story approach work? The self-defining life stories of authentic leaders differ in fundamental ways from those constructed by their less authentic peers. Authenticity stories motivate and reinforce individuals' efforts to achieve goals that benefit others. The crucible stories that authentic leaders fashion to make sense of their life sustain the development of pro-social goals to contribute positively to others. The implication of this finding is that authenticity constructed in a narrative of the self is not simply being yourself, but rather having a purpose greater than yourself.

Carlo Volpi's emotional attachment and pro-social goals were rooted in his early past experiences and his own life narrative.

How to become and remain authentic by evoking the past

When I asked Carlo about the marriage between tradition and innovation outlined on Volpi's web page, he explained, 'Wine is a tradition but people's tastes change, which means coming up with new wines. We must keep up with market trends to find out what young people really want. The key to success is to maintain tradition while following customers' needs to make them happy.'

Carlo says storytelling is a key part of the way he leads his company: 'I tell my story to my employees. And part of that story is that with determination you can achieve whatever you want in life.' Carlo doesn't so much transmit a way of working, but instead a way of life. To him, this is true leadership. Carlo's remarkable life story of triumph over adversity has led him to become a role model for his team. When he hires a new employee, the first thing he says is, 'You are here to learn a job that is good for you.' Carlo prides himself on having made Cantine Volpi a means for employees to develop their careers, and is personally in charge of supervising their training. For example, newcomers are appointed a mentor to introduce them to the values of the company.

I asked Carlo what makes for a successful leader. 'You must be humble with everyone: customers and employees,' he replied without hesitation. Carlo develops authentic relationships with his employees, whom he sees as his colleagues. He aims to be democratic and flexible. For example, some have flexible work schedules if they live far from the winery and have small children.

'The company is a team and everyone must perform. If everyone plays well, the team wins. If somebody does not play well, the team fails,' Carlo explains. Carlo also recognizes his employees' success, delegating and praising good performance. If something goes wrong, he takes the blame because he has selected and trained his team. He also has a profit sharing scheme. At the end of the year, employees receive a bonus related to their performance: productivity, new ideas, and passion. This is especially important for new employees.

In sum, leadership means three things to Carlo: being a visionary, a collaborator and a role model. A leader must 'see something that other people are unable to see', a leader must 'be able to delegate' and a leader must 'lead by example'. He arrives at work each morning at 7.30 and is always on hand. A typical day for Carlo starts with wine tasting with a team of four people who not only put their own wines to the test, but compare them with their competitors'. This typically takes an hour. Then it is time to check and respond to emails. Next comes accounting, administration and dealing with the banks. The rest of the day is spent tackling new problems and challenges.

Using storytelling to craft a company mission

Authenticity stories like Carlo's help us understand their narrators' values. I wanted to see if executives could craft a more uplifting mission statement using the best storytelling. In one of my leadership development programmes with senior executives from a multinational industrial company, I ran the following four-step storytelling exercise to create a renewed mission for the company.

The first two steps involve selecting and writing a story. I ask participants individually to think of a story that reflects 'what it looks like when we are doing our best work' and to write down an outline of the story. Then, participants move into groups to pitch their own story and choose one that best represents what the company does and its core values. As a group, they write down the complete story in about 500 words.

The last two steps involve analysing each group's story and the collective storytelling. The group identifies specific places and people; when the company makes a difference, and acts, and what changes happened for the better as a result. During the collective storytelling, all stories come together to represent the three elements of the mission statements: the customers (places and people); the company actions (what the company does); and the impact (changes for the better). The result is a more complete, personal and inspiring company mission.

The authentic identity of an Italian winery

Now in his late fifties, Carlo isn't sure if his son Marco, in his mid-twenties, will follow in his footsteps: 'I don't know what Marco will do. You can only work at the winery if you are passionate about it' – which means understanding and mastering what 'good' wine is. Carlo says Marco needs experience outside the winery to better appreciate and understand the outside world. Winemaking is now a global business, with competitors in China, South America and Australia, as well as Europe and the United States. 'Which is why you need to work with your soul, not only with your brain,' Carlo argues.

When I ask Carlo about his legacy, he looks at Marco, inviting him to continue the saga. For him, legacy means keeping the winery alive: 'Keeping the identity of the family and its passion for wine means keeping the name of the winery.' Marco does not seem ready yet, but his younger sister has just joined the Wine Society at Bocconi. Who knows, perhaps she will lead Volpi into its next phase?

Rewrite your life story: how satisfied are you with yourself and your life?

Consider the extent to which you are satisfied with yourself and your life story. Indicate to what extent you agree or disagree with these statements using a scale from 1, 'Strongly disagree', to 5, 'Strongly agree'.

1   When I look at the story of my life, I am pleased with how things have turned out.

2   In general, I feel confident and positive about myself.

3   I like most aspects of my personality.

4   I made some mistakes in the past, but I feel that all in all everything has worked out for the best.

5   For the most part, I am proud of who I am and the life I lead.

6   The past had its ups and downs, but in general, I wouldn't want to change it.

7   When I compare myself to friends and acquaintances, it makes me feel good about who I am.

What does it mean to be a high scorer? According to Carol Ryff, a higher scorer 'possesses a positive attitude toward the self; acknowledges and accepts multiple aspects of [the] self, including good and bad qualities; and feels positive about past life'. In contrast, a lower scorer 'feels dissatisfied with [the] self; is disappointed with what has occurred in past life; is troubled about certain personal qualities; and wishes to be different than what he or she is'. How can you rewrite your life story to improve your authenticity and satisfaction with life?

10 ways toward authentic leading through storytelling

1   *Feel comfortable with your origins.* Your life story is the most powerful resource to help find your passion. When you tell life-based stories, you create an emotional bond with your followers and build community. This point is also emphasized by Rob Goffee and Gareth Jones in *Why Should Anyone Be Led by You.*[6] For example, Carlo Volpi shared his story of personal hardship when he lived through tragedy, losing his

father when he was 15, then his older brother seven years later and had to take charge of the company.

2   *Do what McAdams called a 'life review'.* The process of reflecting upon, elaborating, editing and extending one's life story. Passion is rooted in our life experiences. Our life story is the source of our inner energy. Carlo's experience was 'The winery was mine. It was very strong in my mind, my soul and my body. And this was one of the things that gave me the strength to go on.' He grew up around grapes and wine. The dreams we hold passionately have a backdrop in our personal experience.

3   *Be the main character of your story.* Make sure you show agency and credibility in which you are the thread of the narrative that, like a road movie, is a journey of self-discovering and personal transformation. Authentic leaders are not passive receivers of events; they are in charge of their life. Carlo says, 'I was very curious and I wanted to understand the winery inside out by working with the most experienced employees.' This active approach gave him a solid grounding in all aspects of the business.

4   *Identify patterns in your life-story.* By looking at high points, low points and turning points, discover thematic lines and basic motivations like affiliation, control, power or love. For example, a turning point for Carlo was the conflict with Bruno about the future of the company. In the end, Carlo decided to buy out Bruno and become the sole owner of Cantine Volpi. We need a story to move on, to get a sense of unity and purpose with our life's ups and downs. The narrative self gives us a sense of continuity in an otherwise seemingly chaotic life.

5   *Transform bad scenes into good outcomes.* You can't change your life, but you can rewrite your life story. Turn the downs into positive learning. Produce narratives of your life in which negative events result

in positive consequences, sustaining the hope that hard work today yields benefits for the future. For example, when Cantine Volpi started losing local customers, Carlo had readied himself for the international market by attending international wine fairs where he learned 'the different mentality of the international market'. The construction of a progressive life story is an important component of leadership development.

6 *Listen to the emotional tone of your narrative*. Evaluate the events trajectory along the positive–negative continuum. Do not be afraid to reveal your weakness. The most important lesson is to recover after failure. Create a progressive narrative that link events in such a way that your story communicates a positive evolution over time. Carlo Volpi's story is one of success, ending with positive emotions such as passion and enthusiasm. He invested in innovation while retaining a passion for tradition.

7 *Be aware of your values and moral stands*. Behavioural integrity is anchored in your childhood attachment. Our life story helps us identify our enduring values and purposes, what kind of character or personality we have. The disclosure of these values and purposes become clearer during crucible events and changing events during our life. For example, Carlo's leadership mantra, 'If you want to be a leader in the market, you must see what other people are unable to see', becomes clearer during the period of internationalization. Our core values give us a sense of coherence and openness.

8 *Decipher your ideological settings*. Write a 'polyphonic novel' as your life story. Through your role models and connections, find the voices and social contexts where your moral stands have been forged. Put yourself in context: voice a community or be part of a larger group such as a generation, which is connected to others. For example, Carlo is

associated with the reputable suppliers for organic wines meeting the strict rules for organic status, even getting the certification to sell in the United Kingdom. Bridging within our communities gives us a social identity.

9   *Create followership.* Select portions of your life story to create an uplifting mission for personal and organizational identification. Be prototypical: highlight in your stories the similarities with your group in terms of background, values and preferences. Carlo tells his story to his employees and part of that story is that 'with determination you can achieve whatever you want in life'. Carlo doesn't so much transmit a way of working, but instead a way of life. To lead authentically, we need a life story that justifies our leadership – our right and ability to lead.

10   *Keep others in your heart.* Show commitment to pro-social goals, working hard to do good things for others and supporting generative efforts. For instance, Carlo Volpi went on to rescue not just a family business, but his family's identity for generations to come. In doing so, you provide a common purpose. Knowledge about our life story creates fulfilling expectations and ultimately validates our leadership in the eyes of followers.

'We live life forward but understand it backwards,' says Boas Shamir. The second chapter of Steve Jobs' life is 'love and loss'. His 'loss' is redeemed by 'love' – 'I still loved what I did ... I was still in love ... I decided to start over.' Carlo Volpi's life story starts with family tragedy and ends with a wonderful and successful family business with an internationally recognized name.

Conclusion to Part 1

Resolving the protean-authenticity paradox in the narrative self

The underlying assumption within the literature on authentic leadership is that we see ourselves as one-dimensional. However, our true self may include a variety of identities, a belief some theorists have called the protean self, after the Greek sea god Proteus, who appeared in many forms.

Occupational therapist Susan Harter, who has written extensively on self-esteem, offers one potential solution to the paradox of the protean self and authenticity, advocating the role of autobiographical narratives:

> In developing a self-narrative, the individual creates a sense of continuity over time, as well as coherent connections among self-relevant life events, each of which can be experienced as authentic ... Moreover, narrative construction is a continuous process as we not only craft but also revise the story of our lives, creating new blueprints that facilitate further architectural development of the self. In doing so, one's life story can also emerge as a true story.

The protagonists in the preceding chapters are clearly protean: Rafael de la Rubia –athlete, entrepreneur and musician; Hiroko Samejima moves from different entrepreneurial roles – designer, founder and developer of her start-up andu amet; and Carlo Volpi is both a member of a large, traditional Italian family and the leader of a family business as director of the Cantine Volpi winery.

How do they manage their protean selves while remaining authentic? Let's look at their type of narrative, their identity negotiation work and their use of polyphonic voices. Often, managing the protean self requires some identity negotiation work, especially with those people who are close to us. They are used to our most salient identity and are likely to be surprised (or resistant) to the appearance of a different self. We can manage the protean self better when using a polyphonic narrative that evokes a larger social group or collective.

In a narrative of the self emerging out of struggle, Rafael de la Rubia constructs a strategic storyline where he anticipates and overcomes challenges. It looks like his career and identity transitions have been planned and unfold just in time. It is during periods of transition that Rafael must negotiate his identity with significant others. For example, he does identity negotiation with his daughter when the time comes to make his musician self more salient than his entrepreneurial identity. His daughter probably feels more comfortable with the stable entrepreneur she has known all her life, rather than the emerging musician. Implicit in Rafael's life narrative is the organizing principle of social class. His story becomes coherent and legitimate when the reader understands that coming from a humble background means he has spent half of his life making ends meet and now has the luxury to pursue his dreams in the second half of his life.

In a natural-born leader narrative, Hiroko Samejima transitions from her well-established role of designer at Chanel to the role of start-up founder. Yet, as with Rafael de la Rubia, she also must negotiate her new work identity with her family. Hiroko must convince her parents that this is a good idea and that she has the moral obligation to pursue this new professional identity. To achieve that, she presents a polyphonic narrative with the voices of her generation and her culture. Hiroko puts herself in the context of Japanese society, echoing the voices of young Japanese consumers who want to set themselves apart from mass-production through slow-fashion. As a result, she moves across entrepreneurial roles smoothly, displaying a harmonious rather than obsessive passion focused on a single role. In the process, she develops into an authentic leader.

In a learning-from-experience narrative, Carlo Volpi becomes an authentic leader by learning the secrets of winemaking, working his way up from the bottom to decision-making positions. This involved a fair share of identity negotiation with his cousin and business partner, Bruno. During this learning period, Carlo developed a big picture of the winery from the vineyard to the market. When negotiating with Bruno, Carlo points to the context of the international market and the organic wine industry as future opportunities for the family business. This facilitates Carlo's move from a family role to a business one. In the end, he managed to move his business forward while staying on cordial terms with Bruno.

Michael H. Kernis and Brian Goldman, who have researched authenticity in management, also endorse a strategy that reflects a multifaceted self. As we have just seen, the apparent contradiction between one's true self and multiple selves can be resolved by considering the idea of what they call *functional flexibility*:

> Functional flexibility involves having confidence in one's ability to call into play multiple, perhaps contradictory, self-aspects in dealing with life situations. An individual high in functional flexibility believes that he or she will experience little anxiety or difficulty in calling forth these multiple selves because they are well-defined and can be enacted with confidence.

When we identify our multiple identities, we are more aware of our strengths and weaknesses and understand better our contribution to teams, organizations and society. More than that, we begin to appreciate the contribution of others different from us.

PART TWO

THE *HABIT* OF LEARNING: GROWING INTO YOUR AUTHENTIC BEST SELF FROM ZERO TO CEO

Authenticity is less about being your best self and more about growing into yourself. Thus, the second element of authenticity is the habit of learning. Bill George argues for 'being yourself; being the person you were created to be' rather than 'developing the image or *persona* of a leader'. I take a somewhat different perspective to this static understanding of authenticity and offer a dynamic view of the self. While I would not deny that people have some enduring attributes of ability and character, they also change over time to be true to their best selves.

Have you ever wondered, for example, how authentic leaders come about? Usually, we think of them as a product of innate charismatic qualities. But the making of an authentic leader is a work in progress. In my research, I have found that most authentic leaders have a 'growth mindset', a term coined by Carol Dweck to define the underlying beliefs that people have about learning as a continuous lifelong process. When people believe that they can learn new skills and abilities and that effort will make them more successful, they are more likely to put in extra time and energy which eventually leads them to stay true to their authentic self.

This requires passion, but also tenacity and persistence, especially when facing adversity. Authentic leaders are constantly asking questions and challenging the status quo because they want to improve. Many of the authentic leaders I have met have faced and overcome difficulties in life by developing confidence and resilience. Rakesh Aggarwal, Dena Schlutz and Angel Ruiz are authentic leaders who have made learning a habit.

This second part of this book is about authenticity and growth over time. Leaders come into their own in times of crisis and change, resulting in post-traumatic growth. When the history of past success collapses, we need to reinvent ourselves. But change might threaten our authenticity. How do we reinvent ourselves, our team and our organization and stay true to ourselves?

Here are three inspirational stories of authentic leaders who reinvented themselves, and in the process not only stayed true to themselves but also turned around their teams and organizations: Rakesh Aggarwal, an entrepreneur with a growth mindset who never stops innovating; Dena Schlutz, a rancher's daughter with a rapport that builds relationships and futures; and Angel Ruiz, a fighter whose mental toughness makes him a natural survivor.

You will learn lessons on how to keep a growth mindset and embrace resilience, building authentic relationships with others and fostering mental toughness. You can practise some easy exercises to identify your strengths and put them to work for you. You will also find short surveys to help you become more aware of your personality. Do you follow promotion or prevention regulation focus? Are you an internal or external locus of control? Do you practise ego-centric, other-distorted or balanced authenticity?

4

Renewal: Develop a Growth Mindset and the Habit of Learning

We cannot limit ourselves to continuing along the path we have already cleared . . .

AMANCIO ORTEGA

In 2015, Amancio Ortega briefly overtook Bill Gates as the second-richest man in the world. Many readers may wonder who Amancio Ortega is. Aside from discreetly putting his billions to doing good deeds, he is also the creator of global fashion retailer Inditex, which owns Zara, Maximo Dutti, Oysho, Bershka and Pull&Bear. In her book *The Man from Zara*, Covadonga O'Shea tells Ortega's life as a rags-to-riches tale. The son of a railway worker and a housemaid from a small town in northern Spain, he left school at 14 and moved to the port city of La Coruña to work for a local shirtmaker where he learned to make clothes. It is said that a shopkeeper who refused to give credit to his mother to buy groceries for the family motivated him to work even harder to provide for her.

Today, the lifestyle of the 80-year-old retail magnate reflects his humility and determination. He still wears a simple 'uniform' of blue blazer, white shirt and grey trousers. The day I am writing this, 7 June 2017, Amancio Ortega donated €320 million to the Spanish state health system to fight cancer. He rarely speaks to the media, but in a 2007 interview he said, 'I never allow myself to be content with what I have done, I have always tried to instil this in everyone around me.'

Rakesh Aggarwal: from India to CEO of a milk factory (Australia)

Authentic leaders like Rakesh Aggarwal have an entrepreneurial spirit with a growth mindset and a habit of learning. Like Amancio Ortega, they never stop innovating. They can adapt to new circumstances and they articulate life principles that teach the people around them a way to live. They develop a systemic view of their company and the industry in which they operate and this overall picture gives them the flexibility needed to learn, change, adapt and progress.

Rakesh founded Longwarrry Food Park, producing Gippy Milk for the Asian market. After securing funding and coping with the global financial crisis, an unforeseeable challenge surfaced: a fire damaged a section of the factory and its equipment. It cost $5 million to repair and halted operations for seven weeks. 'My desire to continue to grow was foremost in my mind. During all these problems, we did not lose faith in the future of our business and kept investing in the business to increase capacity.'

His humility and determination made him a hero to the media: 'The man who ignored the banks and turned a mothballed milk factory in Longwarry into a successful export-oriented dairy manufacturer has sold his company for $67 million,' reported local newspaper the *Baw Baw Citizen* in February 2015.

On 1 January 2015, the plant, in Longwarry, a small town located some eighty kilometres east of Melbourne, was bought by Italian dairy giant

Parmalat. Rakesh stayed on as managing director, but he had realized his vision of taking the company to the next level, which required a bigger investor. Raised in a traditional Indian family, he had followed the mantra of living within his means.

I was introduced to Rakesh through his niece Arti Aggarwal, a student of mine who proudly talked about her uncle's business in Australia. When I initially talked with Rakesh in February 2016, he had just completed his working day, but appeared fresh, lively and spoke proudly of his accomplishments.

Rakesh says tenacity is the key to his success. Even under the most difficult circumstances, he held on to his entrepreneurial spirit and vitality to keep moving forward. He learned to delay rewards by pursuing not just his own interests, but seeking to make a long-lasting impact on his business and future generations. A sense of ownership, emotional attachment and personal responsibility is part of his leadership role.

Longwarry Food Park, Victoria, Australia

Longwarry Food Park is an entrepreneurial story punctuated by a potentially disastrous crisis. Rakesh Aggarwal's story was featured in several business magazines as an example of 'how innovation revitalized a dairy company' as reported by *Smartcompany*. The article highlighted how 'opportunities are created when leaders find innovative ways to manage risk'.

The Longwarry story began in 1992, when Rakesh decided to leave India after finishing his degree in engineering and head to Australia to work for a powdered milk factory owned by Bonlac Foods. 'I wanted to have a good life for the family, my wife and two children,' he says. 'The first six months were quite hard; we were new to the country. My youngest son had broken his leg when we arrived to Australia and my wife barely spoke English.'

After five years with the company, Rakesh was restless and decided to set up his own engineering consulting company, naming it Saurin, after his sons Saurabh and Rohin. Customers thought the two-man engineering consultancy was a much bigger business. This first experience of success boosted his confidence. 'I was quite good at what I did,' he says, which gave him the motivation to try new things.

Meanwhile, Rakesh's previous employer hit problems. By the beginning of the new century, Bonlac Foods was forced into selling off its loss-making plants. The plant was closed because it was 'too small, too labour-intensive, and too energy intensive', he explains. Rakesh saw a business opportunity to rescue the company he had worked for in its glory days by using state-of-the-art green technology to make the company's operations more efficient and environmentally friendly.

PHOTO   4.1 *Rakesh   Aggarwal, founder and CEO of Longwarry Food Park (Australia).*

Facing challenges and delaying rewards

Financial challenges

Rakesh put in a bid for the company in August 2001. His plan was to update its technology to increase capacity and efficiency. It was a good strategy, but it stumbled at the first hurdle. He explains, 'I went to practically every bank in Australia,' but the banks refused to back the bid seeing the factory as too much of a risk.

Furthermore, Rakesh had no previous experience in running a factory. 'Banks did not want to lend me money for the purchase because I did not have experience in the field, which put in question my ability to pay back the loan,' he recalls. Set on achieving his goal, Rakesh divided the business into three segments – the agricultural land, the machinery assets and three buildings – and secured three separate loans. He refinanced his mortgage and secured a high interest loan using the land the factory was located on. Along with his own personal savings and help from family, in December 2001 he was eventually able to buy the entire factory.

The no-competition ban

This should have been the start of a period of exciting growth at the company. But Rakesh faced a second challenge: a restriction imposed by Bonlac meant that he could not produce milk for the first three years of operation. Instead of viewing this as a setback for both the business and his vision, Rakesh turned it to his advantage: 'In the first three years, I used the land as a real estate business to generate income. Space for parking trucks also generated some revenue,' he remembers.

While this took care of the interest on his loans, Rakesh focused on updating the dairy producing technology and revamped the existing outdated machinery with green technology. By 2006, the plant was finally in good enough condition to increase its manufacturing capacity. His innovative and affordable in-house automation improved productivity at lower costs, and would not have been possible if he had not used the time to implement the necessary updates.

Renamed Longwarry Food Park, the company managed to reduce its energy usage by 30 per cent and its water usage to less than half of the industry standard.

As Australia's first and only private powdered milk company, from 2005 to 2008, there was significant growth and success for Longwarry Food Park. Rakesh's initial strategy was to purchase milk on credit from local dairy farmers. In the end, 38 farmers accepted his proposal. Longwarry Food Park entered Australia's competitive, cooperative-controlled dairy industry. After the first year of production, the company recorded AUS\$17 million in sales. By 2007, annual sales increased to \$41 million, with exports accounting for more than 90 per cent of sales. Longwarry Food Park was recognized as one of Australia's fastest-growing businesses by *Business Review Weekly*.

The global financial crisis

Then came the global financial crisis in 2008. 'Nobody was prepared for it,' says Rakesh. Many orders were cancelled. Prices plummeted by 60 per cent. Longwarry Food Park's revenues plummeted from \$41 million to \$32 million. The challenge was keeping the cash flow when customers could not pay. Rakesh had to negotiate with them and hold on to his long-term vision. The survival of the company was in his hands.

Once again, Rakesh preferred to see a difficult situation as an opportunity and focused on the company's reputation as a 'clean and green' source of food and fibre. This set it apart from competitors and helped the company receive some much-needed credit. He arranged long-term contracts with customers based on lower prices. 'We were the only dairy company in Australia that made a profit that year,' says Rakesh.

He also learned from the global financial crisis. It prompted a change in the business strategy. 'Once we had been through it, we realized business is irregular and we needed to expand.' Prior to the crisis, the company focused exclusively on milk products that were highly sensitive to changes in domestic and international demand. After the financial crisis, Rakesh developed a diversification strategy to avoid exposure to dynamic shifts in export markets, introducing new products such as fresh milk, UHT (ultra-high temperature) milk and cream cheese. This strategy was developed with his son Saurabh, a former UBS investment banker, who had recently joined the family business.

These measures proved to be successful, and Longwarry Food Park returned to prosperity and growth. During this period, the plant went from using 400,000 litres of milk to more than one million litres. Rakesh was confident that the company could continue to grow by 25 to 30 per cent per year.

For almost a decade, Rakesh learned to delay rewards by seeking to realize his grand long-term vision of growth and prosperity. He achieved his financial goal by securing three separate loans that allowed him to own the entire operation. Then, he patiently waited for three years to conform to a non-competition ban, using this time to update old machinery with green technology.

The Stanford marshmallow experiment

In the late 1960s, the psychologist Walter Mischel conducted a series of experiments at the Bing School at Stanford University about delayed gratification. How do human beings regulate their behaviour to delay immediate satisfaction for the sake of better future consequences? Mischel and his team assessed children's delay of gratification behaviour during a period of approximately six years (1968–74) in a series of experiments that came to be known as the 'Stanford Marshmallow Experiment'. This test has been replicated countless of times (e.g. Figure 4.1) with the same basic question: 'If you could eat *one* marshmallow right now, or *two* marshmallows after waiting fifteen minutes, which one would you pick?'

FIGURE 4.1 *A replication of the Stanford marshmallow test: self-regulation is the key to success.*

A total of 653 children participated in at least one experiment. The researchers assessed the ability of three-to-five-year-old pre-school children to delay gratification as follows:

> Children were escorted individually into an experimental room in the Bing School, played briefly with some toys with the experimenter, and were told they would play with them more later. The child was then seated at a table on which there was a bell, and was shown reward objects determined by pretest to vary in desirability (e.g., one small marshmallow vs two) ... The experimenter indicated that she or he had to go out of the room then but that 'if you wait until I come back by myself then you can have this one [pointed to the two marshmallows]. If you don't want to wait you ring the bell and bring me back any time you want to. But if you ring the bell then you can't have this one [two marshmallows], but you can have that one marshmallow.' ... The experimenter left the room and returned when the subject rang the bell or reached a predetermined criterion time (usually fifteen minutes).

Some of the children resisted the temptation to eat a treat (marshmallows or cookies) but others didn't. What happens when the children waited for the reward? Researchers found that children waited much longer for the two marshmallows when they were distracted from the reward. That is, instant gratification was delayed when the reward was not physically available to the children.

Finally, came the most important question. Was delaying gratification predictive of the future success of these children? Mischel at Columbia University and his research team sent letters to the parents about ten years later. The researchers mailed a survey with questions regarding the coping and competence of their now adolescent children to the parents whose addresses could be located. They managed to put together a matched sample of 185 children. Mischel and his colleagues reported the results of their follow-up study:[1]

> Preschool children who delayed gratification longer in the self-imposed delay paradigm were described more than ten years later by their parents as adolescents who were significantly more competent. Specifically, when these children became adolescents, their parents rated them as more academically and socially competent, verbally fluent, rational, attentive and able to deal well with frustration and stress.

A second wave of follow-up data was collected about three years later by the researchers.[2] The purpose was to identify the psychological conditions under which children's gratification delay is more likely to predict future behaviour. An important variation in the original marshmallow experiment was whether gratification was more visible during the delay period. The interesting finding was that exposure to the reward reduced the delay period. When the rewards were exposed, children who delayed longer were rated higher by their parents on successful competences, such as 'thinks ahead, is attentive and able to concentrate and uses and responds to reason', and lower on ineffective habits, such as 'is unable to delay gratification' and 'tends to go to pieces under stress, becomes ratty and disorganized'.

These follow-up studies provide very important lessons as to what makes someone like Rakesh such an effective and authentic leader. The first is that self-control and tenacity is the key to success. The second implication of these studies is that physical cues are important and that people must learn to divert attention from the immediate reward or must transform mentally the rewards to achieve better outcomes in the future. The third – and perhaps most important – implication of these studies is that authenticity often works in ways that we do not understand. One of the core attributes of authentic people is self-regulation. But, do we all regulate our behaviour in the same mode?

Tory Higgins, Professor of Psychology at Columbia University, identified two modes of self-regulation: promotion versus prevention. The *promotion* system is motivated by advancement and growth; in contrast, the *prevention* system is motivated by security and fulfilment of responsibilities.

Based on Higgins's original formulation, a team of psychologists – Penelope Lockwood of the University of Toronto and Christian Jordan and Ziva Kunda of the University of Waterloo[3] – conducted a series of studies to understand the motivation of promotion and prevention individuals. The interesting results can be seen in Figure 4.2. The authors demonstrated that promotion-focused individuals are motivated by role models that highlight strategies for achieving success. In contrast, prevention-focused individuals are motivated by role models that emphasize strategies for avoiding failure.

What are you? Promotion or prevention regulatory focus

Lockwood and her team developed a survey with eighteen propositions that are relevant to promotion regulatory focus (e.g. 'I frequently imagine how I will achieve my hopes and aspirations') or prevention regulatory focus (e.g. 'I

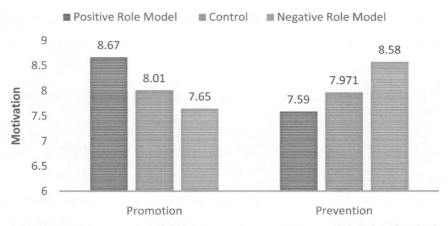

FIGURE 4.2 *Motivation of promotion- versus prevention-focused individuals after exposure to a positive role model, negative role model or no target.*

am anxious that I will fall short of my responsibilities and obligations'). You can use this scale from 1, 'Not at all true of me', to 9, 'Very true of me', to indicate the number that best describes yourself.

1   In general, I am focused on preventing negative events in my life.

2   I am anxious that I will fall short of my responsibilities and obligations.

3   I frequently imagine how I will achieve my hopes and aspirations.

4   I often think about the person I am afraid I might become in the future.

5   I often think about the person I would ideally like to be in the future.

6   I typically focus on the success I hope to achieve in the future.

7   I often worry that I will fail to accomplish my academic/professional goals.

8   I often think about how I will achieve academic/professional success.

9   I often imagine myself experiencing bad things that I fear might happen to me.

10   I frequently think about how I can prevent failures in my life.

11   I am more oriented towards preventing losses than I am towards achieving gains.

12   My major goal in school/work right now is to achieve my academic/professional ambitions.

13   My major goal in school/work right now is to avoid becoming an academic/professional failure.

14   I see myself as someone who is primarily striving to reach my 'ideal self' – to fulfil my hopes, wishes and aspirations.

15   I see myself as someone who is primarily striving to become the self I 'ought' to be – to fulfil my duties, responsibilities and obligations.

16   In general, I am focused on achieving positive outcomes in my life.

17   I often imagine myself experiencing good things that I hope will happen to me.

18   Overall, I am more oriented towards achieving success than preventing failure.[4]

Rakesh Aggarwal clearly falls into the promotion side of regulatory focus. He imagines himself attaining his hope of a better future for his business and his family. He has the motivation to try new things, innovate and fight if necessary to advance and achieve success.

Fighting fire with authenticity

Disaster struck in the early hours of 21 February 2012: at 2am Rakesh received a call from his son, Saurabh, saying there had been an explosion at the factory. By the time he arrived, firefighters had the blaze under control. The fire, in the powdered milk section of the factory, was due to a dust explosion. But the safety measures put in place worked, and all employees had followed the established protocol. The fire cost $5 million and forced a halt to operations for seven weeks.

It was a major setback, but Rakesh refused to admit defeat. 'There were no milk products to sell; so again, we had a cash flow problem.' He had to keep his commitments to suppliers and employees without the cash flow from sales until operations were running again. 'There were three things I had to work through besides getting the factory back in operation,' he recalls: suppliers, workers and customers.

Suppliers are critical in the dairy business and he could not afford to lose the best farmers in the area. If they started selling to other factories, he would have lost them for good. So he became a broker to keep them on his side. He kept buying milk from them and selling it a loss.

Rakesh explains: 'Firstly, there are suppliers of milk to us. I couldn't stop buying milk from them even if I can't use it. If I don't buy milk from them during that time, I would never be able to buy milk from them again because they would go and supply to some other company. So, we bought milk from them and sold it at a loss to other companies to process the milk'.

Then there was the key question of the staff. Longwarry is in a rural area and it takes up to a year to find and train a new employee. This investment-in-employee approach puts a premium on keeping well-trained and motivated workers who identify with the company. The workforce was willing to help. Rakesh convinced the insurance company to hire his own people to fix the factory. He explains:

The second challenge was that because the factory wasn't operational, what was I to do with the workers? Do I keep paying them or do I terminate their employment? The business is in a remote location and it is not easy to find people. I did not want to let my employees go. But we had no idea how long it would take to get the plant back up and running. So, what I did was to speak to the insurance company and I said that we need to clean the plant and do work on the factory. Allow me to use my own people, which will be cheaper than bringing in outsiders, it will be faster, and we keep people employed. They agreed. So, we used our own people to clean the factory and get it ready for the operations. That means I did not have to terminate their contract. The plant was completely rebuilt in a record time because these people are highly committed to the business.

Rakesh once again had to resort to his negotiation skills with the bank to ask for a loan to repair the damage. This turned out to be easier, based on his past success during the financial crisis. He recalls:

The biggest challenge was the customers. They thought that because of the fire, the quality of the product would be compromised. So, they stopped buying from us. I had a warehouse full of milk powder which I couldn't sell. It created a cash flow problem and we had to go to the bank to get special funding.

Rakesh needed to inspire confidence among his suppliers and so decided to resell raw milk to competitors at a loss. This enabled Longwarry Food Park to continue its association with the local farmers who had first helped the factory become prosperous. He was also concerned about the welfare of his employees, who had worked countless hours to ensure the factory's success and had always remained loyal to the company. He knew that his decisions as a leader in the face of this crisis would affect both revenues and the reputation of the business.

During this time of crisis, redefining priorities was critical. Long-term financial goals were put on hold to fix immediate problems. Two new product lines were stopped until the factory reopened. Revenues for the year of the fire fell from $85.7 million in 2011 to $75 million in 2012. However, in recognition of the company's commitment to its employees, it received several awards and, since the crisis, Longwarry Food Park has continued to grow and expand by introducing new products and new production facilities.

Authentic leaders have an internal compass

Rakesh dealt with the fire crisis at Longwarry by following his internal compass, prioritizing long-term reputation over short-term revenues and keeping in mind suppliers, workers and customers. His behaviour and problem-solving was regulated by what he believed was right. Authentic leaders evaluate and regulate their behaviour using their own 'voice' as a benchmark for their internal compass or *promotion* system.

In Chapter 1, I described my *Authenticity and Well-being* study to show that authenticity relates to subjective well-being. It helps to understand how authenticity relates to our self-regulation. The same 127 MBA students indicate the degree to which each of the propositions of the promotion versus prevention regulatory focus reflected their own behaviour in the MBA programme. In general, participants reported a promotion self-regulation (e.g. follow their hopes and aspirations) to a greater extent than a prevention self-regulation (e.g. worry about falling short of their obligations).

The most important thing that we found in this study is that heartfelt authenticity was positively associated with the *promotion* regulatory focus and negatively associated with the *prevention* regulatory focus two months later. This suggests that when we have a promotion regulatory focus, meaning we are motivated by considering new possibilities and feel comfortable with ambiguity and change, we feel more authentic to our true self. In contrast, when we have a prevention regulatory focus our main motivation is to avoid failure and disappointment of others. As a result, we feel less authentic. What happens when we feel true to our authentic self?

In 2016, during a sabbatical at the European School of Management and Technology (ESMT) in Berlin, Laura Guillen and I led a follow-up study to understand how promotion versus prevention regulatory focus relates to an authentic leader identity, seeing oneself truly as a leader, and in turn, what kind of leaders we are.[5] In a multi-source field study, we assessed regulatory focus and authentic leader identity with 153 focal leaders participating in an executive education programme. Then, two months later, leaders were asked to send their colleagues an online survey to assess their visionary leadership style. In total, 1,451 colleagues evaluated our participants, an average of nine people per participant.

We found that leaders with high-promotion and low-prevention regulatory foci have a more authentic identification with the leadership role and in turn are perceived as visionary leaders by others. When leaders regulate their behaviour through the *promotion* system, motivated by their own hopes and standards, they are more likely to see themselves as true leaders with an emotional attachment to their leadership role. In turn, this truly authentic identity of leadership is noticed by their peers, subordinates and bosses, who view the leader as more visionary, inspiring others to look for new business opportunities.

The habit of learning and innovation

Rakesh inspires people to look beyond existing boundaries. Innovation is the core of his business, he says, while keeping in mind the needs of multiple stakeholders: customers, farmers, and the workforce and their families. This has been the secret of his company's 30 per cent growth from 2005 to 2008.

Some seventy employees are responsible for the four product lines, working in three shifts, keeping the factory running 24/7 to produce close to 1 million litres of milk a day. A self-managing team of four people operates each product line with one 'leading hand' in charge of the group. The operation is supported by twelve administrative members. Longwarry produces fresh milk for the domestic market as well as powdered milk products for export.

Longwarry is part of a small community in West Gippsland of 120 farmers and about 200 families, who depend on the milk company. As an active member of the community, Longwarry sponsors a local school football and basketball team, as well as offering scholarships to high school students and inviting specialists to work with farmers to improve the operation of their farms. The company supports employees who want to volunteer their time at the expense of the company in community services like firefighters. A monthly barbecue and a Christmas dinner dance help to create a bond with the workforce.

Continuous innovation and training is part of the daily routine of supervisors and operators. 'We are an innovating business, so we are always changing, trying to find ways of either saving energy or doing it faster and more quickly, which means people have to be undergoing training all the time,' explains Rakesh. To achieve this, he has created 'orbiting' meetings as part of the daily working routine, informal chats at the beginning of each shift. The supervisor discusses what is working and what could work better, potential changes and plans with each team. This can take as little as ten minutes.

Rakesh explains how being an innovator was key for success. 'In big companies, people tend to be risk averse, while in my own business I could afford to take risks,' he says. 'We are not afraid of experimenting.'

Most employees hired by Longwarry are completely untrained to work for a factory that is fully automatic. 'Training is not an event that happens once or twice a year,' Rakesh explains. He and his team devised what they called a 'standard operating procedure' (SOP). These are documented single sheets with pictures on how to operate each function of the factory. These SOPs are in each work area. Every single operation in the company from printing to operating an automatic machine is translated into a picture with instructions – a SOP. For every change implemented in the plant, a new SOP is created. During the day, supervisors work closely with employees, reinforcing training and new skills using some 115 SOPs. Each supervisor has a mandate to instruct and/or review with every employee at least two SOPs a day. This takes about fifteen minutes a day and ensures that every employee has the skills required for the job.

When Rakesh interviews a new employee, the first things he talks about are innovation and growth. 'My expectation from you is that you need to be innovative,' he tells interviewees. 'Once the dedication to learning is there, we move them on into a seeded position within the company.'

Employees are encouraged to experiment with new ideas. Rakesh has an open-door policy: if an employee comes up with a new idea, he/she is able to come to him directly for discussion. 'We let people try things out if we believe it will improve productivity,' says, adding, 'I listen to people and implement the idea.'

That said, most innovation at Longwarry comes about through more formal channels. Regular brainstorming meetings are held to consider ideas. 'Anybody can contribute,' Rakesh says, and 'I put my ideas into the mix.' After a couple of days for individual reflection, a final team decision is made and an implementation plan is developed. In the end, 'the idea came from the whole team'.

'I want others to participate in the decision-making,' says Rakesh, who believes that people can change substantially and become better with practice and training. With a growth mindset, he delegates responsibility to lower level management and employees.

Experiential exercise: how to develop a growth mindset

In her book, *Mindsets: The New Technology of Success*,[6] Carol Dweck, who teaches psychology at Stanford University, identifies what she calls growth and fixed mindsets. People with a fixed mindset believe that intelligence and other skills are something you are born with and cannot be changed. For example, if you have a fixed mindset facing a difficult maths exam, you are likely to tell yourself something like 'I am not good at this, what's the point?' In contrast, people with a growth mindset believe that you can always substantially change how intelligent you are and that the harder you work at something, the better you will be at it. For example, when facing a challenging exam, a person with a growth mindset like Rakesh Aggarwal thinks, 'I can get better, I must keep learning, let's just study fifteen minutes every day.'

Consider the following growth mindset plan suggested by Stanford University's applied research centre.[7] Cultivating a growth mindset might be tricky when you are used to a fixed view of your abilities. Think of a time when you overcame a learning struggle and solved a problem. Take note of your hard work, strategies and help from others. Then you can write a letter to your younger self about this learning-related struggle. How did it make you feel? How did you overcome it, and what did it teach you?

Proud to be associated with an authentic story

A growth mindset and the habit of learning leads to a fair share of challenges but also continuous improvements and success to feel proud about. Authentic leaders make their followers proud of being associated with them and their successful stories. When I asked how Rakesh keeps his employees motivated, he underscores one key factor: 'Being part of a successful business story is the key,' he says. 'It gives them a feeling they are working for a company that is well known.' Whereas the dairy industry overall is a declining business in Australia, losing about 4 per cent; Longwarry grew at a rate of 30 per cent over a three-year period, attracting visitors, politicians and the media to the plant.

The ongoing conversation between employees and the leader of the company has strengthened since the fire. His office used to be at the headquarters, 200 km away from the factory. Following the disaster, Rakesh decided to move his office closer to the factory and his workforce so as to monitor progress in getting the company back on track. Rakesh's typical day includes a walk through the plant, speaking to every employee about work and sometimes about their family. He knows whose children are not well or whose are going to school and university.

Longwarry is also regularly in the news as the recipient of awards, including the Fastest Growing Private Business in Australia in 2008; Exporter of the Year in 2011; a Gold Medal in 2012 from Sydney Royal; and listed in the Top 500

Private Companies in Australia 2014. Employees at Longwarry are looked up to by their neighbours and friends. They are part of its success. The workforce is very proud to be working at Longwarry. Among all these awards, the Exporter of the Year award in 2011 from the government of Victoria received a lot of media attention. Longwarry exports about 90 per cent of its products to more than thirty countries in the Middle East, Asia, Africa and South America. A total of 70 per cent of exports go to Asia, where demand for dairy products has increased. At the event, Victoria's governor, Alex Chernov, said, 'This is against all trends and the economic problems of the dollar, underlining something so important for the future of this region and this country, research.'

In December 2014, Longwarry was sold to Parmalat Australia for $67 million. Rakesh believes that Parmalat was attracted by Longwarry's export-oriented strategy. For example, 'If you go to any major city in China, in any supermarket you will find Gippy on the shelves,' says Rakesh.

In January 2015, Longwarry formally became a subsidiary of Parmalat. Rakesh stayed on as managing director. When I asked about this decision, he acknowledged that it was not an easy one. But he reasoned that 'to get our business to the next stage of growth, we needed an investor, an investment that we as a family couldn't make'. Thinking back over the two cycles of difficulties, the global financial crisis and the fire, made Rakesh see that this was the right time to sell the business and achieve the company's mission. 'It was the time to get out of the business and let somebody else take the company to the next level,' he explains. There were many people interested in buying the business. 'Milk is going to do very well in the future; it's no longer milk, it's white gold,' he says.

Longwarry's long-term growth was at the heart of Rakesh's decision. A bigger investor able to handle cash flow was needed. Raised in a typical Indian family, he followed the mantra of living within his means.

Looking to the future, says, 'I would like to stay with the business as long as possible. This is what all my blood, tears and sweat have gone into and I would like to see the growth.' Rakesh continues to run his research company Saurin Group and has his own vision for the Australian dairy industry. 'Dairy is an important and sustainable business model in Australia,' he says. 'We as a country must encourage dairying as a profession and keep it growing to be the food bowl of Asia and the rest of the world,' Rakesh told the *Baw Baw Citizen* in February 2015.

Rakesh likes to tell the story of his fifteen-second meeting with Tony Blair during an official visit to Australia. Impressed by Blair's image of self-confidence, Rakesh asked him his secret. Blair responded, 'You just pretend you are confident.' Sometimes, faking confidence is part of the authenticity script.

During difficult times at the company, Rakesh would always appear calm and composed as if he had everything under control. But underneath this appearance of confidence he admits he was filled with doubt and was anxious. His self-confidence may not have been genuine, but his preparedness to take control of the situation was.

This mental toughness in the face of adversity comes in part from assuming the responsibility of leadership and then acting like a leader. There's an element of acting here, with the leader faking self-confidence to hide any feelings of doubt. But the price of being a leader, says Rakesh, can be loneliness: 'At the top, you cannot share certain things with anyone, so as not to worry them.'

Like an award-winning actor, Rakesh appears to me like an authentic confident leader strongly motivated by advancement and growth.

Authenticity and personal growth

Carol Ryff's work includes personal growth as one of the key elements of a person's sense of psychological well-being. Growth refers to a person's orientation towards self-improvement. In Chapter 1, I described Alex Wood of

Manchester University's study on the relationship between authenticity and two psychological well-being dimensions – autonomy and environmental mastery; and in Chapter 3, the relationship with self-acceptance. In their study, the authors also found a significant positive correlation between feelings of authenticity and personal growth and a negative correlation between feeling inauthentic and personal growth. This is another example of the nuances of authenticity.

You can take a moment to evaluate the extent to which you agree or disagree that these statements apply to you, using a scale from 1, 'Strongly disagree', to 6, 'Strongly agree'.

1   In general, I feel that I continue to learn more about myself as time goes by.

2   I am the kind of person who likes to give new things a try.

3   I think it is important to have new experiences that challenge how you think about yourself and the world.

4   In my view, people of every age can continue growing and developing.

5   With time, I have gained a lot of insight about life that has made me a stronger, more capable person.

6   I have the sense that I have developed a lot as a person over time.

7   For me, life has been a continuous process of learning, changing and growth.

8   I enjoy seeing how my views have changed and matured over the years.

What does it mean to be a higher scorer on growth? A high scorer 'has a feeling of continued development; sees [the] self as growing and expanding; is open to new experiences; has [a] sense of realizing his or her potential; sees improvement in [the] self and behaviour over time; is changing in ways that reflect more self-knowledge and effectiveness'. In contrast, a low scorer 'has a sense of personal stagnation; lacks [a] sense of improvement or expansion over time; feels bored and uninterested with life; feels unable to develop new attitudes or behaviours', explains Ryff.

10 ways to stay authentic making learning a habit

1 *Cultivate a growth mindset.* Try new things and remember that the harder you work on something, the better you become at it. Make learning a habit. Rakesh has a feeling of continued development and growth for himself and his company. When the fire damaged a section of the factory, his thinking was, 'My desire to continue to grow was foremost in my mind.'

2 *Develop a strategic view of your career.* When we see ourselves over time, we are more likely to grow and change in ways that make us effective. For example, Rakesh developed a long-term view of himself, his company and the industry in which he operates. This strategic system view gives him an overall picture needed to learn, change, adapt and progress. He never loses faith in the future.

3 *Engage in self-determination behaviour.* Monitor time and progress to accomplish your goals following your internal compass and voice. His self-determination made him an unsung hero in the eyes of the media: 'The man who ignored the banks and turned a mothballed milk factory in Longwarry into a successful export-oriented dairy manufacturer has sold his company for $67 million.'

4 *Be persistent and delay rewards.* Passion needs to be coupled with persistence. Rakesh's tenacity is key to his success. Even under the most difficult challenges, he held persistently to his goals. He learned to delay rewards by pursuing not just short-term goals, but by seeking to make a long-lasting impact on his business and future generations.

5 *Develop your leadership out of struggle.* Recover confidence in your abilities after a struggle, emphasizing the moral choices that you make. For example, when Rakesh found out that he could not produce milk for the first three years, he updated the existing dairy machinery with green technology. As a result, the company became more environmentally friendly and it managed to reduce its energy usage by 30 per cent.

6 *Learning out of struggle.* Appreciate how your views have changed and matured over the years. Thinking of the time you learned to solve a problem, you can focus on the subsequent positive consequences. When Rakesh faced the financial global crisis, he learned how to be better prepared in a volatile business environment by changing to a more diversified strategy.

7 *Avoid an 'if it ain't broke don't fix it' motivational style.* A *prevention* regulatory focus makes you vigilant to minimize failure at the expense of innovation. When we operate in a prevention mode, we are less likely to feel authentic and to enact a leadership role in an authentic way. Leaders with a prevention regulatory style appear less inspirational and visionary. Executives in big companies who fall into the prevention system tend to lose the entrepreneurial spirit. In contrast, Rakesh is not afraid of experimenting, taking risks and making innovation the hallmark of his company.

8 *Craft your goals via aspirations.* As opposed to the prevention regulatory focus, a *promotion* mode makes you centred on achieving your goals and aspirations. When we operate in a promotion mode, we are more likely to feel authentic and make leadership a part of our true selves. Leaders with a promotion focus engage in change-oriented and unconventional behaviours that further their own boundaries and those of their followers. After the fire, Rakesh convinced the insurance

company to do something unusual – hire his own dairy workers to fix the factory.

9   *Instil a growth mindset.* Sharing your growth mindset with others creates a culture of innovation and growth. Keep a learning orientation and search for opportunities to share your hopes and aspirations with your colleagues and significant others. For example, when Rakesh interviews a new employee, the first things he talks about are innovation and growth. 'My expectation from you is that you need to be innovative,' he tells interviewees. A learning orientation is the seed to grow within the company.

10   *Become a role model for learning and growth.* When we act by the principles of personal and professional growth, we become a role model leading by example. For instance, Rakesh's efforts are recognized by Victoria's Minister for Manufacturing, Exports and Trade: 'You are setting an excellent example for a more sustainable and prosperous future.'

With an exceptional growth mindset, Amancio Ortega has grown from 'zero to Zara'. Innovation defines Zara's corporate culture. And beyond business, Ortega is defining his legacy: 'My desire is that the results of my life experience, both personal and professional, may reach all those members of the society who might be in special need of backing and encouragement.' Likewise, Rakesh Aggarwal's renewed desire is summed up by his view that 'We as a country must encourage dairying as a profession and keep it growing to be the food bowl of Asia and the rest of the world.'

5

Relational Authenticity: Foster Authentic Relationships

I had no idea that being your authentic self could make me as rich as I've become. If I had, I'd have done it a lot earlier.

OPRAH WINFREY

In 1997, *Life* magazine listed Oprah Winfrey as 'America's most powerful woman', and almost two decades later, *Forbes* listed her among the most powerful 100 women in the world, ranked number 14th in 2014. The same year, her personal wealth surpassed $2.9 billion, making her the richest self-made woman in America. What's the secret of her success? 'Being your authentic self,' she says. The *Oprah Winfrey Show* was genuinely different. Debora Tannen, the author of *You Just Don't Understand: Women and Men in Conversation,* analysed Winfrey's style in *Time* magazine:[1] 'She didn't create the talk-show format. But the compassion and intimacy she put into it have created a new way for us to talk to one another.' With an incredible empathy, Winfrey created 'rapport-talk' rather than 'report-talk', changing the traditional focus on information. 'She turned the focus from experts to ordinary people talking about personal issues.'

Learning and reinventing herself, she builds authentic relationships with others. 'Oprah exhorts viewers to improve their lives and the world. She makes people care because she cares,' says Tannen. Her influence is such that she can turn an unknown book into a bestseller[2] or help Barack Obama win an election[3] through what is known as the 'Oprah Effect'.

Dena Schlutz: from stay-at-home mom to real estate CEO (United States)

Inner motivation is often seen as a form of inspiration, but it can also be rooted in desperation. By using their desire to learn, create aspiration out of desperation, authentic leaders like Oprah Winfrey reinvent themselves, rising from zero to heroes. Authentic leaders learn how to stay in top psychological condition to avoid the downward emotional spiral that often comes with adversity.

These people use adversity to make a personal transformation. They may face severe challenges in their everyday lives, but they are confident and optimistic about the future. They create a personal narrative of constructive self-disclosure within which they are an ordinary hero. They create epic journeys that link life events in such a way that their story turns into a positive message. Caring for others, these unsung heroes are never alone; their approach is to play as part of a team.

Dena Schlutz is a successful real estate entrepreneur in Colorado. But this is only the latest episode in what has been an extraordinary string of experiences and careers.

As a rancher's daughter growing up in the north-west of the state, Dena learned responsibility at an early age:

My parents gave me and my sister a lot to do. We had to take care of the sheep, we had to cook, we rode four wheelers and horses. My sister and I even drove the truck although we were too small to reach the pedals and the steering wheel at the same time. We improvised, one steered and gave out orders while the other pressed the gas and brake pedals. I was taught to do what needed to be done.

The hard work on the ranch did not ensure its success. On her sixteenth birthday, Dena stood with her mother in bankruptcy court – just the two of them. At the age of thirteen, Dena's father abandoned the family when things went south financially with the ranch. Dena's mother suffered from depression from that point until her death. Her mother filed for welfare for a brief period.

Although times were tough, Dena always had a positive attitude about the future and felt that her childhood adversity gave her the internal strength and confidence to take on any challenge. She graduated in the top 5 per cent of her high school class and was employed from the age of thirteen. And it was this positive, proactive outlook that took her from desperation to aspiration after her young husband, Ivan, who was training to be a pilot, suffered a tragic accident that left him with a severe brain injury. Ivan had always told her that she should not quit school, no matter what.

Two years after the accident, now caring for her husband, she graduated at the top of her class (Magna Cum Laude) and had another baby, her son Logan. Two decades later, I was introduced to Dena by Logan when he was studying at IE Business School in Madrid. Dena landed the job that all her classmates wanted, a job at a Fortune 500 company, Hewlett Packard, with good opportunities for an executive career.

She was described as strong, fearless and easy to work with by her boss and colleagues, and nearly doubled her salary in just two years. She then decided to start her own business, founding Estate Professionals, now one of the best-performing brokerages in the country, specializing in ranches and farms. She was also able to spend time with her family and husband who, during therapy, discovered an artistic side. He began creating bronze sculptures, winning several awards and staging exhibitions.

Today, in her mid-fifties, Dena lives in Colorado with her family, which aside from Ivan, includes three children, two grandchildren and two horses and two dogs. She competes in show jumping events on her Dutch warmblood.

To learn how Dena moved from desperation to inspiration by caring for others, I arranged an interview with her in February 2015. Talking to her on Skype, I couldn't help noticing her beautiful Colorado home, and was particularly attracted by the Western-style decoration and Ivan's sculptures, which I could see in the background. I had many questions about how she had stayed psychologically fit in the face of adversity. For example, what sort of narrative did she create to tell others about the accident? And did the accident make her discover things about herself that she did not know before?

Dena showed a great deal of what psychologists call emotional fitness. She managed to overcome negative emotions. How did she stay positive and energetic? The answer was to build strong relationships at work and to negotiate the flexibility she needed to manage work and a huge family responsibility.

PHOTO 5.1 *Dena Schlutz, founder and CEO of Estate Professionals (USA).*

Ultimately, Dena and Ivan swapped roles, with her taking over the leadership of the family. This change inevitably put the relationship under pressure.

Growing up as a rancher's daughter

Dena was born and raised in Colorado and says she continues 'to be awed by the incredible beauty of this state'. She has deep roots in this land: little wonder she has enjoyed her work as a real estate broker over the last two decades. Dena is proud to have developed close relationships with some of her clients during what she considers one of life's most memorable events – selling or buying a home. She says it is a privilege for her to be a part of that with her clients.

Dena's early years shaped her way of seeing the world and she identifies with the culture of hard work, having learned at an early age the value of making a life for herself. Dena was the youngest of four children and was given responsibilities both at school and at the ranch from an early age. She enjoyed learning new things and remembers the feeling of personal satisfaction when she accomplished something after a hard day's work.

'My father raised sheep, and he would leave me and Sandy, my older sister by three years, on our horses, in Wyoming in the middle of the wilderness to take care of 2,000 sheep.' Her upbringing taught Dena to act independently and to believe she could do anything.

At school, Dena was a diligent student who took everything seriously. 'She was the most hardworking of all the kids in the family,' her sister Sandy says. She performed well academically, and her dream was to go to college. However, the family's finances didn't permit this. But in her mind, Dena always knew she would get her desired degree in finance and advance beyond that.

Dena and Ivan Schlutz: facing adversity together

Dena married Ivan at the age of twenty-three. They dreamed of starting a family together and looked forward to Ivan's career as a pilot. Dena had just started her degree programme at the University of Boulder, Colorado, and was ecstatic to be in school full time. 'I had always wanted to go to college. But the planets had never aligned to allow me,' she says. Dena was also working part time as a legal secretary in Denver to pay for her education, making $30 an hour in the 1990s.

Ivan was a commercial pilot working on the side as an aircraft mechanic at Vance Brand airport in Colorado. He was on the fast track to get a job with a commercial airline. To support his flying career, the couple had moved often, living in Utah, Las Vegas, Salt Lake City, California and finally Colorado. Ivan was on his third round of interviews with an important commercial airline. He was close to getting his dream job when fate struck.

On 29 September 1990, Ivan had had a serious accident at work. During routine maintenance work on a small propeller plane, he dropped his screwdriver. He bent over to pick it up, and when he stood up he bumped the propeller causing the compressed air in the cylinders to kick the propeller through a stroke as if the engine was starting. The propeller struck his head so forcefully that it shattered the left side of his skull. A co-worker found Ivan on the floor bleeding and unconscious.

At the hospital, Ivan was responsive, but the right side of his body was paralysed from the brain injury. The doctors did not know if he would make it through the invasive surgery he needed or if he would be able to walk again afterwards. They shared these concerns with Dena and asked for her permission to perform the difficult surgery. Dena remembers the burden of responsibility of deciding about another person's life. This was a critical moment for her – she realized then that her role in life had changed forever: 'I remember thinking, wow I am the one who is making a decision about another person's life. It was a surreal experience. There was this terrible fear that he was not going to live. It was a very difficult time.'

Before entering the operating room for his emergency surgery, Dena remembers him telling her, 'Do not quit school no matter what happens to me.' During the operation, Dena took her books and started studying for her mid-term exams for the next week. 'If I couldn't quit school, I thought I'd better do well,' she says. Ivan was in surgery for about three hours. When the doctors came out, all they would say was, 'We'll have to wait and see.' Somehow Dena found the ability to focus on studying while waiting for Ivan in the recovery room.

After two weeks in intensive care, the pressure in his brain began to subside. Ivan was able to move his left arm, although he was nearly fully paralysed on his right side. Dena was very anxious and remembers watching him struggle with his movements and thinking, 'This is the way it's going to be.' Ivan then went through a demanding rehabilitation programme for a couple of years to try to improve his movement, cognitive processing, speech and memory.

Life after the accident

After his release, Ivan was in a wheelchair, later learning to walk with a cane. 'How is the future going to work? What do I need to do to prepare myself?' were among the questions racing through Dena's mind as she entered a new stage in her life. But as her sister Sandy points out, 'Dena is the type of person who no matter how difficult the situation she manages to improve it.' The accident would trigger Dena to find even more inner motivation.

Dena turned to her 'rancher's daughter' philosophy. The unexpected is always happening on a ranch, she says: 'The weather may suddenly change, putting you in a difficult situation where you have to figure out how to finish the job.' Her task now was to figure out how to plan for her future and that of her family. First, she had to prepare herself to appeal to employers and be competitive in the workforce. 'I was taught to do what needed to be done. I had always performed best under pressure in competitions with my horses or in school, so the pressure of being the head of the household felt comfortable to me,' she affirms. By now, Dena was starting to feel more confident with taking on the leadership of the family and starting a new career.

During the first two years after the accident there was a lot of physical and psychological therapy. Things were slow and painful, but Ivan had a positive outlook on life, which kept him strong. The couple settled into a new daily routine. She would take him to therapy on her way to school and his parents would pick him up from physiotherapy and take him home. His family's support was crucial in allowing Dena to continue with her studies. Slowly, Ivan regained full mobility in his right side. But his dream of becoming a professional pilot was over. Ivan would not fly again and now needed to reinvent himself, in the same way that Dena had to readjust her life. Things could never be the same for either of them, but that did not mean they could not turn out well: Ivan discovered an artistic talent he had previously been unaware of.

After being struck on the left side of the brain, which is mainly responsible for speech and logic, the right side, the more artistic, had taken over. Ivan began having strange dreams and seeing images he felt compelled to recreate in some way. To improve his dexterity, Ivan had been given clay to work with. 'He just got bored squeezing the piece of clay day after day,' Dena recalls. One morning, during rehab, he picked up a piece of the clay and transformed it into a beautiful piece of small sculpture. 'He really enjoyed doing it and eventually he made something that looked really good,' says Dena, surprised at this new facet to Ivan's character: 'I had no idea he had any artistic ability.'

By now, Ivan had recovered significantly, and was able to walk. At the same time, he began to feel that something was missing in his life. The couple then decided to start a family. For Dena, the timing was not ideal: she became pregnant in her junior year of university, while her husband was still recovering and while she was still in school full time. In the end, things worked out. This time, the planets aligned and Dena passed her last exam two days before her baby was born. 'The baby was a great motivation for my husband. As a father, he found a new identity,' Dena says.

When I asked Dena about her inner strength, she replied modestly: 'I didn't think that what I had done was anything special until other people told me. I just did it because there was no other choice.' People have since asked her how she kept on going forward, juggling the rehabilitation, the new baby and senior level classes. She now realizes she had not thought about it that way: 'I just did the things I did out of necessity.'

Her focus during this time was on keeping going rather than thinking about what had happened: 'I did what I had to do each day and in each moment.' She says she was not aware she was doing anything unusual: 'Anyone in my position would have done the same.'

A professional career

Two difficult years after the accident, Dena had achieved her lifelong dream of going to university, graduating with high honours; she had helped her husband recover from a life-changing accident and was now a mother. She felt empowered and ready to handle anything life could throw at her. 'It was instinct to just do what needs to be done, rather than worrying about how hard things are,' Dena says.

Now she needed to get a good job to pay back her $36,000 student loan and to take care of the baby. She found a job close to home with Hewlett Packard, working in accounting. With a starting salary of $38,000, Dena's commitment and hard work soon gained her the respect of her boss and colleagues. Her performance was excellent and she was quickly promoted, with a significant salary increase. After only two years, she was earning more than $55,000 in 1995, with a promising career ahead of her.

Dena enjoyed every aspect of the job. The only problem was that she was expected to work up to sixty hours a week, making it hard to balance her home and work responsibilities. Her husband and the baby were alone at home all day, and she says she would feel guilty. So, Dena asked her boss for a more flexible schedule that would allow her to be more productive for the company while taking better care of her family. She would work Tuesday through to

Saturday and then spend Sunday and Monday at home to take care of the family. She was granted the flexibility she needed on the spot. To her colleagues, this was a stand-out moment, reflecting the trust her boss had in her.

Closing the gap in feedback and self-perception

To stay true to your authentic self, you need more than heartfelt authenticity. A true assessment of authenticity comes from evaluating the gap between our own perception and third-party feedback. The smaller the gap, the more authentic we feel in your relationships. For example, Dena had a strong trusting relationship with her boss and colleagues.

Yet most of us tend to think a little too highly of ourselves. Researchers have consistently found that we tend to overestimate our own performance and skills. We think we are nicer and smarter than others see us. This creates a challenge for us when accepting critical feedback: even our most friendly colleagues are likely to perceive us as having more weaknesses that we would attribute to ourselves. Because receiving feedback from peers calls into question our self-views, it is very likely that some of us will develop psychological defence mechanisms to avoid 'emotional fallout'. Who is open to honest feedback?

We addressed this question in a study I conducted with my research team,[4] involving 169 men and fifty-two women with an average age of thirty and with around six and a half years of work experience who were assigned to 'learning teams' as part of an MBA programme over the course of an academic year. At the end of each term, students' peers provided feedback on leadership qualities. As later published in the *Harvard Business Review*,[5] the results, depicted in this HBR video,[6] revealed that all students started off by rating themselves higher than they were rated by their peers. Everyone thought more highly of themselves than their peers did. But with each assessment, getting critical feedback encouraged reflection, making people's self-image more realistic.

However, not everyone responded to feedback in the same way. As you can see in Figure 5.1, women more quickly aligned their views of themselves to match others' opinions. By the end of the year, the average woman saw herself almost exactly as her peers saw her on three out of four skills. For example, confidence was 3.84 (self-rating) vs 3.67 (peer-rating) in January; 3.64 vs 3.44 in April; and 3.42 vs 3.47 in June.

Men showed a different pattern. Confidence began at 3.99 (self-rating) vs 3.70 (peer-rating) in January; 3.92 vs 3.46 in April; and 3.84 vs 3.64 in June. After receiving critical feedback, women were quicker to revise their self-confidence and other leadership skills, while men continued to think highly of themselves.

The gender gap in self-perception and feedback stunned us. Why this difference? One possibility was that women are socialized to be more sensitive

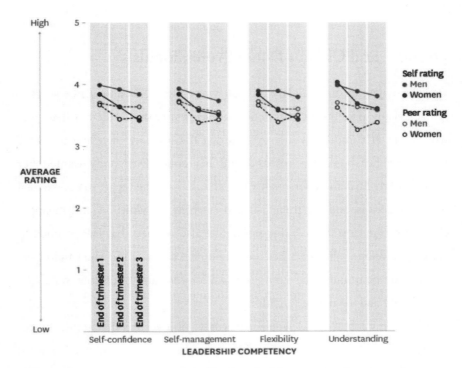

FIGURE 5.1 *Closing the gap in feedback and self-perception for men and women.*

to other people's opinions. Women's greater openness and sensitivity to peer feedback is a mixed blessing. It increases their self-awareness and authentic leadership. Women may be more in touch with who they are and therefore are able to learn. But it may also block the same confidence it is intended to boost, discouraging women from taking on new business challenges. At the same time, men's tendency to overestimate their abilities, ignoring what others are saying, is hardly a prescription for success in the long run. How can we learn from others' feedback to strengthen our authenticity?

Here's one way. Make a list of the people you work with and ask them for feedback on some critical skills such as time management, getting buy-in, or self-confidence. Check the gap between your acquaintances and yourself. Then, reflect about your reactions to the feedback you have just received. What is the gap in feedback and your self-perceptions? Are you an overestimator or an underestimator?

Founder and CEO of Estate Professionals

Dena managed an increasingly difficult work–life balance for three years. 'I didn't feel any anxiety and pain until three years after the accident, when I was working at HP.' Suddenly, she says, she felt the pressure of trying to please everybody: her boss, her husband and her child. Everybody wanted her attention. 'My husband's personality had changed and he wasn't so easy to deal with,' she recalls, adding, 'things started catching up with me, and raising a child drew me close to breaking point'. She also learned that HP planned to close its Loveland office near her home and relocate, meaning she would have a one-hour commute each way every day or relocate to another state. She decided she had to change something.

'I loved my job at HP; I would never have quitted had the circumstances been different,' Dena explains. But she also had to adapt to balance her work and her family responsibilities. The solution was to draw on the entrepreneurial spirit she had inherited from her family and so she decided that if she was going to have to work so hard, she should do it for herself. There was another key factor: 'My boss, Dave Willet, a true leader, was put in charge of another department,' she remembers, which made the decision to leave HP a little easier.

Dena was determined to create the flexibility she would need to allow her to enjoy her personal life and believed that starting her own business in real estate was the perfect way to do so. She had always been interested in property, and her skills in organizing, long-term planning and strategizing could be put to a good use, this time on her own terms. Her mother-in-law Hilda Schlutz, a Cuban immigrant and serial entrepreneur herself, encouraged and supported Dena.

Her sister Sandy thought otherwise, believing that HP offered a much easier career path for Dena. She was also worried she wouldn't be able to make enough money in real estate; but she also understood how important a flexible schedule was to Dena.

Dena sounded everybody out, listening to their views on her decision. For her, it was important to do a job she could be proud of: 'I was going to lead people through the biggest investment they'll ever make. I am proud to have a good education and I'm ready to work for myself.'

It turned out to be the right choice. Dena founded Estate Professionals and ran it successfully for twenty years. She worked from home and she had more time. Her sister Sandy now believes that Dena's work in real estate has enhanced many of her best qualities: 'sticking to something, of not giving up; her ability to adapt and change; and her ability to be more flexible. She is never afraid to try things . . . making new things work.'

Dena's day starts at 5.30am with meditation, exercise, a planning session and then appointments with her clients. Driving is a big part of the job and winter snow can be a problem on the roads at times. She works a lot from her home office so that she can be close to her family while still accomplishing what needs to be done to provide exceptional service. Her time and energy is divided between her business and her family and she spends little time socializing. Her best friend from childhood lives in California, a Harvard PhD and stock trader.

'I'm proud to say that over all my years working for myself, I have a 100 per cent satisfaction rate among my customers. I don't just ask my clients about how well prepared they are to make the purchase, I also ask them about their biggest fears and I make sure they know that everything will be done for their benefit,' she affirms. She strongly believes that the key to her success is never forgetting that buying a house is one of the biggest investments most people will ever make.

Dena's strategic advantage is developing trust with her clients. As she notes, 'My business is driven by referrals and word of mouth. I value the incredible loyalty from my customers and feel honoured that they consider me part of their extended family.'

In 2014, she grossed $6.5 million, and in 2015 doubled that figure. She is proud about what she has accomplished and that she wakes up every morning full of energy and enthusiasm. She loves doing what she does. When I asked her about where this inner passion and energy comes from, she has no doubt: 'It is my family.'

Giving authentic praise

We have seen above the importance of being open to critical feedback to grow into your authentic best possible self. But this is just one side of the coin. What happens when people share positive experiences?

The work of Shelly Gable,[7] a psychology professor at the University of California, Santa Barbara, explains four ways to respond to someone who is sharing a positive experience. As you can see in Figure 5.2, the four conversational styles can vary along two dimensions – active versus passive

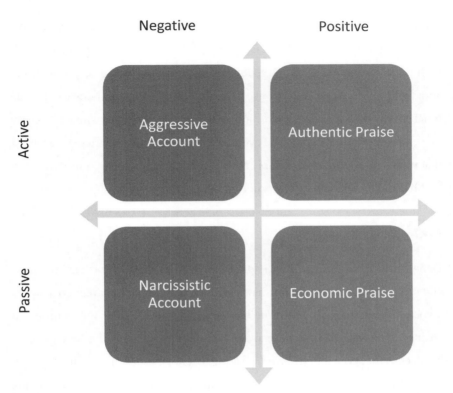

FIGURE 5.2 *Authentic conversational style is positive and constructive.*

and positive versus negative. Here's an example in a product development team: Ruth tells her peer, Alex, 'Hey, I have just completed my assignment for the new product.'

Authentic praise: 'That is great. What did you have to do? How long did it take you? How do you feel? What do you have to do next?

Economic praise: 'Good job.'

Narcissistic account: 'I am reading this interesting article on the internet. Come and see . . .'

Aggressive account: 'It took you a long time. Hope you did not make any mistakes. I finished my last assignment two days ago.'

Authentic conversations have enormous implications for developing positive relationships with others. We can actively focus on the other person with enthusiastic support, showing genuine concern about what he/she is doing and feeling. This authentic praise strengthens friendships between people much more than a simple 'Good job' comment. In contrast, when we overly focus on ourselves, ignoring the event, we respond with a narcissistic account that undermines the relationship, or even worse, an aggressive communication that harms the relationship by pointing out negative aspects.

Ivan's artistic career

Dena Schlutz practises authentic praise, providing support for her husband's emerging artistic career. Being a pilot for Ivan was not just a career goal, it was a vocation and a family tradition: his father had been a pilot for commercial airlines. Although Ivan has recovered from the accident, he suffers from headaches that prevent him from working to a normal routine. He has his own flexible schedule and works in his art studio at home where he can create his sculptures. Much of his work is inspired by native American themes, and includes a statue dedicated to volunteer firefighters across the nation.

He works mainly on a commission basis, with his mother helping him with art galleries and finding ways to showcase his new work. Leaving a legacy of his life through is artwork is what keeps him moving and creating new works. His work has received awards and sold for thousands of dollars around the world. But for Ivan, art is more than just a career, says Dena: 'After all the perils that he has overcome, I think that his art symbolizes his optimism and his passion for life.'

Ivan understands that his art is the result of a major change in his life. 'My inspiration comes from all the people that have helped me get to where I am today,' he acknowledges. He is particularly grateful to Fritz White, who taught him the foundations of sculpting over the course of seventeen years. But Ivan's desire is to go beyond self-expression. 'I believe that it is very important for an artist to give back to the community,' he says, explaining that his art focuses on the unnoticed. 'I create my sculptures to call attention to things that other people overlook.' His art and life story have been featured on CBS's *The Ordinary and the Extraordinary*, TBS Superstation's *Ripley's Believe it or Not* and *The Oprah Winfrey Show*.

What is your relational authenticity?

If we think of authenticity as a dynamic process of growth into our best self in balanced relationship with others, it is possible to understand how some people like Dena can be rated by others as genuine and authentic.

Wang Yi Nan, a psychology researcher at Beijing Normal University in China, has developed what he calls the Relational Authenticity Survey to assess this ability to establish authentic relationships.[8] The key idea here is that your authenticity does not emerge against others (ego-centric authenticity), nor through striving for the approval of others while concealing one's true self (other-distorted authenticity). But rather, authenticity comes from achieving 'harmonious unity between [the] true self and relational self'. Unbalanced authenticity in either direction reduces subjective well-being. You can rate the following statements from 1, 'Does not describe me at all', to 5, 'Describes me very well'.

Balanced authenticity

1 I am fully aware of when to insist and when to compromise.

2 I always find the ways to reconcile my needs and other's requirements.

3 I would neither give up the real me nor make others hard to accept me.

Ego-centric authenticity

1   I usually tell the truth without being concerned about how others will think of me.

2   I just speak my mind without concern for others' feelings.

3   I always offend people speaking frankly.

Others-distorted authenticity

1   I always hide my true thoughts for fear of others' disapproval.

2   I usually try to cater to others.

3   I do not dare tell others the truth due to caring for their feelings.[9]

What does a high score mean in terms of high balanced authenticity? Wang writes,

A typical individual with high-to-balanced authenticity, but low ego-centric and other-distorted authenticities would neither deny their own natural inclinations in return for the approval of others nor rigidly adhere to uncontrived inclinations at the expense of others.

Building authentic relationships

When I asked Dena about her strengths, she responded confidently: 'There isn't a situation that could come up [that] I wouldn't be able to deal with,' adding: 'I believe I can create relationships with anyone.'

Dena's team includes her family, her business coach associates and employees at work. Building high quality relationships, Dena has stayed psychologically fit, learning new habits, entering new routines and evolving over time while staying true to her authentic self and life principles. Or as she puts it, 'Get up and do it.'

In the face of adversity, Dena says she never felt a sense of crisis or that she was doing anything extraordinary. 'Life is like that, with its ups and downs, and you live every moment that you have,' she argues. It was only when she started to tell her colleagues at HP about her husband's accident that people reacted as if she were some kind of heroine. 'People were always complimenting me and heaping praise on me. They would tell me how strong I was,' Dena recalls. It was not the first time she had been in a really difficult situation and it was second nature to handle it as required, which turned out to be quite extraordinary.

Dena found to her surprise that she had become a role model to some of her colleagues at HP. For example, Tracey Reichard, who worked closely with Dena, says she learned two big life lessons from her. First, she learned that 'a person needs to play to their strengths', an approach to life that works particularly well in life-changing situations. Tracey says she first assesses a situation and then tries to make the best out of it. After witnessing Dena's path, she says, 'you are stronger than you think but you just must be courageous, set out on your path and go for it'.

Second, Tracey values 'taking your priorities into account – work and family'. Tracy saw how this helped Dena to change the course of her future. 'She looked at who she was and took the time to see what was the next step to take,' she says, remembering how Dena persuaded her bosses that she would be productive and have time for her family if she could change her schedule. Tracey was pleasantly surprised that the management team allowed her to do that. 'Dena was willing to try things that way, she was very creative, and she managed to make people see her point,' says Tracey.

How did Dena develop these high-quality relationships at work? When Dena was at HP, 'she never, ever complained. She just accepted things bravely,' Tracey explains. One of Dena's many social skills is making others feel comfortable. 'If there was ever tension at the office, Dena was the person who put people at ease. She asked a lot of questions and shared what was really going on. And when she was approached with a problem, she never made a person feel bad or dumb. She would attack the problem instead, trying to find a solution,' remembers Tracey.

I asked Dena what others could learn from her strength. Her wisdom reminded me of the 'three baskets of life' that I teach my students: yourself, your work and your family. 'You have to keep in mind the commitments that you make to people, to organizations and to yourself,' Dena told me, adding: 'You have to learn to balance those things, to make life worth it.'

Dena believes 'you can have it all, if you work for it.' After all, she could have chosen the security of a job at HP, but she gave all that up to be her own boss and be with her family. 'You have to find creative ways to do what you want,' she suggests. Dealing with adversity, she found out who she could really be, increasing her self-confidence to the point where she now feels there is no mountain she can't climb. She could overcome obstacles while taking advantage of every opportunity she found along the way. 'I kept fighting and held on for the family,' she says proudly. She was the little seed that stood its ground to become a proud oak tree. Giving up would have been divorce, but 'you don't give up when things are important'.

She encourages those around her to follow her approach to life. 'My goal is to make the world a better place by being honest, hardworking and delivering excellence.' She regularly volunteers to help youth organizations such as the Boy Scouts, the United States Pony Club and the Fellowship of Christian Athletes. To keep in shape, she likes to do yoga, biking and horse riding.

Dena is also aware that over the years she has been able to draw on the strength and wisdom of others. Her boss and mentor at HP gave her some words of advice that have stayed with her: 'As you make decisions each day, ask yourself this question: how will this decision affect my life when I am 100 years old?' For Dena, success in life means 'No regrets, be proud of the life you have lived, the way you lived it. What really matters in the end is the image you have of your life and yourself. When I'm 100 years old, I want to be able to look back at my life and be proud of what I have accomplished personally, and for others. That's what drives me every day.' Dena is also an example of how women can find ways to overcome the invisible barriers to full participation in the workplace.

Growing with self-confidence

The critical thing about authentic leaders is that they are not static. What sets them apart is that once they figure out their strengths, they want to grow, seeking new opportunities and building strong relations with others. Yet, growing with self-confidence may be easier for men than women.

A Hewlett-Packard internal report shows that men apply for a job when they meet just 60 per cent of the requirements, but women only apply when they are confident they can meet 100 per cent of them. Critical feedback from peers is intended to fix this issue, but surprisingly, as we saw in our feedback study, the so-called gender 'confidence gap' may become wider.

How can women turn self-confidence into a competitive advantage for personal growth? To address this question, with my colleagues at ESMT and INSEAD, we conducted a study in a large multinational software development company.[10] A total of 297 computer engineers completed an online survey to evaluate their positive relationships with others. Then, a wide range of stakeholders, including supervisors, peers and internal clients, evaluated the engineers' self-confidence, performance and influence in the organization.

The results were predictable. Successful performance makes both men and women appear self-confident in the eyes of their supervisors. But, the interesting question is: did they get the same credit for their self-confident appearance? Men and women are not equally rewarded for their self-confidence. There is one more social requirement for women to fully realize the benefits of their self-confidence – caring. The implication of these results is that if women are to succeed in a biased world, it is not enough to simply encourage them to be more competent and perform better. Women must go out of their way to care about others, which I think may be a positive thing, as I explain in my *Harvard Business Review* article.[11]

Positive relationships with others

Carol Ryff points out the importance of warm and trusting relations with others for our subjective well-being. She says, 'Self-actualizers are described as having strong feelings of empathy and affection for all human beings and as being capable of greater love, deeper friendship, and more complete identification with others.'

Wang's study on relational authenticity examines the correlations with positive relations with others. There are two interesting results of this study. The first is that there is a strong positive correlation between balanced authenticity and positive relations with others. The second interesting thing is that, of course, as people show ego-centric authenticity, the relations with others are less positive. But the same negative correlation is found between other-distorted authenticity and relations with others. This means that seeking the approval of others at the expense of one's inner tendencies does not give you the expected return of better relationships.

You can take a moment to evaluate your relations with others indicating the extent to which you agree or disagree that these statements apply to you, using a scale from 1, 'Strongly disagree', to 6, 'Strongly agree'.

1   Most people see me as loving and affectionate.

2   I enjoy personal and mutual conversations with family members or friends.

3   It is important to me to be a good listener when close friends talk to me about their problems.

4   I feel like I get a lot out of my friendships.

5   People would describe me as a giving person, willing to share my time with others.

6   I know that I can trust my friends, and they know they can trust me.

7   My friends and I sympathize with each other's problems.

What does it mean to score high in terms of positive relationships? A high-scorer 'has warm satisfying, trusting relationships with others; is concerned about the welfare of others; capable of strong empathy, affection, and intimacy; understands [the] give and take of human relationships'. In contrast, a low scorer 'has few close, trusting relationships with others; finds it difficult to be warm, open, and concerned about others; is isolated and frustrated in interpersonal relationships; not willing to make compromises to sustain important ties with others'.

10 ways to stay authentic and build trusting relationships

1   *Play to your strengths.* Be aware of your competences: this is the first step in the learning process. For instance, Dena's sister Sandy believes her work in real estate has enhanced many of her best qualities: 'sticking to something, not giving up; her ability to adapt and change; and her ability to be more flexible. She is never afraid to try things, of making new things work.' Tracey, a colleague at HP, learned from Dena that 'a person needs to play to their strengths', an approach to life that works particularly well in life-changing situations.

2   *Maintain an optimistic outlook.* Turn bad news into opportunities. Take a proactive attitude to stay emotionally fit, positive and energetic. Fall back into your well-established natural strengths. Dena relied on her 'rancher's daughter' philosophy of self-improvement through learning. After the accident, she had to learn how to become someone who can get a job.

3   *Keep the level of pressure at a motivational range.* Moderate pressure is critical to maintain focus and emotional stability in the face of challenges. Authentic leaders have an internal motivation that keeps them going; they never give up. This is exactly how Dena is described by her sister: 'No matter what the situation is, she's always that way, never gives up.'

4   *Visualize your best possible self.* Identify your strengths to imagine how they can help you achieve your authentic best possible self. This increases your optimism and your expectations for the future. Dena had always been interested in property, and her skills in organizing, long-term planning and strategizing could be put to a good use, this time on her own terms.

5   *Be open to honest and constructive feedback.* Critical feedback encourages reflection, making your self-image more realistic. Welcome valid and well-reasoned comments that involve positive and negative aspects. Make sure you avoid the hubris effect. Overconfidence kills learning – incorporate new information into your self-concept, avoiding rationalization and inflation of your self-image.

6   *Give authentic praise.* Don't underestimate the power of offering authentic support when sharing positive experiences with others. Dena shows this authentic support to her husband Ivan. His art is more than just a career, says Dena: 'After all the perils that he has overcome, I think that his art symbolizes his optimism and his passion for life.' Believe in the norm of reciprocity because people feel a moral obligation to treat you the same way you treat them.

7   *Develop balanced authenticity.* Empathize with others and respond to them by turning passion into compassion. For example, Dena was described as strong, fearless and easy to work with by her boss and colleagues. These positive relationships with others at work made her so successful that she doubled her salary in just two years. She was also

granted the flexibility she needed on the spot. To her colleagues, this was a stand-out moment, reflecting the trust her boss had in her.

8   *Show self-confidence in your abilities.* Self-confident people show conviction in their ability to make decisions, organize and execute action plans. They show an inner motivation. Dena enjoyed learning new things and remembers the feeling of personal satisfaction when she accomplished something after a hard day's work. She keeps in mind her commitments to people and organizations but also to herself. Dealing with adversity increased her self-confidence.

9   *Grow with self-confidence and get credit for your competence.* Invest in both competence and warmth. Being gregarious, easy going, social and helpful to others will help you to reap the benefits of your competence. Be alert to social cues shifting ways of handling things to adapt effectively to new situational demands. Dena was determined to create the flexibility she would need to allow her to enjoy her personal life and believed that starting her own business in real estate was the perfect way to do so.

10   *Invest in building authentic relationships.* Positive social networks that confirm your identity increase mutual respect and cooperation. For example, Dena develops trusting relationships with her diverse group of clients. These testimonies give faith to her authentic and genuine leadership and her caring, empathetic, extremely motivated, honest and positive attitude towards her work.

Compassion and intimacy has taken Oprah Winfrey a long way to become one of the most influential people in America. Winfrey's life philosophy of 'doing the best at this moment puts you in the best place for the next moment' is also followed by Dena Schlutz, who faces adversity with confidence 'moment by moment'.

6

Resilience and Vulnerability: Be in Control of Your Own Destiny

It is important to be comfortable being authentic . . . I probably didn't learn that until later in my career.

KEVIN JOHNSON

Kevin Johnson took over as CEO of Starbucks on 3 April 2016 after three years as COO. He believes being authentic allows people to do their best work. For Johnson, a clarifying moment in figuring out the importance of authenticity came when he was diagnosed with melanoma several years ago. 'That sort of prompts you to step back and say, "what's really important in life?", he told *Business Insider*.[1] Even more importantly, Johnson believes that being authentic means you must show vulnerability. He says:

I think everyone on the planet shares in the same set of human experiences. We've all experienced joy and sorrow, we've experienced the struggle of trying to achieve something and the challenges of overcoming obstacles. And, I think sometimes as you get older in life and more experienced, you're more comfortable acknowledging in an authentic way some of the vulnerabilities.

Vulnerability is a difficult but powerful way to develop authentic relationships. Some people fear it will result in a loss of power because it reveals our weaknesses. However, it can benefit leaders, allowing them to develop trust with their employees and other stakeholders.

Angel Ruiz: from Cuba to CEO of Ericsson North America (United States)

Likewise, Angel Ruiz displayed his vulnerability to his colleagues and subordinates by sharing with them the many challenges he faced in life. In the late 1960s, a 12-year-old Angel arrived in the United States from Cuba unable to speak a word of English, beginning a narrative of courage. His early experiences developed in him an extraordinary mental strength and resilience that prepared him for other monumental challenges later in his life. Nearly three decades later, he fought a lengthy and brutal battle with cancer. During the last months of chemotherapy, he was promoted to CEO of Swedish-based Ericsson in North America. He accepted the new position on the spot. His mission was to steer Ericsson's operations through the telecom bust of 2001.

Angel has tasted triumph. He has survived and succeeded. But I have the feeling that what he really enjoys is the process of finding a new challenge to overcome. He lives perpetually in survival mode. A combination of vulnerability and mental strength makes him authentic in his leadership and life. He is a fighter and his new battle ground is now Ericsson Latin America.

Angel accomplished something extraordinary, and the story of how he did it is a marvellous illustration of the second of the elements of authenticity: making learning a habit. He discovered that by setting small but critical new behaviours in how he approached business and life challenges, he could overcome many obstacles. Angel succeeded because he learned how to be resilient, share his vulnerability and stay authentic to himself.

A tale of courage and survival

Ruiz's story was featured in *Dallas Magazine* in January 2016. His proud son, a former student of mine, sent me the link. I was fascinated when I read the piece. A year later, Angel was in Barcelona to attend the World Mobile Congress, so we set up a meeting on 2 March 2017 and then a second one the following day.

Angel had just turned sixty. He talked to me in Spanish and immediately we felt the connection. He has a genuine interest in academic life. Before we started the interview, he asked a few quick questions about my research and teaching. After only ten minutes, it felt like we had known each other for a long time.

'In an industry like telecommunications, everything is constantly changing,' Angel said. 'Even the leaders of big corporations change jobs frequently. For example, just two months ago, Hans Vestberg, the president and CEO of Ericsson left the company.'

He had worked for Angel from 2001 to 2002 when Vestberg was chief financial officer of the company's North American operations. Amid the hustle and bustle of the World Mobile Congress, the pace of change appears to be even more rapid. Angel talks slowly, as though trying to compensate for the speed of change, taking his time to reflect, as well as citing specific examples to illustrate his points.

Experiential exercise: what are your strengths?

What makes some people like Angel thrive while others fall behind in the face of adversity? Angel developed his authenticity and leadership by turning bad news into opportunities with a positive outlook, showing exceptional resilience.

Martin Seligman[2] of the University of Pennsylvania is considered the father of positive psychology – the scientific study of how strengths enable individuals and communities to thrive. In his *Harvard Business Review* article, 'Building

Resilience', Seligman studies a critical problem: 'Failure is one of life's most common traumas, yet people's responses to it vary widely. Some bounce back after a brief period of malaise; others descend into depression and a paralyzing fear of the future.' The key difference is how people play on their strengths.

What are your strengths? Seligman presents a survey of twenty-four positive character traits such as curiosity, integrity and persistence that can make us strong in the face of adversity. Take a moment to rank the following sample of ten statements from 1, 'Very much unlike me', to 5, 'Very much like me', to identify some of the areas where you shine:[3]

- I find the world a very interesting place.

- I always identify the reasons for my actions.

- I never quit a task before it is done.

- Being able to come up with new and different ideas is one of my strong points.

- I have taken frequent stands in the face of strong opposition.

- I am always willing to take risks to establish a relationship.

- I always admit when I am wrong.

- In a group, I try to make sure everyone feels included.

- I always look on the bright side.

- I want to fully participate in life, not just view it from the sidelines.

Once you have identified your key strengths, you can write your own 'strengths in the face of challenges' story—a situation in which you successfully use your strengths to solve a problem or help someone.

Looking to the future, you can also write about how your strengths can help you grow into your best self. This exercise, called 'Best Possible Self' (BPS), has been shown to boost people's optimism and increase their expectations about the future:

Your best possible self means imagining yourself in a future in which everything has turned out as well as possible. You have worked hard and you have managed to realize your life goals. You can envision it as satisfying all your life dreams and development of all your best possible potentials. Think of and write down your goals, skills, and desires you would like to achieve in the far future for one domain in your life (personal, relational, or professional).

A group of researchers at Maastricht University[4] conducted a longitudinal study to understand the effects of visualizing your Best Possible Selves (BPS). In one experiment, they compare the experimental group that practices the BPS exercise for five minutes a day over two weeks with a control group that comes up with a daily activity.

Think of your schedule of the past 24h and go over it calmly. Think of the activities, meetings, etc. and go more deeply into the conversations, discussions, thoughts, or mood you may have had.

PHOTO 6.1 *Angel Ruiz, CEO of Ericsson North America (USA).*

The experimental group reported a significantly larger improvement in their optimism compared to the main group. This may seem obvious, but it isn't. We tend to think of our daily activities much more often than we think about our future best self.

From Cuba to the United States: building resilience

Angel's forward-thinking mentality is a great example of resilience in dealing with adversity. He was born into a lower-middle-income family in Cuba in 1956. His first years of life under Castro were anything but easy. His father, Angel Arturo Ruiz, worked as a warehouse supervisor for ITT, but he lost his job when he filed paperwork in 1963 for himself and his family to relocate to the United States. He then had to make a living doing construction work and cutting sugar cane. His family could apply for an exit permit because his mother's sister had emigrated to the United States in the 1950s. It took the Ruiz family five years to get the necessary permission to leave the country.

Before leaving in 1968, Angel spent the night sleeping on the floor of Havana Airport with his parents and younger brother, Carlos, waiting for thirty-six hours for one of the two daily flights to the United States. Once the family landed in Miami, he says he and his brother ran to the vending machine to get a ham sandwich, a Coke and a pack of chewing gum. They eventually settled in Baltimore where they lived with Angel's aunt. 'When we arrived in the United States, nobody in the family spoke a word of English,' Angel recalls. 'And I started seventh grade without speaking the language.'

His father could not find a job in telecommunications and so he worked as a supervisor at a spice company. His mother, Brunilda, took a temporary job in a factory that made synthetic flowers. But Brunilda was determined to make the best life for herself and her family. She wanted to start her own beauty salon, although it meant passing a dermatology exam in English. She prepared for the test by memorizing answers even though she did not understand them.

Brunilda passed the exam and for over twenty years was the breadwinner of the family, running her successful business in Orlando, Florida.

Angel has learned two important lessons from his parents. His mother's determination and discipline was an invaluable role model when facing adversity; from his father, he inherited an orientation towards achieving results. 'Say what you will do and do what you said you would do, because if you don't, you will lose credibility with that person,' remembers Angel. These values have been important in his executive career. Discipline and results-orientation have been the two cornerstones of his leadership.

The family's economic situation had not improved by the time Angel started college. His parents could not afford the tuition fees of a large university and so he attended a community college while he worked in the same company as his father to pay for his education. Five years later, he got a grant to help pay for his electrical engineering studies.

First jobs: learning to lead

In 1978, Angel started his first job in telecoms as an engineering trainee in the electrical department at Bethlehem Steel. One year later, he came back to Florida to work at Computer Science Corp. As a hardware engineer, he worked on a project for the NASA space shuttle at the Kennedy Space Center.

But the real beginning of his telecoms career was at C&P of Maryland, one of the original companies of the Bell system. There, he faced his first leadership challenge. The 24-year-old found himself supervising a unionized work crew of sixteen men much older than him: some were in their fifties and sixties and with a lot more experience in the company.

What did he learn from this early managerial experience? Many of my own MBA students face a similar challenge today. They fear being young leaders having to lead more experienced workers. Similarly, Angel found it difficult to earn their respect. Back then, 'when you came to work at any company of the

Bell system with a B.S. you were assigned a supervisor role whether you had any supervising experience or not', Angel recalls. The unionized environment made it more difficult for him.

The productivity and motivation of the work group was low and Angel found it challenging to report these poor results to his own boss. 'I couldn't pick up a tool, or they'd file a grievance', Angel recalls. Several times, a small group of employees broke into his office to see the performance reports he had written. He also dealt with a three-week strike and crossed a picket line. Angel takes this as a learning experience of how respect does not come automatically from your position, as well as the importance of exercising influence without authority.

It was this experience that precipitated Angel's decision to enrol in a Master's degree in Management. He was accepted to a Master's in Administrative Science in the night programme at Johns Hopkins University, which he completed while working at C&P. When he graduated in 1983, it was time to put his degree to use, so he moved back to Orlando to work as a senior project manager at United Telephone of Florida. He had recently married his wife, Miriam, and the couple was happy to be close to their families. Only six months later, Ruiz's ambition and performance earned him a job offer as a product manager from a small digital communication company in Plano, Texas. Now with a two-year-old daughter, Desiree, he had his wife moved to Texas where their second child was born in 1989, a son named Arius. Angel believed he could get a better job and a better life with hard work and focus on what is known as the internal locus of control.

Are you an internal or external locus of control person?

We all differ in our belief of how much control we have over our lives. In the late 1960s, the psychologist Julian Rotter conducted a series of experiments on how human beings acquire new skills and knowledge.[5] Some of us believe that rewards are contingent on our own behaviour or attributes: an internal locus of control. In contrast, others feel that rewards are controlled by forces outside of themselves and may occur independently of their action: an external locus of control.

Consider the short version of Rotter's original measure of internal versus external locus of control and indicate the statement that best describes how you feel.

1   ...

    a. Many of the unhappy things in people's lives are partly due to bad luck.

    b. People's misfortunes result from the mistakes they make.

2   ...

    a. One of the major reasons why we have wars is because people don't take enough interest in politics.

    b. There will always be wars, no matter how hard people try to prevent them.

3   ...

    a. In the long run, people get the respect they deserve in this world.

    b. Unfortunately, an individual's worth often passes unrecognized no matter how hard he tries.

4   ...

    a. The idea that teachers are unfair to students is nonsense.

    b. Most students don't realize the extent to which their grades are influenced by accidental events.

5   ...

    a. Without the right breaks, one cannot be an effective leader.

    b. Capable people who fail to become leaders have not taken advantage of their opportunities.

6 ...

    a. No matter how hard you try, some people just don't like you.

    b. People who cannot get others to like them don't understand how to get along with others.

7 ...

    a. I have often found that what is going to happen will happen.

    b. Trusting to fate has never turned out as well for me as making a decision to take a definite course of action.

8 ...

    a. In the case of the well-prepared student, there is rarely, if ever, such a thing as an unfair test.

    b. Many times, exam questions tend to be so unrelated to course work that studying is really useless.

9 ...

    a. Becoming a success is a matter of hard work; luck has little or nothing to do with it.

    b. Getting a good job depends mainly on being in the right place at the right time.

10 ...

    a. An average citizen can have an influence on government decisions.

    b. This world is run by the few people in power, and there is not much the little guy can do about it.

11 ...

    a. When I make plans, I am almost certain that I can make them work.

    b. It is not always wise to plan too far ahead because many things turn out to be a matter of luck anyway.

12 ...

    a. In my case, getting what I want has little or nothing to do with luck.

    b. Many times, we might just as well decide what to do by flipping a coin.

13 ...

    a. What happens to me is my own doing.

    b. Sometimes I feel that I don't have enough control over the direction my life is taking.[6]

Subsequent research has revealed several positive consequences for people with self-control. For example, children who believe that their actions make a difference have higher self-esteem and build more resilience. Students able to control their moods make better academic progress. And adults with an internal locus of control are more likely to change jobs and improve their physical and mental health. More recently, however, one study led by Christy Zhou of Duke University reveals the possible dark side of self-control – the burden of responsibility.[7] In a series of experiments, it is demonstrated that people with high levels of self-control report a greater burden from the reliance of co-workers and romantic partners who develop higher expectations of them. This burden of responsibility from others can lead individuals with high levels of self-control like Angel to feel less satisfied with their interpersonal relationships.

Ericsson North America: leading without authority

Angel became impatient with his current position, believing he could deliver better results. As a typical internal locus of control personality, he had the feeling he could do more and more in less and less time. Searching for better opportunities, Angel joined Ericsson in 1990; first as a senior product manager. Then he moved into project management for the next six years, learning the important lessons of leading without authority. To put it in his own words,

'Project management is the epitome of having all the responsibility with very little authority, because in a project no one really reports to you. You have to motivate your team to perform when you are really not their manager.'

So how did you motivate your employees? I asked Angel. 'Communication is paramount,' he replied. 'Motivation comes from knowing what we are trying to accomplish as a company. This is a collective effort.' Angel likes using metaphors. He compares leading the mobile industry to American football's Super Bowl. 'We are in the middle of a fierce competition and you have to have the best players in every season.' He believes that the type of knowledge that is needed is changing so rapidly that if a company does not continuously look for and hire the best talent, it is at a clear competitive disadvantage.

During this period, one of his mentors taught him 'to inspect what you expect'. This might sound like micro-management, but Angel takes it as a planning strategy to be better prepared for potential trouble. He expects the best, but is well prepared for the worse. In a competitive environment like the mobile telephone industry, this level of alertness and ability to act quickly helps him to actively search for talent and resources to achieve the best results. 'I lead toward achieving results: actions speak louder than words.'

He also believes that people are inherently good workers, and you need to create the context for them to succeed. 'You cannot just expect them to get results without the guidance of a leader,' he says, adding: 'Just like an orchestra conductor, the leader is not the best player, but the one who knows who, what and how each musician needs to play to create a beautiful melody.' As in an orchestra, many hardware and software tasks are highly sophisticated. The job cannot be completed unless the leader creates the context and monitors progress. As a hands-on leader, Angel believes that confidence in employees must be accompanied by discipline and guidance.

As a believer in a results-oriented approach, he has no problem with distance working. For many years under his leadership, people have worked from home. 'The problem was that many employees overworked,' Angel says.

Angel's achievements did not go unnoticed by management, and he soon rose through the ranks at Ericsson. In 1995, he was promoted to Director of Business Operations and the family relocated to Columbus, Georgia. Three years later, Angel moved up the ladder again, this time relocating to Atlanta. In 2001, Angel was offered the position of Executive Vice President of Ericsson North America.

The trust of results-oriented leaders facilitates distance working

Why did Angel do so well? When I met him, he expressed a strong belief in achieving results. Consistent with his internal locus of control, Angel is a good example of a results-oriented leader who put technology to work for the well-being of employees. Technology is no longer a barrier for distance work, but leaders' attitudes may be.

Distance working is, obviously, a radical departure from a physical presence in the traditional workplace. For example, telecommuting means giving employees' greater autonomy. This means that employees are not rewarded on the number of hours in the workplace, but rather on their results.

A few years ago, I conducted a study with my research team to understand what we called 'results-oriented leadership'. We examined the leadership style of 122 CEOs in Spanish firms in 2002.[8] CEOs completed a survey that asked them, 'Does your company offer telecommuting for a certain number of hours a week?' There were also questions about their results-oriented leadership style. For example, 'I make clear what my subordinates can expect from positive results.' In addition, we collected information on the firm's tenure, size and degree of internationalization.

The expected results of this study show that smaller and international-oriented companies are more likely to offer distance working because they are more open to new practices and technology. The most important thing that we found was that younger and international companies are more likely to offer telecommuting to their employees if they are led by a CEO with a high orientation towards results. This is a very well-known principle in organizational psychology – leaders act as catalysts of transformational change.

The lesson is clear: leaders who believe that employees are not internally motivated and will not work as hard unless they are closely supervised may resist using distance learning technology and lose their best talent. Authentic leaders communicate an internal locus of control and sense of personal agency to others. The digital transformation requires trust in employees, giving them control.

Beating cancer: the courage of vulnerability

Angel says he differentiates himself from leaders who look for solutions outside the company when they face a major problem. To mobilize people in such situations, some leaders hire a consultant or create a task force to avoid friction and conflict. But Angel believes that this approach can backfire because the leader is seen as not being personally involved and that this can create a lot of scepticism and push-back. As a result, he or she may waste time on side issues rather than addressing the fundamental problems. To stay authentic in leadership and life, says Angel, 'you should face problems head on'. And that's what he did when he had to face his biggest challenge.

In November 2000, he was a healthy 44-year-old with an athletic figure. He had worked out with heavy weights all his life. But – and here Angel kindly advices me that the details of the illness are unpleasant – he began to notice blood in his stools.

When he first went to the hospital, the doctor performed a procedure called a sigmoidoscopy which searches for problems like cancer in a more limited part of the colon than a colonoscopy. This is the procedure insurance companies allow as a pre-screening because it is about three times cheaper. The results found nothing wrong and Angel was misdiagnosed with haemorrhoids. The sigmoidoscopy did not detect his cancer, which was deep into the colon. Angel's doctor told him go back home and enjoy Thanksgiving.

The symptoms continued. It was Christmas, and Angel went home to Florida to visit his parents. It was during this family gathering that his mother disclosed to him the family history of cancer. Seven of her nine siblings had died of cancer, along with her mother. Like many people of her generation, she was brought up to avoid disclosing health problems. 'Being from Cuba, the culture dictates that we are very proud and no one speaks about this kind of disease in the family,' Angel explains.

After the Christmas reunion, Angel immediately went back to his doctor. He explained the newly found family history of cancer so that the insurance company could approve the colonoscopy. Ruiz's doctor had to exaggerate the health issue to get the insurance company's approval. The result of the colonoscopy detected a tumour located four centimetres above where the previous procedure had stopped. The cancer was at stage three, meaning it had spread into Ruiz's lymph nodes. The statistics show that the chances of survival are about 20 per cent, but the tumour was not large and it had not broken through the wall of his colon. 'This was the first thing that saved my life,' Angel recalls.

When the doctor told Angel he had cancer, his mind went to a 'dark place' but he soon reacted with his customary results-oriented approach. 'What do I do?' he asked himself. This was his toughest battle and he was a tough fighter. He went through all the stages of psychological trauma. First, denial, then, when he accepted the illness, he became depressed for a short while. Then, he got angry, asking himself 'Why me? I am in good shape. I have worked out all my life. Is it fair?' Until finally, 'I became obsessed with how to beat it.' An internal-health locus of control has been linked to improved physical and mental health in people with cancer.[9]

Angel's doctor advised him to have surgery right away to remove it and to find an oncologist prepared to treat him with aggressive chemotherapy. Angel and his wife Miriam did not have time to search for the best doctor, and so he took the first doctor who was available: he was lucky. The following day he had surgery. A foot-long section of his colon was removed, along with twenty-five lymph nodes, fifteen of which were cancerous.

Two weeks later, he started to look for an oncologist. Following his doctor's advice, he located a specialist called Dr Franco who was from Nicaragua and lived in Atlanta. Angel tried to get an appointment but the doctor's assistant told him the doctor was too busy to see him. Then, Angel called back later to the doctor's office in person and this time he spoke to the receptionist in Spanish, telling her he was a relative of Franco's visiting from Nicaragua. When Dr Franco came to the phone. Angel spoke to him in Spanish, explained the situation and apologized for the lie. The doctor agreed to see him.

When Angel went to see him, Franco recommended that Angel try a potent anti-cancer drug called LPT 11. This experimental treatment was part of a clinical trial. But it was very hard to join because patients had to be chosen randomly from a computer. 'Of course, the computer did not pick me,' Angel says.

Angel went for help to Linda Armstrong, who was working for him at Ericsson. Linda was Lance Armstrong's mother. The cyclist had been through cancer several years before. Linda put Angel in contact with Lance's doctor, who would administer the same drugs that Dr Franco was using in his clinical treatment. But the doctor was based in Portland, Oregon, which is 2,600 miles from Atlanta. The distance would have made it almost impossible for Angel to get the treatment. Anxiously, Angel went back and persuaded Dr Franco, who finally agreed to put him on the clinical trial.

The trial consisted of a three-drug chemotherapy cocktail. One of the drugs produced such severe dehydration that it would kill some of the women and children involved. Angel needed twenty-four treatments. He went on Friday morning for two hours during which roughly a half-gallon of the poisonous fluid was pumped into his body. Franco's recommendation was clear in Ruiz's mind – 'The greater your ability to take the drugs, the greater your chances of living.'

For the first two weeks Angel could go home alone after his treatment. By the third week, he felt so weak he needed to be driven. After that, he would take two weeks off between treatments. When he went back home on Fridays, his wife Miriam would cook a Cuban soup with vegetables. Then she would take the children, 12-year-old Desiree and Arius, aged nine, to the park to let Angel deal with the pain. 'She was very supportive,' Angel says, 'but this was a personal battle.' In the end, it took him nine months to receive the full twenty-four treatments. But he did it.

During this time, he stayed very focused and in control of the illness, reading a lot to help him understand what was happening to him. Angel believes that feeling in control helps recovery. He also worked out as much as possible even though his body was very weak from the chemotherapy. He wanted to burn as many calories as possible to help his metabolism burn cells faster. He thought if he did that the chemotherapy would kill any new cancer cells. Of course, he knew that it is hard to accelerate the metabolism to match cell growth, but he had the feeling of being in control. He used many such mind games to motivate himself to work out for two hours a day and stay focused.

I asked him how he found the mental and physical strength during this difficult time. 'Different people do different things. I kept working because it kept my mind occupied. I went to work some days and others I worked from home.' He still travelled on aeroplanes; he even went to Sweden. Cancer becomes a 'psychological war', he recalled; 'the point is to find something that helps you stay focused'. 'Once you are diagnosed with cancer, you never feel psychologically safe,' Angel asserts. There was a period when each time he had a check-up he would almost have a nervous breakdown, certain the doctors would find something. 'Each scan was psychological torture,' he recalls. But he now no longer needs treatment. If you are in remission for seven years, there is a very good chance that the cancer will not come back, he explains.

Angel's family also helped him in his recovery. 'The family had to be patient with him,' his wife Miriam recalled. 'But it also affected us in a positive way, because he tried harder to do more things with us. In his mind, this was his opportunity to do more with his wife and kids.' In August 2001, the family took a trip to Spain, visiting Madrid, Seville and Toledo. 'He wanted to make sure that he spent time with those who he cared about the most,' Miriam said.

CEO of Ericsson North America: taking on new challenges

Still with three more months of chemotherapy ahead of him to treat the colon cancer that was diagnosed as 'incurable', Angel was offered the post of CEO of North America. To my surprise, Angel recounted how 'They called me and I accepted on the spot; it was a great honour and a great job.' He did not ask for an offer or the terms; he just accepted it. In February 2001, Angel was appointed CEO of Ericsson North America.

The challenge he faced was considerable, but again he succeeded. He recalled that before he was at the helm, nobody had lasted for more than two years in the post. Angel was required to significantly reduce his unit's workforce within the first two years. He did it following a transparent criterion of performance and competence. When he took over at the company, it had about 10,000 employees in the United States and Canada. His business unit (focus on customers) had about 3,600 people. By the middle of 2003, the company's workforce had been trimmed to 3,500 employees in the United States and Canada and his unit was slimmed down to 1,164 people.

During his fifteen-year tenure as a CEO in a rapidly declining market, the operating margin improved by 3 per cent in the first year, and then between 9 per cent and 20 per cent over the rest of the period. He witnessed how out of the ten competitors that once shared a market with Ericsson, some have shrunk and others are merging. For example, Nokia acquired Alcatel-Lucent in 2016. 'Working in a telecom, you are constantly under high pressure and every day you have to fight to get the talent you need.' But, he has managed his business, which is now one of the survivors.

Angel attributes this remarkable result in part to emphasis on communication. He wants to make sure that everyone understands the strategy of the company. They need to know 'what they are getting into'. Twice a year, he holds a town hall meeting with what he calls 'the extended management team' which includes the top 160 people in the company who work for him. The purpose is keep a close relationship with them so they can inspire their subordinates.

Every year in September, the annual strategy is hammered out. Once the strategy is defined, he prepares webcasts for employees and managers to explain it. He believes that each employee – even in the lower ranks – must understand the company strategy. Only half-jokingly, he says, 'If I ask you what the company strategy is, you'd better know.' Using his love of metaphor, he says the strategy of the company is like a music score: 'If you find the right employees, it is like creating music.'

Angel's policy is to interview everyone who is going to report directly to him, which is about fifteen people. In addition, he interviews everyone who is going to work for these fifteen people. The purpose is to look for someone who fits with the company, with the industry and with the team. He honestly believes that Ericsson North America is not for everyone – 'only if you like to win'.

Leading by example in the digital era

Communication is surely part of the reason why Angel has been so successful. But his success is also based on being a role model. Leaders set an example of what is expected in the company. For instance, adopting telecommuting can be influenced by top leaders. Why, we ask, do some organizations adopt alternative work arrangements? What kind of role do top leaders play, if any? The answer has always been that firm characteristics such as size and industry determine the adoption of new practices. But, I also believe that authentic leaders, who behave in accordance with their values, serve as role models.

With my research team, I examined how senior leaders' authenticity influences the use of technology to facilitate the work–life balance.[10] The findings showed that firms are more likely to offer telecommuting to their employees when senior managers 'walk the talk' and serve as role models for the work–life balance.

In 2005, with the support of the European Union, several Spanish regional governments conducted a survey to evaluate the extent to which companies allowed employees to work from home. A total of 2,388 firms were randomly chosen and participated in a telephone survey, stratified by industry and firm size. Participating companies ranged from organizations with fewer than five employees to those with more than 200 employees and belonged to a wide array of industries including manufacturing (27.1 per cent), construction (12.9 per cent), retail and hospitality (31.3 per cent), finance (6.7 per cent) and health and education (22.7 per cent).

Who answered the survey? Executives working at decision-making levels: CEOs (68.2 per cent), general managers (20.2 per cent), owners (9.6 per cent) and others (2 per cent). They were asked to what extent (1) 'key decision makers were convinced of the value to employees of supporting family-friendly HR practices', (2) 'key decision makers displayed good role-modeling behaviours on how to balance work and family life and thus provided an example to other people in the organization', and (3) 'key decision makers felt a personal commitment to implementing family-friendly practices designed to meet employee needs'. This 3-item scale captures leaders' authentic regard for work-life issues.

The fascinating thing about authentic role modelling is how pervasive it is. A company's provision of distance working is more powerful when its top leaders believe in the importance of a work–family balance and enact it as a personal commitment. More importantly, we found that leaders' authenticity augments the positive influence of global high-knowledge firms. As shown in

FIGURE 6.1 *Provision of teleworking in global knowledge-based firms by leaders' authenticity.*

Figure 6.1, authentic leaders drive the adoption of telecommuting in global and knowledge-based firms where distant working is instrumentally valued.

What this means is that the authenticity of top leaders plays a critical role in the adoption of technology-aided human resource practices. The adoption and use of these novel practices is not driven solely by utilitarian logic; it also requires the authentic conviction of senior managers.

Authentic and charismatic communication

Angel Ruiz believes that what separates authentic and non-authentic leaders are their convictions, strength and the perseverance to carry on. His conviction and strength is clearly communicated to others with passion. He is a great communicator, using similes and metaphors to get his message over. Waking up in the morning with passion is what keeps Angel moving in an industry where success is the reward of a few. 'The survival rate is low, given the global competition and the entrance of new players in the market,' he says. Passion is the cornerstone of his life. He recalls Steve Job's message that if you get up in the morning and do not see a sparkle in your eyes when you look in the bathroom mirror, it is time to change.

'As your competitors realize you are getting better, they adjust. Like in any major-league sport, when a team wins the championship, the next year the rest of the teams get the extra motivation to beat the champion because they are playing with the best,' he says, adding: 'As a result, the better you become at something, the harder the competition will work to challenge you. In short, it's tough at the top. The question becomes how you do get better, renew the company and still stay true to your core values.'

So, I put it to Angel, what is the final purpose and the mission of the company? 'I am fortunate that I am working on something important. Let's just imagine our lives twenty years ago, and think what we do with our phones today. For me, it is a luxury to sit on a plane and be able to work, for example.'

To illustrate Ericsson's mission, Angel told me about his experience in a small village in Kenya. The head of a community of fifty people explained the impact of having just one phone. It has changed the economic and social situation of the village, which depends on perishable products that have to be taken 10 kilometres every day and were exposed to the uncertainty of the weather conditions. If it rained they did not have the proper means to protect their goods and they would be ruined. Now, they were able to call ahead to find out what the weather was like and how many buyers were in the market that day so that they could plan and be better prepared. This story goes to the core of Ericsson mission: the networked society. Everyone is connected to improve people's lives.

Examples of authenticity in the networked society

As you can imagine, stories of authenticity in the networked society are a source of inspiration. Consider the following examples from the above study on the work–life balance. I analysed in-depth interviews with ten human resource managers to better understand the importance of leaders' authenticity in the adoption of technology-based working. Three themes were recurrent in the interviews: open communication, results orientation, and role modelling.

Open communication

Several HR managers emphasize the importance of managers' attention and responsiveness to work–life issues via an intranet company survey. For example, 'top management is involved in the decision making and adoption of work–life balance policies. This initiative originated with the first climate survey which indicated the need for a plan on flexible work arrangements.'

Results orientation

The HR manager of a large company reports that 'the company trusts employees' responsibility and results-oriented management'. This results-oriented culture facilitates the adoption of teleworking.

Role modelling

One manager notes that 'the general director lives in Paris and he teleworks fulltime. He only comes to Spain one week per month. The two maxims of the company are trust and responsibility. Under these premises, the general director assumes that each employee is independent to manage his/her work. The employees, on the other hand, respond with complete commitment [to the company].'

Showing vulnerability

Angel faced many challenges – from his humble upbringing in Cuba to his revival of Ericsson in North America – that have shaped his leadership and his life. Through it all, Angel shared his vulnerability and resilience, serving as an example for others. Brené Brown in her landmark book *Daring Greatly*[11] says,

'We must go into the arena, whatever it may be – a new relationship, an important meeting, our creative process, or a difficult family conversation – with courage and the willingness to engage . . . We must dare to show up and let ourselves be seen. This is vulnerability.'

Angel has talked about his personal battle with cancer many times. 'If I can help anybody who is going through a similar situation to get through it faster, better or more easily, it is worth it,' he says. In remission since November 2001, he felt very fortunate to be talking to me. Colleagues at work have come to him for advice. He talks about it, coaches them and tries to help. Some have made it and others have not. He thinks that the difference sometimes is the attitude. 'Some people do not take the disease head on and instead ignore it,' Angel says. His fight with cancer reflects his personality. He likes to be in control.

When I asked Angel how he would like to be remembered, he brought up his father's lesson in life – 'I did what I said I was going to do.' Even though he acknowledged that some people might find him hard to work with because of his intensity and obsession, he sets guidelines to achieve great things together. He would like to be remembered as someone who got results and treated people fairly. Angel believes that people want to be associated with winners who do the right things.

'Best people, great focus, flawless execution – from good to great. If you get these three things, you can get the company to a great place,' Angel insists. He believes that if you put your mind to it with the right people working on a task in a focused way, you can accomplish almost anything.

But for Angel, what really differentiates the leader who has accomplished so much year after year in a sustainable way and another who has not, is the strength of his or her life story. The single most important factor is resilience. Authentic leaders can accurately read the environment and adjust their behaviour. This ability to adapt all the time will eventually make an authentic leader great because he or she is able to perform in a range of situations. The difference between great leaders and mediocre leaders is the ability to figure out what needs to be done in a particular situation and set new habits to execute and achieve the collective goals. Great leaders get things done regardless of the odds and the challenges they face, says Angel. It is not enough to have a good heart with positive emotions: to stay true to your authentic self in leadership and life you need to generate positive habits consistently.

Typically, Angel is looking ahead and is concerned with the development of the next generation of leaders. He believes that leaders-to-be need to understand that crafting their unique authentic leadership style is part of the challenge. 'Because the environment is constantly changing they need to try to succeed not by copying other successful leaders. Their role is to figure out by themselves what needs to be done to succeed,' Angel concludes.

Ericsson is a huge company, employing 120,000 people in 180 countries. But the big problem is that the market cap was about $35 billion two years ago and it is now down to $17 billion. 'It is a very challenging situation,' Angel explains. In August 2016, Angel picked a new battlefield – Latin America – and is now focused on helping Ericsson's Latin American division, which had a negative 12 per cent operating profit last in 2016. He knows how to win tough battles by staying true (almost to the point of obsession) to his authentic, disciplined and fair self. He is focused on getting Latin America 'back into the black'.

10 ways to stay authentic through resilience and vulnerability

1 *Have control over your life.* Remember that authenticity comes from the Greek word 'authentes' – being the agent of your own destiny. Engage in self-controlling behaviour by monitoring the focus, time and progress in accomplishing your goals. Leaders who emphasize an internal locus of control increase hope and work satisfaction. Even during his fight with cancer, Angel stayed very focused and in control of the illness. He believed that exercising and reading helped him

understand what was happening. This feeling of being in control helped his recovery.

2   *Build resilience and mental strength.* Do not fall into the trap of overgeneralizing after adversity. What is interesting about Angel's story is that his early experiences developed in him an extraordinary mental strength and resilience that prepared him for other huge challenges later in his life. His mother's self-determination to make the best for herself and her family was an important role model for him.

3   *Visualize your best possible self.* Identify your strengths to imagine how they can help you achieve your authentic best self. Thinking of your authentic best possible self increases your optimism and your expectations for the future. Angel played on his strengths of discipline, a hands-on approach and persistence to successfully overcome the many challenges he had to face, with a forward-looking mentality.

4   *Express vulnerability.* When leaders express their vulnerabilities, they more fully engage with their followers. Your employees look up to you for inspiration and guidance. Practice self-disclosure by sharing similarities to make salient common identities that raise a positive affect with others. Angel has talked about his personal battle with cancer many times. When you share how to overcome obstacles, others will see you as trustworthy, reliable and influential. Through revealing vulnerability, employees more readily identify with their leaders.

5   *Construct a story with heroic elements.* Share your stories of your self-sacrifice. Successful leaders find strength in their life story. Angel kept a positive outlook in conveying his own story. Playing on your strengths is self-affirming but experimenting with your weaknesses is a tale of courage. In 2016, I completed my first triathlon, and the most important lesson I learned was that vulnerability can strengthen empathy.

6 *Create a results-oriented culture.* When you give your employees greater freedom to organize themselves, they cannot be rewarded based on their physical presence in the workplace. Instead, you must be willing to reward them based on their results and performance. As a leader, you need to practise tough empathy – tough on results and easy on people. Angel actively searches for talent to achieve the best results, providing employees with autonomy and guidance, like a football coach or an orchestra conductor.

7 *Develop strategic-systemic thinking.* Because events are interconnected, your short-term goals should serve your long-term aspirations. For Angel, the strategy of the company is like a music score: 'If you find the right employees, it is like creating music.' To achieve this, communication is crucial. Everyone needs to understand the strategy.

8 *Break the brick wall.* In a competitive environment, agility is decisive. You need to break old habits and learn quickly. It is important to be alert and learn from your mistakes. Angel learned that gaining the respect of subordinates does not come automatically. Instead, leaders must earn the trust of their followers through positive relationships.

9 *Practice behavioural flexibility.* Have a broad range of responses and adjust your strategies to different circumstances while preserving your integrity and trustworthiness. Authentic leaders can accurately sense the environment and enact their authenticity while adjusting their behaviour. Angel follows his father's advice – 'say what you will do and do what you said you would do'. This way you will gain credibility in your leadership.

10 *Look to future generations.* Thinking of the next generation provides a purpose greater than yourself. Angel is concerned with the development of the next generation of leaders. He believes that the

most pressing challenge leaders-to-be have is to figure out for themselves what needs to be done and how to be true to themselves.

Comfortable with being authentic, Kevin Johnson looks outside Starbucks to find talent and inspiration. Like Angel Ruiz, he emphasizes 'blending that talent the right way and creating the environment for this group to work as a team based on trust, transparency and teamwork'.

Conclusion to Part 2

Resolving the growth-authenticity paradox in the possible self

Authentic leaders show consistency between their true self and behavioural choices. However, as we have seen in the examples of Rakesh Aggarwal, Dena Schlutz and Angel Ruiz, authenticity does not mean behaving in the same way. Instead, it involves the balancing and resolution of the growth–authenticity paradox.

Contemporary academic scholars agree on a broad definition of authenticity. For example, Michael Kernis of the University of Georgia and Bryan Goldman of Clayton University argue that authenticity is more than just 'knowing yourself and acting accordingly'. Authentic people are open to new experiences, strive to have fulfilling interpersonal relationships and take a non-defensive stance towards evaluative information. Herminia Ibarra of London Business School writes about the 'Authenticity Paradox',[1] pointing out how 'a simplistic understanding of what it means can hinder your growth'.

The protagonists in this second part of the book clearly experienced growth by reaching their best authentic self after adversity: Rakesh left India to rescue a mothballed milk factory in Longwarry, Australia, overcoming unforeseeable challenges, from the global financial crisis to a fire at the factory; Dena Schlutz moved from stay-at-home mom to a successful entrepreneur after her young husband suffered a tragic accident; and Angel Ruiz, a natural survivor, left Cuba with his parents for a new life in the United States, survived colon cancer and turned around a battered Ericsson.

How do they grow and still stay true to their authentic selves? All three flourished after adversity, building resilience with a combination of optimism, positive relationships and mental toughness. In this process of growth, they became more self-aware of their strengths and limitations, passionate about what is important, open to the contributions of others and sensitive to leaving a legacy. Although leaders may experience incremental growth, it is when facing crucible challenges that personal and professional growth is more noticeable. Let's look at how they manage growth and authenticity, making learning a habit in order to strive for their possible selves.

Rakesh Aggarwal developed his authenticity and leadership role out of struggle, resolving the dilemma of mixed emotions. In each situation, leaders have a choice to enact and express certain behaviours. For example, a leader may authentically experience conflicting emotions such as fear and hope in the face of organizational adversity. Enacting one's true self in such situations calls for leaders to decide how they might express this complex authenticity. This mixed reaction of anxiety and confidence was what Rakesh experienced after the fire in the factory. The lesson here is that without self-knowledge he would probably have been unaware of just how confident he really is and how much he wants to communicate this to others in order to find the best solution. Managing this tension, Rakesh enacted his true 'situated' self and developed stronger relationships with all stakeholders, staying optimistic about the future.

Developing authentic relationships at work and at home, Dena Schlutz relied on her mental toughness as a rancher's daughter to keep a positive outlook after her husband's accident. Dena exercised 'balanced authenticity' in relationships to emphasize the reconciliation of her own inclination and the desires of others. Authenticity does not mean giving our own desires priority over the wishes of others. Instead, a healthy balance between the self and others' focus is the key to authenticity in relationships. But as in the case of Rakesh Aggarwal, Dena also faced the dilemma of fear and excitement when deciding to leave her executive job at HP to start her own business. She decided to enact her balanced authenticity to stay true to her own interest in being proud of her work while at the same time considering the desires and needs of her family. As a result, she grew into her best self in business and the family.

Comfortable with being authentic, Angel Ruiz has undergone transformational learning. Deeply self-referent aspects of himself serve as anchors to learn new habits and grow, expanding his behavioural repertoire. The key to his authenticity has been to develop a wider range of behavioural strategies to choose from and enact, depending on the situation. We can become chameleons and still be authentic, as long as our behavioural repertoire represents the essence of our true self. For example, Angel developed a leadership style based on moral values and an internal locus of control that gave him extraordinary mental strength when facing organizational challenges such as downsizing. It was this mental strength that was critical when winning his battle with cancer, keeping him focused and optimistic. In the end, expressing his vulnerabilities through these many challenges made him a stronger authentic leader in the eyes of others.

Authenticity is a work in progress. Other leaders show us that being and staying authentic is a dynamic process that takes time. Oprah Winfrey wishes she'd done it a lot earlier; Amancio Ortega urges us to go outside our limits to continue growing; and Kevin Johnson is sorry he did not learn the importance of authenticity earlier in his career. We can develop our authenticity when we grow into our best possible selves.

PART THREE

HARMONY IN AGENCY AND COMMUNION: BE TRUE TO YOURSELF AND OTHERS BY BUILDING AUTHENTIC CONTEXTS

The danger in limiting authenticity to the dictum of 'be yourself' or 'grow into yourself' is narcissism. Which is why I add a moral dimension, so that authenticity is only reflected when both one's own self and that of others are recognized and respected. This is the third element of authenticity – harmony – which I discuss in this part of the book.

The authenticity equation

It is important to put the three elements of authenticity – heart, habit and harmony – in perspective. I describe their interrelationships in what I call the Authenticity Equation. It suggests that the first two elements of authenticity – heart and habit – add up to increase a person's authenticity. However, the last element – harmony – has a multiplicative effect to predict authenticity. This means that if the harmony element equals zero, the resulting authenticity will also be close to zero; even when the person scores well in the other two factors. The challenge to authenticity is then to realize one's inner desires in harmony with others.

$$\textbf{Authenticity} = \frac{\text{Heart Factor} + \text{Habit of Learning}}{2} \times \text{Harmony}$$

The final characteristic that is important for authenticity is to be true to others beyond the here and now. Authentic leaders find harmony in agency and communion, achieving the balance of being true to one's self and to others over the long term. For example, many of the leaders I have interviewed are concerned about how they are going to be remembered twenty years from now or whether their companies will be successful in fifty years.

In the following pages, I will introduce the Schwörer family from Germany, who are proud and passionate about leading the PERI construction company and bequeathing a legacy that improves people's lives, and whose commitment to the more than 7,000 PERI employees worldwide teaches us leadership lessons on how to stay true to business and employees.

Next is the fascinating story of Vista Alegre, much more than just a tableware company founded in Portugal in 1824, told through Francisco Rebelo, a millennial who combines the achievements of the past and the dreams of future generations.

And finally, Ana Botín will remind us that leading Santander, one of the largest banks in the world with more than 190,000 employees, can be as simple, personal and fair as striving to help people and businesses prosper.

In the process, I hope you will learn lessons on how to lead by example, building authentic structures with and for people; how to foster a community that allows your employees to express their authenticity within the constraints of an organization; and how to leave a legacy by leading with a social purpose. You will also find a few quizzes to diagnose the authenticity of your organization. Does your company make a point of letting employees know how much it truly cares about them? Are the things you value in life similar to the things your company values? And is your organization concerned for the welfare of others and the environment?

7

Exemplarity: The Epidemiology of Authentic Leadership

It is always good to work with people who make you feel insecure about yourself. That way, you will constantly keep pushing your limits.

SUNDAR PICHAI

Google CEO Sundar Pichai's meteoritic rise surprised many. He 'doesn't exactly seem part of the brash, big-ego club of Silicon Valley's top leaders', reported *Quartz India* in 2017. His low-profile leadership style earned him the reputation of a nice guy who could pull teams together and get work done. Who is Sundar Pichai? He grew up in a two-bedroom apartment in India, studied metallurgical engineering at the Indian Institute of Technology and then won a scholarship to Stanford where he earned his MS, then did his MBA at Wharton Business School.

His leadership mantra is 'Let others succeed'. In an interview during his visit to India featured in *Quartz*, he remarked:

I have an outstanding leadership team. It's learning to let go and really empowering people at all levels of the organization, and trusting them to doing the right thing.

As a leader, a lot of your job is to make those people successful. It's less about trying to be successful [yourself], and more about making sure you have good people and your work is to remove roadblocks for them so that they can be successful in what they do.

Sundar Pichai's collaborative leadership works well in the digital economy with knowledge workers. Can we translate this empowerment and authentic leadership to conservative industries like construction?

PERI Group: building social scaffolding and diffusing a collective identity (Germany)

Authenticity is in high demand. A generational shift has also reinforced the authentic personal nature of CEO power like Sundar Pichai's: millennials want to follow people they admire not only for their work, but also for their personal and moral stance; they want to see the social impact of their work and demand meaningful challenges and growth opportunities from their leaders.

In short, if you're a CEO looking for success with the new workforce, you'd better provide more than a pay cheque. Authentic leaders who create social scaffolding have lasting impact. To build authentic power, CEOs need to change the way they relate to employees. The usual focus is on short-term transactional relationships. However, to achieve lasting authentic transformation, CEOs need to develop meaningful and empowered relationships. They must go further and craft trusting networks that build social capital to create an authentic organization.

PERI is a great example of an authentic organization. One of the world's largest manufacturers of formwork and scaffolding, it takes its name from a Greek prefix meaning 'around'. Just as the suburbs stretch around a city, PERI provides the formwork used to pour concrete as well as the scaffolding of a building. Founded in 1969 by Artur Schwörer, PERI's headquarters are in

Weisserhorn, a small town near Ulm in southern Germany. Its main business is the design, manufacture, rent and sale of formwork and scaffolding modular systems. The solutions it offers to its clients are competitively priced, rapid and ensure maximum quality and safety. The company employs over 7,700 employees and generated revenues of €1.3 billion in 2016.

Artur Schwörer's desire to be independent from the shifts of the construction economy motivated him to grow the business in other countries. With German reunification, PERI first moved into East Germany in the 1990s. At that time, PERI decided to open new subsidiaries in Eastern Europe and other parts of the world. This made PERI the global market leader. This was a period of learning fast, overcoming difficulties and bouncing back to grow quickly.

Over the last ten years, PERI has grown from 35 subsidiaries to 64 worldwide groups operating in seven regions, in addition to 120 logistic centres. The reason for this extraordinary internationalization is PERI's innovation, which has made it a world leader in the development of new products in its sector: PERI has developed pioneering systems in Europe for vertical formwork on pillars and horizontal aluminium for laying concrete. PERI's projects demonstrate the complexity of the company's operation, its customer focus and its innovative vocation.

In June 2017, I talked to Alexander Schwörer, the current CEO of PERI, to try to understand the secrets behind the company's extraordinary growth and success. Educated in the United States in the 1990s, Alexander took over the US subsidiary in 1999 and founded a PERI subsidiary in Canada. In 2003, he returned to Weissenhorn as managing director of the PERI Group. He is proud and passionate about leading a company that leaves something behind and improves people's lives. 'We are proud to participate in projects like the expansion of the Panama Canal or the airport in Madrid,' he says. He enjoys his business because it allows him to transmit this passion to others.

PERI's expansion into the United States, for example, has exported an employee-first philosophy that resonates with a millennial workforce. Offering

PHOTO 7.1 *Alexander Schwörer, CEO of PERI (Germany).*

career development paths and being part of the most impressive construction projects, PERI USA is an attractive employer for straight-out-of-college engineers who are seeking progress in their careers.

PERI Spain

I first heard about PERI in 2005, when I wrote a case study about its pioneering human resource policies and its investment policy in employees' well-being in its Spanish operations. The kind of initiatives PERI has in place are unusual for the construction industry. At that time, its managing director had inculcated PERI's value-oriented management in the Spanish subsidiary. Located outside Madrid, the modern building decorated with artworks was surrounded by pieces of scaffolding in basic colours –yellow and red, ordered like so many objects of art.

As the daughter of a construction worker who saw her father working on unsafe scaffolding, I was fascinated with the values of PERI Spain. The mission of the company was to make the process of fitting formwork and scaffolding safer and the life of construction workers better. The company was making not only safer structures but also collective activities. It ran classes in gymnastics and English, organized sporting activities in football and tennis and put on social events for employees and their families, such as its Father Christmas party with presents for children aged three to ten. The company made it possible for its employees to include sporting activities within their work schedule. Employees had a variety of fitness schedules to choose from. Some work out between 7am and 9am, while others used the gym between 2pm and 5pm. The gym was also open on weekends.

Ten years later, I contacted the new managing director of PERI Spain, Jorge Morell, for an update. I wanted to find out not only about the evolution of the subsidiary in Spain but also about the origins of the PERI management philosophy and its future.

Jorge joined PERI Spain in 2012, attracted by the values of the company – 'Excellence and people are in the DNA of PERI' – and in 2015 he was promoted to Market Unit Director of Southern and Western Europe. He is deeply committed to the company. In his new role, he is the interface between PERI headquarters and its operations in Southern and Western Europe. As a result, he travels from Madrid to Munich fortnightly to craft and implement new corporate strategies.

In November 2015, Jorge gave a talk as part of my Master's programme, discussing the competitive advantage of the company, and specifically its health and safety policy. PERI's accident rate is much lower than the construction industry's average. The sector consists of many small firms that subcontract workers for larger construction companies. Unfortunately, some of these workers lack the training necessary to work on site, which leads to accidents. In contrast, PERI's workers are not allowed to go on site until they have been trained. PERI offers training courses in manual load handling, fire prevention and the use of forklift trucks. Workers who show a special interest in an area can enrol on an apprenticeship supervised by a foreman. Attention is also paid to safety measures: the latest generation of scaffolding incorporates protective handrails.

PERI Spain has been through some tough times in the recent past. A construction bubble that began in the 1980s in Spain burst in 1992. The managing director at that time had to cut employees' salaries to cope. He promised that when the company recovered, PERI would pay them back, with a bonus on top. And when the company emerged from the crisis, he kept his word.

Jorge and I met over lunch, and I asked how PERI Spain survived the recent global economic crisis. He believes that the emphasis on investing in employees' well-being through professional development and social projects helped during the tough economic times. There were mass layoffs in 2014, but the safety and excellence of the work were not compromised. Transparency, equity and communication were at the core of this painful process of downsizing. 'Safety indicators actually improved during crisis,' Jorge says. Safety procedures are integrated into the training of staff members. There is no supervisor inspecting every single step; instead, employees are responsible for their own safety and that of their team members. Employees' health and work–family initiatives remained unchanged during the crisis: for example, flexible working hours stayed in place. Staff continued to use the gym and sports facilities, although they had to do without gym monitors. This culture of safety, caring, empowerment and learning helped to overcome the difficult times. PERI Spain is now undergoing a revival.

Founding story: the origin of authentic principles

Who created PERI? *Artur Schwörer: A Portrait* describes the founder of PERI as 'An engineer, a great entrepreneur and an extraordinary person.' Born into a large rural family, he transitioned from a joiner's apprentice to a global market leader. His biographer reports that 2,500 people came to say goodbye on 21 April 2009 'to a man whose remarkable life and work touched and shaped their own'.

Schwörer came from a family already operating in the construction business. At the age of twenty-two he helped his older brother Hannes move into the prefabricated wooden housing business, which quickly became the star product in the successful family business. But he was uncomfortable with his brother's authoritarian leadership style and so the 35-year-old Schwörer decided to start his own company, PERI, from scratch. This break was a difficult decision and could have alienated his parents and siblings. But Schwörer did not fall out with his family. His youngest brother recalls his positive nature: 'He was always happy. It was Artur who would comfort his sisters when they had their hearts broken.'

His employees described him in his biography: 'He is charismatic. Maybe it is because he loves people. He looks at them without prejudice. Maybe it is because, despite his sparkling career and his material wealth, he is completely free of arrogance, and trusts others.' This unsung hero combined his charisma with a strong dose of humility. 'His modest demeanour may partly be because a serious illness in his youth left him deaf in his left ear. He suffers from this handicap during business meetings, but mostly acts like everything is fine.'

Illness as a young boy influenced his personality. Introverted and reflexive, the 17-year-old wrote these notes reproduced in his biography:

The serious illness that would affect me for the rest of my life started innocently enough. In the autumn of 1946, when I was thirteen years old, I was eating unripe apples from roadside trees. I developed a stomach ache. At first, it didn't seem that bad. I went to see the doctor, who diagnosed appendicitis. Since the French had seized the surgical clinic in Tübingen, I was taken to the eye clinic up the hill, where I was examined and driven to the women's hospital. Unfortunately, several patients on stretchers were already queued up in front of the surgery room. I had to wait. I had serious peritonitis. It took six weeks for me to recover from the peritonitis and diphtheria. Finally, I was allowed home.

And the suffering continued:

> After about four weeks – I was on my way back from the ambulance to my room – I passed out in the corridor. This time the diagnosis was meningitis. The head of the ENT department removed my entire left inner ear, injuring my facial nerve in the process. As a result, my face was heavily paralyzed. My sister Hedwig told me later that she wanted to cry when she saw me at the hospital with my crooked mouth; in her opinion, I had always been such a handsome boy.

Years later, Schwörer revealed how this early life experience with illness affected him. 'Only being able to hear on one side has seriously affected me throughout my life and significantly changed how I behave with people. After that I never felt comfortable in large crowds again. Later, at receptions and other company events, I would always feel uncomfortable about the fact that those standing on my left could never have a conversation with me.'

Schwörer recovered from the illness and continued at secondary school. However, coming from a modest family, he could not go to university. He began his apprenticeship as a carpenter after graduating from secondary school. Schwörer's father and elder brothers needed his services for the family business. After finishing his apprenticeship, he enrolled on an engineering course in Rosenheim, a decision that his father approved in the hope he would later join the family business in sales.

On the positive side, his university years enhanced his self-confidence. He earned a degree as a wood industry engineer. 'My previous education had been minimal, so I was extremely hungry for knowledge, not only about my major but also about other subjects. I spent a lot of time sitting on benches reading up on history and philosophy,' wrote Schwörer. His thirst for knowledge was a lifelong inspiration and passion to support young people educationally in their formative years.

Schwörer became an independent thinker and the rebel of a traditional Catholic family. He married a Protestant, Christl Baeuerle, which his mother disapproved of. But Schwörer was firm in his decisions. Christl was excited about everything he loved like music, design and sailing. He remembers their first date: 'I demonstrated what my new stereo could do, playing a movement from Beethoven's Ninth Symphony on it. That evening was the beginning of a fairy tale whose happy ending was the rest of my life.' In 1967, the couple married and soon became a business team.

At work, conflict with his older brothers increased and Schwörer finally made the big decision to leave the family business where he had worked since his early youth for twelve years. In his diary, Schwörer wrote a letter to his brother Hannes explaining the reasons for this difficult decision:

> You should finally recognize that I have worked and am still working for our company (I suppose I should say your company) with the same enthusiasm, intensity and passion as you. The notes I get from you almost daily show me that you cannot see this. To me, they are disrespectful in both content and tone. As long as you and Hermann feel you need to lord over me and keep telling me what I have done wrong, we cannot have a good relationship. As long as we cannot celebrate our success together, how can we be happy?

And so, Schwörer ended the professional relationship with his brothers and moved on to a new future. He began working as a consultant but soon realized he needed to 'make something'. His strength lies in product development. Given his financial constraints, he thought that building prefabricated housing would require more capital than manufacturing girders. So, he founded PERI to produce the first formwork girders in April 1969. Five decades on, the PERI girder is one of the company's most important products.

In the early days Schwörer took calculated risks and, like Rakesh Aggarwal, he never lived beyond his means. Negotiating with the banks for loans was an existential struggle. Christl Schwörer remembered those early difficulties in an inspirational talk she gave in December 2009: 'It is hard to believe that PERI actually made it through those first few months. We had the highest interest rates and the coldest winter in years, and our distributor was unable to sell our product.' But keeping in mind his vision for the company, Schwörer was persistent. With an optimistic personality, 'he was a forward-looking man, and the future was his for the taking', recalls a long-time PERI employee.

Schwörer's son, Alexander, remembers him as an independent thinker and an inspired designer able to provide innovative solutions to the demands of new architects. This way, he set the success path for PERI. 'My father could think of solutions that were simpler than those at that time,' he says. 'We were successful because we were different; we were always more expensive, but offered the best service.'

The *We are PERI* identity campaign: authenticity spreads through the social networks

PERI illustrates how authenticity can help spread values throughout an organization worldwide, creating an identity in the process. Artur Schwörer started an authenticity epidemic on a global scale. His son Alexander is currently overseeing an identity campaign to instil PERI values in all employees, which takes him to PERI plants around the world where employees follow the same philosophy, guidelines and principles. One of the most important initiatives to spread the authentic identity of PERI is called *We are PERI*, a short film about the company's values and culture using storytelling.

In addition to a film, management has developed a protocol with supporting materials such as PowerPoint presentations and teaching guidance to ensure managers deliver the message: We are PERI. Self-disclosing stories facilitate the 'diffusion' of authenticity through the social network. Alexander tells me that the goal of this identity campaign is to bring the company closer to employees to make them feel they can also show their authentic self.

In February 2017, the launch event of *We are PERI* was held at headquarters in Germany with more than 140 senior executives. 'How would you want to communicate these values to your people?' asked Alexander. To deal with the cultural diversity of PERI, he appeals to values such as proximity to customers, innovation, open-mindedness, family, quality, safety and passion.

Jorge Morel, director of PERI Spain, had just attended the workshop on *We are PERI* in Germany. We arranged a meeting in my office at IE Business School to watch the video. When he arrived around 7pm, immediately after landing, his enthusiasm was contagious. The video includes PERI employees talking proudly about the company and sharing their best moments. The combination of personal stories from across the globe in Asia, Europe and the United States with lively music, beautiful buildings and bright lights makes the film a moving experience. The only female managing director in Lebanon shows her passion for working at PERI and her strength as a boxer; one of the senior engineers at the head office combines his passion for PERI with playing the drums.

Charisma: the spark of an authenticity epidemic

Authentic leaders create a vision that can spread like a virus. A leader's moral values may not be automatically apparent to followers, so a founding story helps articulate the vision in specific moral and ethical values. The vision of the leader follows the rules of epidemics until it achieves a tipping point and becomes widely spread out within the social system. This is the idea behind Malcom Gladwell's masterpiece *The Tipping Point*.[1]

In the late 1980s, Jim Meindl, a social psychologist at SUNY Buffalo, proposed an innovative approach to charismatic leadership called the Social

Contagious Theory of Charisma that was critical in changing the views of many leadership experts. Conventional leadership theories focus on the attributes of the leader or the relationship between leader and followers. In a radical departure from this leader-centric perspective, Meindl shifts attention to the relationships between followers and how their ideas about the leader are transmitted throughout their social network.

Some leaders believe the key to success lies with their own personal qualities. But when forming impressions about their leaders, employees do not base their opinions solely on individual interaction, but are also influenced by the social information available to them. Why was PERI's identity campaign so successful? The critical thing about authentic leaders is that they are not passive sources of information. What sets them apart is that once they figure out their message, they want to actively transmit it like a virus throughout the social network.

Some years ago, I was honoured to have Jim Meindl as my PhD supervisor. As part of a research project on social contagion, we conducted a study to test part of his theory of contagion.[2] We examined the views of 55 employees about their leader, a senior police officer. The participants also provided information about their social interactions with one another – how often they talk and who they consider their friends. Using network analytic techniques, we found that employees' perceptions of charisma followed the patterns of their friendship ties. The police force in question had small and highly cohesive cliques whose members felt similarly about the charismatic appeal of the leader.

There was a kind of epidemic of leadership. That is, the charisma of the leader was in part predicated on people within the friendship network. Friends had similar views of the charismatic appeal of the leader. The most popular individuals, those occupying central positions in the social network, reflected the average view of the leader, whereas those on the periphery had more extreme views of the leader in the organization.

The implication of these results is that people's feelings about their leaders and their vision is in part emotional and socially embedded. They are influenced by their interaction with people in the surrounding network of social relationships. This is precisely why it is extremely important that leaders, in order to be effective, manage the social context to transmit the core authentic values of their organization.

Effective team leaders encourage their subordinates to communicate beyond their work groups. In an effort to understand the benefits of cross-boundary communication, my colleague Maria Kakarika and I analysed the external network of twenty-four work groups comprised of 234 employees of a global manufacturing company based in the United States.[3] The results showed that teams that had a greater number of informal ties with leaders of other groups were more effective because they brought essential resources to the team such as strategic information and political support. As illustrated in Figure 7.1, it is the instrumental ties that team members have with leaders of other groups that make the team more effective because they increase its social capital. Bridging across research groups, we presented the results of this research project in a symposium in Hawaii chaired by Andreas Richter of Cambridge University.

PERI authentic values

My next contact with PERI came via a conference call with Marc Kimmerle, who had joined PERI in 2009 and was now the head of the company's human resource department. Our conversation focused on the values and the culture of the company. Mark believes that the film *We are PERI* reflects the workforce's strong organizational identification.

'How do employees learn about the PERI identity and values?' I asked Marc. He explained the domino effect of initiatives like *We are PERI*: values that start with senior management, moving on to managing directors, supervisors and front-line workers. A taskforce called Culture Team has been created to come up with measures to keep the PERI identity sustainable. The values are shared with employees through an identity campaign

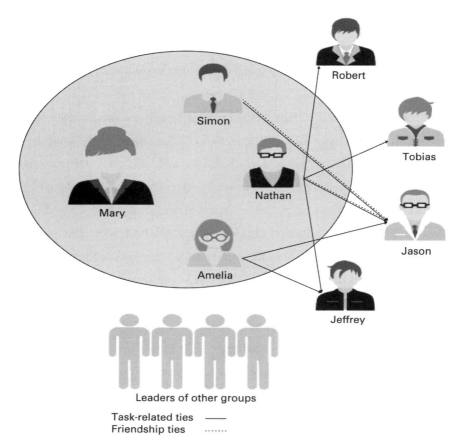

Task-related ties ——
Friendship ties ·······

FIGURE 7.1 *Effective leaders encourage task-related communication with leaders of other groups.*

conducted in phases and that starts with management in Germany. Top management invited the managing directors of subsidiaries to its headquarters. Together, they attended a workshop on what the core values mean across cultures, providing flyers and posters on the values and culture of PERI. Once managing directors understand and agree, the campaign moves on to employees. The homework of managing directors is to transmit the identity of PERI to their teams.

Managing directors of subsidiaries can choose a long or a short version of the PERI identity workshop. The longer, more detailed approach takes about four and a half hours, during which employees actively participate in activities to understand the company's values and its success factors. The shorter version takes about one and a half or two hours, during which there is an opportunity to present the values and success factors and briefly discuss them with employees. In both cases, at the end of the workshop there is a town hall type meeting, typically attended by hundreds of people, at which *We are PERI* is screened. Afterwards people socialize.

Storytelling is used to illustrate the company's values. Marc explained that the founding story is a key part of the identity campaign. At a recent company event, the wife of the founder made an inspirational speech about the success story of the company and her family. 'It was very emotional to see how the company moved from zero to a €1.3 billion-group in just one generation,' says Marc.

The people who appear in *We are PERI* are a diverse mixture of very well-known and experienced people with younger and older employees; people from different cultural backgrounds as well as female leaders. In the film, people are the real protagonists. Marc believes that what sets PERI apart from other companies is that its values are not commissioned by external parties. At PERI, people are the actors on the stage. The final message is 'PERI is not a German company; but rather an international company.'

The film begins with the origins of PERI's values, established by founder Artur Schwörer in 1969, who created the 'light build' concept: the idea that construction work does not have to be tough. Leadership can be exercised through positive relationships with the workforce. A strong believer in the power of 'pull' rather than 'push' to motivate people, Alexander Schwörer told me that his father had written the 'Leading Principle Booklet' explaining the importance and nature of these core values. Marc explains how Artur Schwörer wanted people who were customer-oriented and who showed respect for other employees. He looked for people who supported these core values to reduce the time he spent explaining how the construction business works.

Marc believes that Artur Schwörer was very strategic in defining these core values for the company from the beginning. 'He took the chance, together with his wife, Christl, to start a new company.' In doing so, it was very important for him to develop trusting and positive relationships with employees. This foundational value is described on the company website: 'Cooperation based on partnership and trust is a fundamental value in our company, which therefore also forms the basis of our customer relationships.'

These people-oriented values still exist today and are the core of *We are PERI*. Based on conversations between the family and key company players, the original values have been articulated in a mission statement, four key success factors and four core values. 'Although these values have been renewed and reshaped over the years, they are still at the basis of the company because employees align to them,' Marc explains. The four renewed values at PERI are:

1 Entrepreneurial – keeping an open mind, being gracious and outward oriented, and retaining curiosity about the business.

2 Reliable – working diligently and being fair.

3 Open-mindedness – being respectful and nurturing positive relationships with others.

4 Passionate – showing emotional commitment, dedication and a creative mindset.

Based on these renewed values, there are four pillars that sustain the company and are its key success factors:

1 Customer proximity – problem-solving, customer focused with a local presence in its international operations.

2 Innovation power – understanding what the customer wants and developing new products to meet those needs.

3 Family company – taking a long-term view, financial stability and independence.

4   Highest quality – having outstanding employees and efficient processes that result in the best products and services.

These values and success factors underpin the company's mission in making construction more efficient and safe, while providing the best service to customers.

> We support our customers in the ever-fiercer competition with the quality of our products and services. We measure our achievements against the success of our customers and their satisfaction.

Creating this management philosophy was hard work, says Marc. 'We discussed every word.' The management also came up with a visual metaphor: a house. 'The house is a metaphor that brings everything together,' he says. The basement symbolizes the values, the pillars are the success factors, and the roof represents the mission of the company. If you take a view from the top you can see the complete house. 'It is very remarkable,' Marc concludes. This value-based leadership is the framework used to craft the company's 2025 strategy.

'How do these values manifest themselves in everyday operations?' I asked Marc. The company is committed to safety, innovation and internationalization. Prioritizing safety has given the company a competitive advantage. It has a health and safety department responsible for ensuring that all safety procedures and regulations are in place and followed. PERI managers search for optimization in the workplace, receiving regular feedback at meetings if something happens to people on site or the workplace. There is a discussion and analysis of the situation to evaluate if something needs to change to make the surroundings safer. Also, there is continuous evaluation of ways to make the work easier and ergonomic.

There has also been a huge investment in innovation. The innovation management department employs more than thirty people dedicated to encouraging out-of-the box thinking. They hear suggestions from employees and customers in a bid to better understand what the market demands. Marc believes that this innovative thinking is a large part of what makes PERI a trendsetter in a conservative industry like construction.

Finally, internationalization has helped PERI in dealing with the global financial crisis. This is precisely what 'customer proximity' stands for, combined with a long-term perspective of the business. In 2014, CEO Alexander Schwörer revealed in a newspaper interview that '[a]lmost nine out of ten euros of revenue comes from foreign business'. For example, when the crisis hit Spain and Portugal harder than other regions, PERI focused on the more prosperous markets at that time, such as the Middle East, working on projects in Dubai and Qatar, while the Southern European market recovered.

Positive charisma builds unity within diversity

The charisma of the founder and his son not only helps spread PERI's authentic values but it also builds unity within the great diversity of people that make up PERI. 'Diversity is key to us,' says Alexander, who is proud of the international nature of the workforce and the fact that more leaders in the top management team come from outside Germany, like Canada, South Africa or Spain, working together in a collaborative fashion.

Diversity can be a double-edged sword, offering opportunities and challenges. How can diversity be a strategic advantage? With my research team, we evaluated the last twenty-two years of diversity research.[4] Our critical review revealed four explanations for the effects of diversity in organizational teams, summarized in Figure 7.2. On the positive side, there are two explanations for why diversity is a source of success in organizations. The first is the variety of knowledge in processing multiple viewpoints (information) and the second is the variety of external networks that bring resources and

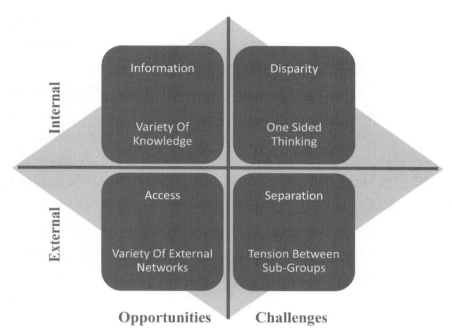

FIGURE 7.2 *Four explanations for the effects of diversity in teams.*

political support (access). Diversity can be a positive influence when differences in perspectives and contacts stimulate a more in-depth understanding of the issues at hand, along with more innovative solutions to problems and decisions.

On the negative side, a third alternative explanation of the effects of diversity relates to social identification and the loyalties of people with subgroups, rather than the principal group, which diminishes feelings of trust and cooperation and increases tension between subgroups (separation). Finally, the fourth possibility is that status differences create one-sided thinking that inhibit the free exchange of information (disparity).

How can leaders maximize the benefits of diversity? This is the question I discussed with Daan van Knippenberg, a top leadership researcher at Drexel University and co-editor of the *Academy of Management Annals*. By the end of our conversation, we agreed to study how leaders can 'manipulate' the cognitive activation (e.g. salience) of certain types of diversity influencing the positive or negative effects of diversity in the team.[5] Based on insights from artificial intelligence research, we proposed a technique to capture the salience of different social categorizations in teams such as gender or race.

What does it mean to manage diversity? We asked 239 employees working in 38 work teams at a large manufacturing company located in upstate New York and New Jersey to complete a survey. Participants indicated the level of charisma of their immediate leader and their perceptions of diversity in the team. In addition, we recorded the demographic composition of the team and computed what is called Blau's Index of Diversity.

The fascinating result was that positive charismatic leaders who go beyond their self-interest for the good of the group can inspire diversity blindness to some extent, avoiding negative biases and promoting an exchange of information in demographically diverse teams. What our study suggests, as illustrated in Figure 7.3, is that the positive charisma of leaders can make people diversity blind to demographic differences such as gender and race. See how the darker line flattens toward zero. This effect can be used to enhance work-related identities such as organizational identity.

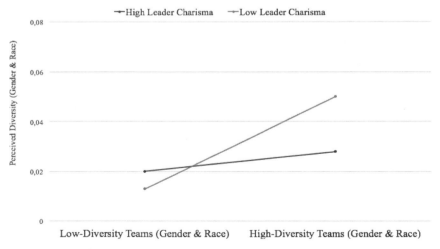

FIGURE 7.3 *Charismatic leaders make people diversity blind.*

How to design an authentic diverse organization

PERI'S support system is akin to a social scaffolding that creates and maintains an authentic organization. The 'Growing with PERI' section on the company website reflects its employee-centred philosophy:

> Our key to success: Development of potential and growth – created by the people in our company. Because behind top products and innovative solutions, there are committed people who work self-reliably and add their strengths to the team. Behind the staff members, there is a management board that knows that every individual in the company counts: their personalities, their capacities, their further development and thus their satisfaction.

I asked the human resource manager about hiring practices, training, communication and well-being initiatives. With a strong international presence, I wondered how PERI integrates its culture across subsidiaries. 'This is a huge challenge; and the selection of the managing director for the subsidiary is crucial for us,' Marc answered. PERI's management wants to make sure the managing director shares the core values of the company. Managing directors must have a strong background in the construction industry with executive experience of running a subsidiary. But the most important requirement is to be in line with the company's values.

In 2012, to further facilitate unity and coordination among subsidiaries, PERI created the position of regional director for each of the seven areas core to the business. For example, Jorge Morell oversees Southern and Western Europe. They serve as the interface between headquarters and the managing directors of the subsidiaries for each region. Beside leadership issues, these regional directors bring the state-of-the-art technical dimension to subsidiaries. With regular training courses for managing directors and strategic engineers in its headquarters, PERI attempts to standardize key technical procedures.

The training courses can last up to three weeks. In addition to the technical aspects, managing directors are inculcated with the PERI spirit and take it back to their teams.

'How does training help support PERI values among staff?' I asked. Marc explained how training is organized to support the values of the organization regarding technical issues, as well as providing cultural guidance to ensure the sustainability of the PERI culture. All PERI's staff can support his or her professional and personal development by participating in numerous internal seminars and workshops at the PERI Academy. They can also advance their training further by enrolling on external courses. The topics covered internally range from technical know-how and software to soft and language skills. These internal seminars include interdisciplinary participation by specialists from different departments and often result in new ideas. The continuous internationalization of the company also provides the chance to expand their intercultural skills by participating in foreign assignments. The human resource department, responsible for rolling out the key PERI values over all management levels, has one priority now – spreading the PERI identity campaign in every subsidiary.

PERI has no organizational climate survey, but employees can voice their opinions through the programme of continuous improvement. Bottom-up communication works through open channels to supervisors and managers. Marc believes that the survey methodology is not the best fit for a company like PERI because of its one-time nature. 'Important issues might not come out in an annual survey,' he says. Communication between staff members and management at PERI seems like a natural flow through daily feedback in the process of work. The management's door is always open and everybody has a chance to discuss issues.

Investment in employees' well-being is a top priority at PERI. 'Healthy employees equal healthy business' is no mere slogan at PERI. The company has created its own health management system to promote employees' long-term health based on three pillars – exercise, nutrition and relaxation. There is a fitness room – the PERIfit Room – in Weissenhorn and many subsidiaries, where sports such as spinning, boxing, back fitness or Zumba are available. In addition to individual activities, there are groups like the bike team sponsored by the company. 'The bike team does a tour from Germany to a European subsidiary once a year,' Marc says. There are also other teams, such as boating, football, badminton and tennis, that meet regularly. These activities are also complemented by talks and seminars on relaxation, stress management and nutrition. To promote healthy eating habits, the company has extended its catering service. 'We are opening a new dining room to offer healthy food at a reasonable price,' Marc explains.

'Work is important, but so is your private life,' reads the website. PERI's management acknowledges that the traditional family model is changing. As a result, the company supports its workforce through flexible working hours and other initiatives. For example, employees can work reduced hours after parental leave to better adjust work and family responsibilities. They can also take time off to care for a family member. As a family-owned company, PERI is committed to accommodating the needs of families.

Because of these human resource policies, PERI has low staff turnover rates. Marc says since joining the company in 2009 he has seen only one managing director out of sixty leave for career reasons.

Shared authentic leadership in action

When I asked Alexander about why he thinks PERI has succeeded, he returns to the bedrock provided by his father's personal philosophy, based on trust and goodwill in people: 'We do not micro-manage, we lead by example, we give our workforce independence and responsibility.'

He compares his leadership role with that of a football manager. 'You need the best people, people who do the job better than yourself,' he says. Using a similar sporting metaphor, like Angel Ruiz in the previous chapter, Alexander emphasizes that the best people are team players. Then, his role as a leader is to pick the best people and motivate them by giving them responsibility to try new things, make mistakes, learn and succeed; and then give them credit and recognition – 'let the world know about their success'. He likes to focus on the strengths of each employee more than correcting mistakes.

'Leadership means inspiring employees to give their best,' says Marc Kemmerle. This means delegating responsibility to his team members. 'They know if they have any issue they can come to me,' he says. A modest leader, he appreciates other people's strengths and contributions: 'I am not convinced that I can do better myself,' he says. Overseeing about thirty people in the human resources department, he assigns them challenging tasks and coaches them as they work through them, the idea being to make them responsible for what they are doing. 'My target would be to make myself unnecessary; this is what I am aiming for,' he says.

'I am happy to be part of this success story,' Marc concludes. The company has passed many milestones since 1969. Just five years later, PERI opened its first subsidiaries in Switzerland and France. In 1984, the first subsidiary outside Europe was established in the United States. Technological advancements in the early 1990s included a self-elevating system using a hydraulic drive without the need for a crane, as well as CAD software for design. The 25th anniversary was marked with thirteen branch offices in Germany, twenty-two subsidiaries around the world and a portfolio of more than 2,000 products.

In 1998, PERI was hired to help with the construction of the Petronas Towers in Kuala Lumpur, then the highest building in the world at 452 metres. The use of the PERI self-elevating system ensured smooth progress. In 2005, PERI expanded its production area by 80 per cent, investing approximately €80 million in the facilities at Weissenhorn. The company's continuity after its founder Artur Schwörer passed in 2009 has been guaranteed by his son

Alexander taking over as president. In 2011, PERI joined the construction project of the century, the extension of the Panama Canal linking the Atlantic and Pacific coasts. Reflecting its commitment to customer proximity, in 2012 PERI launched the online My PERI customer portal.

How to develop shared authentic leadership

Shared leadership occurs when influence is evenly distributed among all members of the group or organization. Leadership shifts from the unidirectional influence of a single person to reciprocal and mutual influence among members of a team in business, politics or sports. It can take multiple forms as members of the team assume specific leadership functions. For example, team members clarify what the team must do to achieve its purposes, taking shared responsibility for goal setting. When group members share resources and knowledge, they exert leadership and learn from one another. This collaborative approach improves performance over time, encouraging mutual confidence in the team's abilities, giving them pride in their team, and earning praise from each other for their efforts and achievements.

Drawing lessons from mountain-climbing teams, Andrew Hill of the *Financial Times*[6] writes about the value of not just following a single mind, but rather considering individual differences in teams. Using music as a metaphor, Richard Hackman, professor of psychology at Harvard University and my mentor during my Fulbright year, studied the benefits of shared leadership in the New York Orpheus orchestra.[7]

To what extent does your organization share authentic leadership?

Consider the following statements, adapted from the Authenticity Inventory by Michael Kernis and Brian Goldman, indicating how people in general feel, think and behave in organizations.[8] Evaluate the extent to which you feel most accurately characterizes the people in your organization using a scale 1, 'Strongly disagree', to 5, 'Strongly agree'.

People in my organization . . .

Unbiased processing

1   . . . feel comfortable considering their limitations and shortcomings.

2   . . . find it very easy to critically assess themselves.

3   . . . find it easy to embrace and feel good about the things they have accomplished.

4   . . . accept the validity of any compliments that they receive.

Behavioural consistency

1   . . . try to act in a manner that is consistent with their personally held values, even if others criticize or reject them for doing so.

2   . . . behave typically in ways that express their personal values, needs and desires.

3   . . . put on rarely, if ever, a 'false face' for others to see.

4   . . . are willing to endure negative consequences by expressing their true beliefs about things.

Relational authenticity

1   . . . make it a point to express to others how much they truly care for them.

2   . . . can accurately describe what kind of person close others are.

3   . . . want to understand the real 'me' rather than just the public persona or 'image' of others.

4   . . . place a good deal of importance on having open and honest relationships.

If we talk about authentic leadership in this way – shared among employees – it is possible to understand how some organizations can be rated as authentic. The first element is unbiased processing, something like shared humility, when people often accept their own positive and negative aspects. The second element is behavioural consistency, acting in accord with one's values, preferences and needs; rather than acting merely to please others. The final element is relational authenticity which presumes people in the organization value and achieve open and truthful relationships with others.

10 ways to stay authentic leading by example

1 *Build personal power, instead of positional power, around your authenticity.* Provide more than a salary by helping employees see the social impact and meaning of their work. For example, PERI offers career development paths and being part of the most impressive construction projects. This employee-first philosophy resonates with a millennial workforce who would appreciate, for example, the passion and legacy transmitted by Alexander Schwörer.

2 *Create authentic structures by and for people.* Employees are most affected by the everyday aspects of running a business: they are responsible and hence have the most at stake. Build a 'social scaffolding' that enhances the well-being of your employees. PERI is making not only safer structures but also a better life for its employees. It runs classes in gymnastics and English, organizes sporting activities, offers work schedule flexibility and puts on social events for employees and their families.

3 *Spend time getting to know others.* Proximity to your stakeholders – customers and employees – helps you to develop authentic relationships. For example, Artur Schwörer spent time getting to know the complexities of new buildings designed by a new wave of

architects. Providing unconventional solutions to new problems is still key to the success of the company. Similarly, trust-based relationships with the workforce keep PERI leaders in tune with the needs of employees, such as the work–life balance.

4　*Engage in socially responsible actions towards employees.* Providing flexible and safety-oriented HR policies demonstrates concern for employees' welfare. This emphasis on investing in employees' well-being through professional development increases employees' engagement and commitment to the company that can help during difficult economic times. The culture of caring, empowerment and learning helped to overcome the difficult times in 2012 at the Spanish subsidiary, where safety and excellence of work were not compromised.

5　*Stay hungry for knowledge.* Lifelong curiosity is contagious. Stay in tune with the people you interact with and listen to their social and developmental needs so that you can create a space where others can learn and grow. Artur Schwörer's 'thirst for knowledge' was a lifelong inspiration, as was his passion for supporting young people educationally in their formative years. Schwörer himself became an independent thinker and the rebel in a conservative industry.

6　*Be vision-driven.* Escape from operationally-driven strategies, because your company cannot survive on processes and procedures alone. You need to act altruistically and strategically. Adopt social agendas not only because they are economically beneficial to the firm but also because of their moral value, that is, because it is the right thing to do. Alexander Schwörer designed a strategic vision for the company where employees play a leading role.

7　*Create a context in which people are at the stage of catching the authenticity virus.* Do not limit your strategic role to defining the vision of the company. Rather, help people 'catch' the authenticity virus.

Encourage a dense social network through which your message can be easily and successfully diffused among all members of the organization. Alexander Schwörer invested time and energy in an identity campaign to help diffuse PERI values.

8 *Make diversity a competitive strategy.* A diverse workforce is a source of potential benefits, but it also brings challenges. Leaders who use their charisma to activate relevant differences as sources of knowledge and networks maximize the potential benefits of diversity, while minimizing the tension because of social and status identifications. The top management team at PERI turn a 'blind' eye to unravelling cultural differences in favour of a higher order organizational identity.

9 *Share leadership with your employees.* Do not over-rely on your expertise and authority. Instead, hire a diverse pool of talent and draw on their expertise to creatively solve problems and make decisions. As with the Orpheus Orchestra, let your employees 'take a solo' sometimes and give them credit and recognition.

10 *Lead by example to build an authenticity climate.* Actions speak louder than words. If you want to create a culture of authenticity, practice the three elements of shared authentic leadership: unbiased processing, behavioural consistency and relational authenticity. PERI is essentially a company built around the principles of authenticity. Top leaders at PERI want to be around people who can do the job better than themselves; they travel around the world to be close to their teams and put a great deal of importance on trusting relationships.

Sundra Pichai is quoted as saying that 'a person who is happy is not because everything is right in his life, he is happy because his attitude toward everything in his life is right'. Artur Schwörer founded PERI with the right attitude, making employees happy, and his values are now transmitted to his son Alexander Schwörer and future generations of executives.

8

Community: Creating Moments of True Authenticity

If the employees come first, then they are happy ... A motivated employee treats the customer well. The customer is happy so they keep coming back, which pleases the shareholders. It's not one of the enduring mysteries of all time, it is just the way it works.

HERB KELLEHER

As former CEO of Southwest Airlines, Herb Kelleher was named the best CEO in the United States by *Fortune* magazine. He is well known for creating a unique culture at Southwest where employees are encouraged to have fun while taking the job seriously. Creating a community among employees is core to their success. 'That's the most difficult thing for a competitor to imitate,' he says. 'They can buy all the physical things. The things you can't buy are dedication, devotion, loyalty – the feeling that you are participating in a crusade.'

And millennials want to 'align themselves with an authentic cause', reports the *Washington Times* recently.[1] 'To millennials, you don't have to be amazing. But you do have to be authentic.' Similarly, the *Huffington Post* says millennials 'are not moved by flashy ads, big promises, and "wow" factor. They want authentic messages, authentic brands and authentic interactions.'

Vista Alegre: the enactment and modelling of authentic leadership (Portugal)

Leadership is about followers as much as leaders. Leaders who have the power to renew themselves are in tune with the needs of their followers. People like leaders who genuinely care about them. When leaders are aware of the social and emotional needs of their employees and respond to them, they are viewed as authentic. Take the example of Vista Alegre, a company whose leaders built a community for its employees in an economically deprived village in Portugal.

Vista Alegre has a rich tradition and history. Following the turmoil after Brazil achieved its independence, Portugal enjoyed a period of prosperity in the 1820s. Taking advantage of this, and influenced by the liberal ideas of the time, Jose Ferreira Pinto Basto asked King Joao VI for a Royal License to build a porcelain-ware factory in the rural north of the country.

In 1824, Vista Alegre was founded: its headquarters and its first factory were some 250 kilometres up the coast from Lisbon, in Ílhavo. The plant produced high-end dinner and tea sets, as well as other tableware. The company quickly grew in reputation and began targeting the luxury market in Portugal and Europe, catering for top hotels and even the British Royal Family.

In 1832, Augusto Ferreira Pinto Basto, the founder's son, travelled to France to learn the secrets of porcelain clay, planting the seeds for the company's international expansion. In 1867, Vista Alegre won awards at the Paris Universal Exhibition. This was a period of rapid growth that included introducing new styles and decorative techniques.

At the turn of the twentieth century the company experienced an artistic revival by adopting styles like Art Deco and Functionalism, adapting to changing aesthetics. In 1964, Vista Alegre opened a museum to showcase the long and rich history of the company as a producer of exclusive pieces. Twenty years later, two landmarks put Vista Alegre in the art market: an exhibition at

PHOTO 8.1 *Francisco Rebelo, consultant at Deloitte London and member of the Pinto Basto family, founders of Vista Alegre (Portugal).*

the Metropolitan Museum of Art in New York and the opening of the Vista Alegre Art and Development Centre in Portugal. During this time, the company was under the leadership of the Pinto Basto family.

A millennial view of Vista Alegre

Francisco Rebelo is a member of the Pinto Basto family. The 25-year-old junior consultant at Deloitte in London aspires to join his family's former business in the future. When I met Francisco, he was a student of mine who had impressed me with an inspiring four-minute video on the history of Vista Alegre. I was convinced he would lead the company at some time in the future. In my class of 2014, he shared a moving story about the history of Vista Alegre:

> Portugal 1824: a powerful country with vast economic growth coming from its many colonies. Ambitious people with entrepreneurial spirit rising from

the many opportunities this exciting time provided. It is around this time that in the north of Portugal, Josep Ferreira Pinto Basto starts imagining a factory to produce the best quality of ceramic. After asking for permission from the King, he is able to set a royal national factory in Ílhavo. With this, Vista Alegre is born.

The original production process was extremely modern and efficient at the time. The factory employed almost 1,700 people and production was constant to meet the high demand for products. Vista Alegre quickly became a synonym of quality and prestige for many. Fast forward 100 years and one can see the process is still very much based on that attention to detail, making use of the great talent that the company has gathered.

To ensure quality in a very competitive environment, Vista Alegre starts all new products by researching and designing a cast which will be filled with the correct blend to deliver a robust product. The piece is then assembled by the sculpture team and taken to the oven. A process that takes several days. Finally, a painter provides the final touches to make this piece available for sale to the general public.

But Vista Alegre has grown to become much more than just a simple ceramic brand. Over the years, the company grew into a family by providing employees with great advantages. It built schools for their children to attend. It invested in sport clubs. It even created a theatre within the factory complex. The factory was located in a poor rural area of Portugal. The company was happy to give these people some help. Vista Alegre built houses for the employees with the biggest needs. A great loyalty developed towards this company.

A few years ago, the company faced great changes. While trying to stay financially afloat, the company invested in new marketing campaigns, new production methods and new employee policies. These changes have an impact on the future of the company and today the company is wondering what to do next.

In May 2001, Vista Alegre merged with the Atlantis Group to make use of potential economies of scale and increase its presence in the global market, creating the VAA (Vista Alegre Atlantis) Group.

In 2009, Vista Alegre Atlantis became part of the Visabeira Group. The family that had nurtured the business over two centuries had no option in the context of the global financial crisis but to hand over the company to a large and diversified investment group. The reasons for the crisis that made the family sell the company were both external and internal. The globalization of the market and the competition of countries such as China made prices fall significantly. Also, there were important cultural shifts in Portuguese society life which made Vista Alegre a seller of 'superfluous' luxury products. An example is how before, when a member of Portuguese middle and high class got married, they would get a set of dishes made specifically for the wedding, as the modern world evolved, this tradition was broken. Internally, there were some disastrous investment decisions that resulted in major losses such as investments in Brazil.

Change of management

Under new ownership, many things changed. In the past, the CEO of the company travelled from Lisbon to Ílhavo once a month to talk to the workforce. The company's leaders cared about the well-being of their employees and invested in them to create a community. Over the years, Vista Alegre had built housing for employees, a school, a theatre and even a sports centre. Over time, the children of older generations of employees joined the company, creating a loyal workforce.

In November 2014, Francisco Rebelo interviewed the workforce, along with past employees and family members, some of whom were no longer working for the company. Many employees complained that the new management only visited the factory when absolutely necessary. As a result, the close relationship between workers and managers had vanished and a breach between the workforce and management had developed.

One employee complained, 'Today, instead of a family working together, this is just a job. They only appreciate the numbers and do not value quality.' Another said, 'The management used to be concerned about us. We were the best in Portugal at that time and we took pride in the company. There was a different connection with the company.' Another observed:

> Before, the work was rewarding. The little that we have they are taking away. What pleasure does work give us? What kind of encouragement do I have? Nowadays they do not invest in us. When the family used to visit they also brought their children. We played football together; now, fewer people come and we don't know who they are.

Most employees felt they had lost ownership over their work. 'With the advance of technology, the company modernized its production processes, making it more efficient and competitive. The workers were given standardized automated tasks to follow, which were simpler and less error-prone. This was in contrast with the previous handmade approach, which gave workers more freedom and a sense of ownership of the work. Employees felt that their knowledge and experience were not being valued,' Francisco explained.

One of the highly skilled team that hand paints tableware recalled:

> I have worked here for almost forty years. My father worked here for fifty-three years and my mother for forty-seven years. My whole family was here. I quickly became the teacher for the new recruits. The director of the company [Francisco Rebelo's grandfather] came every month to ask how the learners were getting on. That showed they valued professional growth.

Under new management, some employees' benefits were eliminated to cut costs. For example, 'the provision of employee discounts to buy Vista Alegre products was stopped, which resulted in many workers not being able to afford these items' and 'long established company traditions such as the Christmas party ended, as did annual gifts', says Francisco. These cuts impacted negatively on the morale of long-time employees. One employee in the moulding area remembered, 'We had our heart and soul here.' Francisco explains how these rituals were a very important part of the identity and culture of the company. 'The family took care of the workers – helping them with accommodation, day-care, sporting activities, school, theatre and church, and also through community activities. These parties had become a tradition in the region,' he said.

When Visabeira took over Vista Alegre, its mandate was 'to tackle various financial issues, while ensuring that existing workers remained productive and loyal to the company'. The result was that the workforce felt disempowered. The human resources manager, who had been with the company for twenty-five years, told Francisco that 'the old management team felt it was not trusted by the new management'. The most notable changes were the replacement of the board of directors and the centralization of key departments such as finance and accounting, marketing, purchasing and human resources.

The new management soon understood it was not capitalizing on its biggest source of knowledge: the old managers and long-time employees. 'The investment group started to understand that the ceramic industry had very particular specifics and was committed to learning these details,' remembers Francisco. Getting in touch with the company's deep-rooted culture, Visabeira's executives managed to reincorporate some existing senior managers who resumed their previous roles on the board of directors. 'Some of the older managers were reluctant to join Vista Alegre again, others were pleased to help and share their expertise.' In the end, 'there was a sense of calm and stability after the return of the old managers; a more collaborative environment was created'.

Vista Alegre's Industrial Director, Teodorico Pais, recognizes the competitive advantage of Vista Alegre's culture: 'The secret of the brand lies in its old values and ancient culture. Lifestyles have changed but we still continue to produce with the same quality and spirit.' Turning tradition into a competitive advantage, 'Visabeira is committed to recovering buildings that tell the company's story,' Teodorico explains. Long-standing traditions and benefits to employees were recovered and remain in practice today, such as the festivities related to Nossa Senhora da Penha, the patron saint of the factory, along with a dinner for retired employees, and the Christmas gift to all employees.

Value congruence to foster authenticity

One way to understand how value congruence of the kind built up at Vista Alegre can foster enduring authenticity is through the theory called the Person–Organizational Fit, which belongs to Jennifer Chatman, a leading management scholar. Drawing on this Perceived Fit notion, Shainaz Firfiray of Warwick Business School conducted an experiment as part of her doctoral dissertation at IE Business School under my supervision.[2] The purpose of the experiment was to try to find out what job seekers value in a job.

The study consisted of a recruitment advertisement scenario in which job seekers (189 MBA students) revealed their attraction to the company as a future employer.[3] The students belong to two generational groups – millennials and Gen Xers – and were randomly assigned to one of the two experimental conditions: work–life benefits and health care benefits.

Work–life benefits: 'In addition to a competitive salary package, we also offer the following work–life benefits to allow our employees to meet business targets while taking their personal needs into account: (1) flexible hours, (2) telecommuting, (3) job sharing, (4) on-site dependent care, dependent care referrals and subsidies, and (5) extended parental leave.'

Health care benefits: 'In addition to a competitive salary package, we also offer the following health care and insurance benefits to our employees: (1) private medical and dental care, (2) illness pay and disability insurance, (3) life insurance, (4) personal accident insurance, and (5) travel insurance.'

Job seekers decided whether or not an organization fitted with their personal values on the basis of the employment benefits it offers. Participants were asked to evaluate their perceived fit between themselves and the potential company. As depicted in Figure 8.1, we found that job seekers perceive more 'value fit' with organizations that supplement pay with work–life benefits in their recruitment materials, in comparison with organizations that supplement pay with health care benefits or offer only a pay cheque. Moreover, millennial job seekers are more attracted to organizations that fit their own values than are Gen Xers.

The lesson of Value Fit Theory is not that authentic organizations should give up change. The point is simply that the things that motivate employees change over time. That is why the case of Vista Alegre is so interesting and potentially relevant to the authenticity problem: it shows us the dynamic nature of creating authentic organizations.

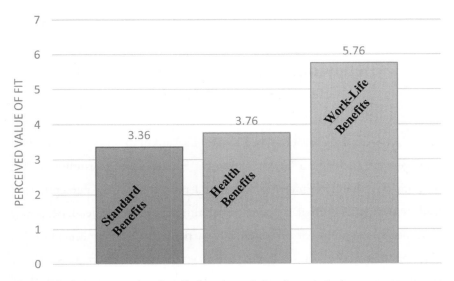

FIGURE 8.1 *Perceived value fit between themselves and the company across benefits.*

Companies that help address employees' true selves in the work and non-work spheres increase employees' perception of value fit with the organization, attract more job seekers and eventually recruit and retain the best candidates because employees can better express their authentic self. What if motivation, instead of following the transactional approach of leadership, follows the principles of authenticity?

Does your company promote value congruence with employees?

Think of the extent to which you agree or disagree with the following statements, indicating a 1 for 'Strongly disagree', to a 7 for 'Strongly agree'.[4]

1   The things that employees value in life are very similar to the things this company values.

2   Employees' personal values match this company's values and culture.

3   This company's values and culture provide a good fit with the things employees value in life.

Behavioural integrity: enactment of authentic leadership

There is a second theory, proposed by Donna Ladkin of Cranfield School of Management and Steven Taylor of Worcester Polytechnic Institute,[5] called Embodied Authentic Leadership, which underscores followers' perceptions of leaders' authenticity. Their key idea is that 'although authentic leadership may be rooted in the notion of a true self, it is particularly the embodiment of that true self that makes leaders appear authentic or not'. Followers use bodily signals such as facial expressions and body movements to draw conclusions about leaders' motives, values and beliefs, and then judge them as authentic or not. Ladkin and Taylor write:

> Leaders with a high level of embodiment who pay attention to their emotions and are tentative to the somatic clues of their bodies and, importantly, to the feedback they receive from the outside world have a better sense of their own identity and therefore fulfil the most important criterion of authentic leadership.

In one experiment, for example, a group of German leadership scholars led by Anna Weischer[6] of the University of Hagen made two five-minute videotapes of an actor playing the role of a 50-year-old CEO. The two videos offered contrasting leadership models: strong and weak.

In the strong enactment of authenticity video, the actor 'fitted his gestures to his statements, matching his facial expressions to his emotions, showing a real smile'. In contrast, in the weak leadership video, 'he seemed to be not so reliable and consistent, somewhat distracted (awkward body movements), and distant (speaking monotonously). Still the enactment was consistent with the portrayal of a CEO.'

The results showed that in the case of the 'strong' leader, participants identified consistency between actions, words and emotions, perceiving the leader as more authentic and transparent, with more behavioural integrity, more open to feedback and with higher self-awareness. The results of this experiment suggest that the leader's ability to 'enact the "true self"' is important influence in followers' judgements of their leader's authenticity.

Can authentic leadership be learned and developed?

There are two implications of this enactment theory. First, if leaders appear authentic to others when they show consistency between their actions, words and internal values, they must generate symbolic interactions for employees to see, such as visiting the workplace and making caring gestures. These gestures generate feedback from followers, who make judgements about the authenticity of the leader. In turn, followers' feedback show the leader 'who he/she is' through the eyes of followers.

The second lesson of the enactment principle of authenticity is that it permits a readier approach to leadership development. An actor can be trained to be authentic in the eyes of others. This is consistent with an emerging theatrical approach to developing leadership qualities. It is not enough to *feel* authentic (the phenomenological state) for others to perceive you as authentic. Leaders must *appear* authentic, showing consistency between gestures and facial expressions through statements, motivations and intentions. The behavioural enactment of authentic leadership can be further reinforced by adding the verbal element of storytelling. In a second experiment, the authors found that when the CEO acting strongly also revealed some personal information about his life, participants rated him as even more authentic.

Francisco Rebelo: a personal account

In 2017, I contacted Francisco Rebelo for an update on how the company kept its core authentic values, or value congruence, and for a more personal account of its history. Francisco was thrilled that I was following up the Vista Alegre story: his personal and professional identity is tied up in it.

The grandson of the CEO who ran the family-owned company until the Visabeira takeover, Francisco's personal account of the history of Vista Alegre brings back memories from when he was nine years old and going with his grandfather to visit the factory and playing with the children of employees.

Listening to the stories of family members over the years, a portrait emerges of the founder of Vista Alegre as a true entrepreneur, a member of the upper classes of the time who saw an opportunity to create a new company. When Jose Ferreira Pinto Basto built a factory in the rural area of Ílhavo, he had more in mind than just a company – he wanted to create a community for his employees. The idea was to give the workforce a sense of place where they would feel proud.

At that time, all products were made by hand. The manufacturing process was highly artistic with little automatization. The workers were proud of what they were doing, particularly the painters, who paid attention to every tiny detail.

'The people who paint and create the designs are very proud of what they do. They are kind of born into it: they consider themselves artists.' But Francisco also notes that the company had to leave its original, artistic ideals behind eventually: 'Once competition started, they had to change this artistic approach to become competitive. The premium that customers paid for that art was too expensive.'

In May 2001, when Vista Alegre merged with Atlantis, there was some debate and discussion in the family. Looking back, the merger brought economies of scale and reintroduced glass to the company's product line. But the merger did not meet expectations and with the advent of the financial global crisis, the company ran into financial problems.

Moments of truth

Vista Alegre employees put a premium on expressing their true self at work. They take pride and ownership of every single piece of porcelain they produce. How can employees express their true selves within the constraints of organizational rules and unpredictable change?

Two Israeli psychologists, Dana Yagil of the University of Haifa and Hana Medler-Liraz of the Academic College of Tel-Aviv,[7] conducted a qualitative study with front-line employees in customer service roles to try to understand what they dubbed 'enduring versus transient authenticity'. Yagil and Medler-Liraz concluded that something like authenticity isn't a dispositional trait. Instead, authenticity is considerably influenced by the situation, or what they called a 'transient' authenticity. Transient authenticity, they write, offers 'a more dynamic view of individuals as varying in the degree to which they enact their true feelings and values ... Based on the notion that self-expression fluctuates owing to changeable and context-specific factors, the concept of transient authenticity refers to temporal expressions of [the] true self.'

The authors found that employees' momentary sense of authenticity in their service encounters with customers is experienced as 'psychological autonomy' and expressed as 'honesty, viewing the task as a personal endeavour, and engaging in close interpersonal interactions'. The advantages of these moments of authenticity include employees' dedication, positive emotions and good interaction with customers.

They also noted a paradox: 'true caring cannot be achieved by rewarding employees for showing it'. Because of the drive of individuals towards authenticity, cases of spontaneous authentic self-expression occur 'even in the restricted service context'. The lesson here is that leaders must strive to build authentic organizations in which employees can express their true selves to meet their basic psychological need of authenticity. This is particularly the case during challenging periods of change, when companies can create moments of transient authenticity.

Managing change: transient authenticity

Francisco Rebelo's research in 2014 had focused on 2009, after Vista Alegre was bought out by the Visabeira Group. Meeting him again in 2017, I was intrigued to hear that he had a different perspective, less emotional and more strategic. 'The company was at a point when it was going bankrupt. It needed someone to come to the rescue,' he explained. Francisco sees the takeover as necessary for the company's survival. 'Visabeira saw an opportunity and went for it.'

During this period of change, Francisco acknowledged that like the rest of the workforce, he had an emotional investment in the company. The employees were used to carrying out their artistic work to the highest standards, but couldn't see the big picture. When he interviewed existing managers and employees at the factory, many said they felt abandoned by the family. People who had worked hard for the company for generations now felt their future was uncertain, a fear Francisco understood: 'Who doesn't understand this feeling of abandon?'

Francisco also appreciates that Visabeira was trying to make the business profitable to give the workforce a future. It introduced cost-cutting measures to solve financial problems and make the company leaner. The result is that for the 2017 financial year Vista Alegre was set to return to profit. Implementing change is often about things getting worse before they get better. 'In the long-run, it was a good strategic business decision, but a painful process on the emotional side.'

But after Visabeira took control of the company, production dropped off and absenteeism increased. Many workers said they were better taken care off under family ownership. 'They were taken back by the drastic change,' explains Francisco: some employees still remember how his grandfather took the time to talk to his employees, asking them about their children.

Francisco remembers how as a child he used to attend the annual company party each May. His family had a house next to the factory, known as the palace. He and his family would be woken up by the firemen's band, which had marched from the factory. The children would be dressed in their best clothes, while his grandfather would head the procession, followed by his grandchildren, the girls bearing bouquets of flowers and the boys with a cane in their hands. After the procession, there was food. 'I felt I was at home because people would treat us very nicely.'

Such close ties between owners and workforce is hard to imagine anymore. With hindsight, Francisco says he now understands the emotional attachment of Vista Alegre's employees to the company.

Without fully understanding the culture of the company and the workforce's strength of feeling about its traditions, it was difficult to implement the necessary changes. Soon the new management from Visabeira decided to interview some of the older managers and employees to better understand Vista Alegre's values and identity.

It worked. Once they understood the employees' view and the strength of Vista Alegre's culture, implementing change was easier. Visabeira's managers followed several successful strategies. They had a town hall meeting to explain the new strategy and to give employees a better understanding of why there was a need for change. They then arranged bi-monthly meetings with employees to share news about the company's progress. They also reintroduced traditions like the Christmas party. The new management team's quick response helped steer the process of change.

They understood the importance of the workforce's need to express their authenticity and the need to respect the culture and traditions of the company while adapting to the times. Visabeira understood how important the Vista Alegre brand and culture were to its success. So much so that they are interested in preserving it, as the company's website notes: 'Nowadays, Vista Alegre is more than a mere industrial unit. It is also part of the Portuguese heritage, boasting buildings of undeniable architectural interest and a repository of social and artistic memories essential to the building of a Portuguese identity.'

Role modelling authentic leadership

Francisco said his dream is to run Vista Alegre some day. Whenever he visits a Vista Alegre store around the world, he loves the fact they have photographs of the factory and his family house in Ílhavo: 'It makes me very proud, although I recognize I have not done anything in the company,' he admits.

He recalls an anecdote from when he was eleven, staying with an American family in the suburbs of New Jersey. When he arrived, the first thing he noticed was three Vista Alegre plates in the cupboard of their living room. He was thrilled. 'It was great going to the other side of the world and seeing a piece of your hometown.' He also took his hosts a book about Vista Alegre, along with a plate.

Francisco says his grandfather was an important role model. Although he passed away when Francisco was fourteen years old, he has fond memories and heard a lot of stories about the company from him. He says the most important lesson was that 'The numbers are important, but the human aspect of the business makes the difference. As CEO, he had a genuine interest in people. He was interested in how people were doing across all levels of the organization.'

Francisco's favourite story about his grandfather is about an employee who lacked the money to send her son to university. Francisco's grandfather immediately arranged an interest-free loan to cover the costs, deducting repayment in small amounts from her salary.

Such a gesture was only possible because the CEO was prepared to make a two-hour trip from Lisbon to the factory to learn about the workforce's problems and then be prepared to do something to make a difference to their lives. As a result, people were committed to the company and were willing to give their best. The workforce cared about the company because the company cared about them. It was not just a job; employees were passionate about the company.

Another significant role model for Francisco was his boss at Deloitte. When he started at the consulting firm, his thinking was: that 'he is a director, I could never speak with him'. But his view changed. 'He is the embodiment of a leader,' he says, explaining how approachable he was. When he had a problem, he was not afraid to ask his manager and didn't feel judged. As a coach, his boss was willing to push him, taking him out of his comfort zone and guiding him, willing to take the time to explain things. Francisco felt valued in the company when his boss asked his opinion about an important project: 'He is open-minded, a person you can speak to. If you have a problem, you should not hide it from your boss.'

Francisco describes himself as 'a leader with a human touch. I will try to understand the numbers and the market, but the most important thing, especially in a consulting firm like Deloitte, is the people. Talking is the only way managers learn and impact on their subordinates and the company. Employees like to see a real person in their leader. When that happens, a job becomes more than a job because you are engaged with your work.'

Am I truly motivated to lead?

Young leaders like Francisco are inspired to copy the behaviour of past and present-day CEOs. Why do we look up to our own leaders? It's probably the result of the way human beings develop their self-conception – in relation to others. For instance, psychologists who study learning and motivation have developed a social comparison theory which suggests that information about the self is only meaningful when compared with relevant others.

But is the social comparison theory true for leadership? Our new research suggests that leaders make two types of social comparisons to develop an authentic motivation to lead and learn more about the leadership role. With my colleagues at ESMT in Berlin,[8] we examined self-to-leader comparisons which indicate the extent to which individuals' views on attributes that characterize leaders match the attributes they ascribe to themselves. For example, when managers are asked to define what being a leader means to them, they use various attributes, such as smart, funny, creative, visionary, eloquent, unique, perfectionist, decisive, sociable, fair, humble, efficient, and so on. Participants then indicate the extent to which they match these prototypical representations of leaders, what we called self-to-prototype comparisons. Participants also indicated the leader who had been the most significant to them in the past and in the present as their role model. They described this individual with ten statements and evaluated how well each of the statements matched their own characteristics. These descriptions included 'encourages people to grow' or 'charismatic', which we called *self-to-exemplars comparisons.*

What this study suggests is that the actual skills leaders have are less important, in the end, in guiding their leadership actions than the positive role models they have encountered in their work experience. We found that the more managers shared the leadership characteristics of their role models, the more confident they felt in applying for leadership positions and the greater their desire to lead in an authentic manner. This does not mean that *know-how* is not important in explaining our leadership effectiveness and authenticity. Once we understand the technical aspect, however, prototypical and exemplar role models can serve in boosting or undermining our authentic leadership self.

Vista Alegre's happy view

In 2014, Francisco titled his research on the company *The Unhappy View of Vista Alegre*, a wordplay on the name of the firm, which translates as 'happy view'. In 2017 he was more optimistic, in large part since the core value of the company was harmony between tradition and modernity. The key success factor emphasized on the company website is 'highly specialized manufacturing activities based on the know-how of its artisans and on its centenarian traditions'. Taste and lifestyles change and designs need to change accordingly. The company has been evolving with changing tastes. For example, attuned to cultural trends, 'the Vista Alegre logo has changed over the company's history to reflect the aesthetic and cultural values of each age. This denotes a constant concern with modernity and an effort to adjust to design evolution and art movements, also reflected in the company's products,' reads the website.

Vista Alegre wants to set itself apart from the Visabeira Group's other business units. This is a question of maintaining an important Portuguese cultural heritage. As a source of social and artistic memories, the Vista Alegre brand contributes to the creation of a Portuguese identity. It is consistently ranked in Portuguese surveys as one of the country's most recognized brands. The company is in partnerships with the best chefs around the world to develop tableware and to come up with limited editions to consolidate the brand's long-term reputation. Vista Alegre's products have graced the tables of the White House and the Palacio da Alvorada, the official residence of the president of Brazil. As an authentic organization in harmony with its context, Vista Alegre has been recognized worldwide: it has been awarded Excellence Status by the prestigious organization Superbrands.

When its workforce demanded greater authenticity from their leaders, Vista Alegre's new management understood the importance of the brand and culture they had acquired and decided to preserve it. Vista Alegre has yet to return fully to its previous splendour, but it is a growing international company, creating not just luxury products but a luxury community.

10 ways to stay authentic when building a community

1 *Care truly about employees.* Leaders who care truly about meeting employees' needs create a psychological community that makes the organization more effective in the long run. Vista Alegre is a company whose leaders built a community for its employees in a depressed village in Portugal with schools, sport clubs, houses and even a theatre.

2 *Encourage value congruence between the company and employees.* The greater the fit between organizational and employees' values, the more effective the business will be. Vista Alegre's values have been internalized by its employees over many years and they are at the core of its culture, history and success.

3 *Practice behavioural integrity.* As a leader, use bodily cues such as facial expressions and body movements that show a match among your behaviour, message and motives. Francisco's grandfather took several trips to the factory to speak to the employees about their work and family. This behaviour was interpreted by employees as authentic.

4   *Enact your authentic leadership.* It is critical to understand followers' perceptions of authenticity. Responding to important social issues with progressive HR programmes, leaders can match the social and psychological demands of employees to more fully express their authenticity at work. Socially responsible investments in employees build a resource that results in a sustained competitive advantage.

5   *Create 'moments of truth'.* Foster employees' expression of transient authenticity. For example, during the process of change in Vista Alegre, long-standing traditions were recovered and remain in practice today. Such rituals and symbols as the festivities related to Nossa Senhora da Penha, along with a dinner for retired employees and the Christmas gift to all employees, foster employees' expression of authenticity.

6   *Address employees' true selves in the spheres of both work and non-work.* This way you will increase employees' perception of value fit with the organization, attract more job seekers and eventually recruit and retain the best candidates because employees can better express their authentic self. When Vista Alegre executives showed concerns for employees' work and non-work needs, they earned their trust.

7   *Signal to job seekers the firm's values and culture.* If you want an authentic image, check that your company effectively promotes its core values to attract and retain talent. It is important to provide information about your organization's values in advertisements and websites. Vista Alegre 'has changed over the company's history to reflect the aesthetic and cultural values of each age' according to its website.

8   *Avoid moral compensation; achieve moral consistency.* Employee investment policies do not compensate for other benefits. Instead, leaders who achieve moral consistency 'bundle authenticity' social initiatives as part of a constellation of 'best authentic practices'. For example, Vista Alegre also funds the restoration of historic buildings.

9 *Engage in self-to-leader comparisons.* Positive social comparisons between yourself and your ideal leaders clarify your own leadership identity and help you to be truly motivated for a leadership role. Francisco Rebelo admires his current boss at Deloitte who, as a coach, encourages Francisco to leave his comfort zone and learn new things.

10 *Be a role model yourself.* Offer inspiration to others by emphasizing similarities that boost their self-esteem and validate their leadership role. When you foster personal identification, your employees bond within the organization.

Herb Kelleher, co-founder of Southwest Airlines, recently shared how to build a humanistic culture for loyalty and success[9] – producing employees with 'a warrior spirit, a servant's heart, and a fun-loving attitude'. Vista Alegre is on its way to return to its glory days by building a community of loyal employees.

9

Legacy: A Climate of Authenticity for Long-lasting Impact

You cannot deliver value unless you anchor the company's values. Values make an unsinkable ship.

INDRA NOOYI

Indra Nooyi is regarded in India as 'a truly global living legend'.[1] In her inspirational speech, Nooyi paraphrases Malcom Gladwell in *Outliers* saying, 'Who you are cannot be separated from where you came from.' She is grateful for her wonderful upbringing in India that allowed her to succeed later in the United States as CEO of Pepsico.

Indra Nooyi gives three lessons that resemble the 3 Hs of authentic leadership: 'Be a life-long student, keeping your childhood curiosity' – the *habit* of learning element of authenticity; 'throw your head, hands and heart into whatever you do' – the passionate *heart* element of authenticity; and 'help others rise' – the *harmony* element of authenticity.

Banco Santander: creating a 'virtuous circle' among all stakeholders (Spain)

Likewise, Ana Botín, Executive Chairman of the Santander Group, has the respect and admiration of the people of her homeland, Spain, and is held in even higher regard in Santander, her hometown in northern Spain. In the 2015 Social Projects Award Ceremony, Ana Botín reminded all employees of the company's social-oriented mission: 'This is the reason why we wake up every day and spend our time at the Bank.'[2]

Authentic organizations must strive for more than just a business goal: they must be in a continuous process of transformation to achieve virtuous harmony among its many stakeholders. Banco Santander has been immersed in a major transformation for two years led by Ana Botín. Its mission is 'to help people and businesses prosper', she explains in the 2016 Annual Report.

Santander's transformation goes beyond achieving results to focus on the process of how to reach those results by considering the communion among its many stakeholders – customers, shareholders, employees and society. The positive relationship between them forms a virtuous circle in which all parties win: 'In 2016, we lent more and improved service to our customers, generating more value for shareholders and supported our employees and communities in a sustainable, inclusive way.'

Banco Santander is a fine example of how to move step by step towards being an authentic organization. 'Our transformation is global and goes beyond metrics. It is mostly about how we organize ourselves and how we behave to succeed in a world changing at exponential speed,' says Botín. Santander's virtuous circle includes 190,000 committed employees who serve 125 million customers, providing dividends to 3.9 million shareholders and helping 1.7 million people in 2016.

My interest in studying Banco Santander against the benchmark of authenticity came out of an IE Business School research project on employer branding in the insurance and financial sector. As an expert in leadership, I was invited to be part of this project whose objective was to understand why these sectors project an impersonal and distant image that in many cases does not correspond to reality. Personally, I can identify with the sceptics' perception of the world of finance, so I decided to investigate the history and the cultural transformation of Santander. It is one of the leading banks in Spain and has the largest international presence, run since 2014 by one of the world most influential women.

Banco Santander's website provides a window onto the company, where values such as 'simple, personal, and fair' reflect its renewed identity. It has just received the Top Employer Europe 2017 seal for its human resources practices in Spain and five other markets. To achieve this certification, it has had to meet the most demanding standards of a survey in which human resources practices such as talent retention, training and staff development plans, management and leadership improvement are evaluated and externally audited, along with career and succession plans, compensation policies and benefits for professionals, as well as the overall company culture. In the sustainability section, Grupo Santander appears as the Global Fortune 500 company that invests most in corporate social responsibility related to education: in 2016, it invested €170 million through its Santander Universities programme to support entrepreneurship, research and development. The Santander Impact Education blog shares customers' experiences with the bank.

My impression of Banco Santander is of an organization undertaking an increasingly positive project of cultural transformation to become an international benchmark for authenticity in a sector that in many people's minds has many negative associations. In addition, the bank is part of my environment. The Santander Financial City, the bank's headquarters on the western outskirts of Madrid, is only ten minutes from my home. I was delighted to be able to interview two senior managers of the bank and learn the details of their transformational leadership towards authenticity.

On 7 March 2017, when I arrived at Santander's headquarters, the first thing that struck me was the three cement columns with the words 'simple' 'personal' and 'fair' inscribed in each one of them.

The executives who welcomed me explained that they were in the process of moving, pulling down partitions and removing doors to turn the building into a more open layout. I felt privileged to hear how this cultural transformation has originated and is being shaped day by day from the CEO down to all 190,000 employees.

History of Banco Santander

Santander's history is present in the bank's culture and business. The bank was set up in the northern coastal city of Santander in 1857, 160 years ago. The bank had an international mission from the get go, created as it was to finance the commerce of northern Spain with the Americas. This international mission lasted over the years. For decades, the bank remained local within Spain. The first office outside Cantabria was in nearby Palencia in 1926. In the 1940s, expansion began with some offices in Mexico, Cuba and Argentina, always following Spanish commerce. Then, in the 1970s, the first banks were bought in Latin America, in Chile, Puerto Rico, Argentina and Brazil. In the 1990s, further expansion in the region was led by Ana Botín.

Following the merger with BCH in 1999 came an important phase of expansion. This merger provided the bank with the clout it needed to maintain its international expansion.

Starting in 2000, the bank began a period of acquisitions in Europe – in Germany and Scandinavia, as well as the United Kingdom, where in 2004 it bought Abbey, investing in Sovereign in the United States the following year. Next came the acquisition of Banco Real in Brazil, greatly strengthening the bank's presence there.

These acquisitions followed clear strategic guidelines to consolidate the bank's presence in the ten key markets where it operates: five in the Americas

(Brazil, Mexico, Chile, Argentina and the United States) and five in Europe (United Kingdom, Portugal, Spain, Poland and Germany). This geographical footprint reinforces the bank's presence in Latin America and Europe. For example, in Germany Banco Santander focuses on car financing, and is now Germany's fourth-largest bank in consumer finance assets. Within this process of diversification, Brazil and the United Kingdom are the largest markets.

The DNA of Banco Santander

Over the course of its 160 years of history, the two basic parts of Banco Santander's DNA have been its international diversity and commercial banking.

'Geographic diversification in Europe and the Americas gives us a highly attractive and differentiated profile,' Ana Botín told shareholders at the bank's Annual General Meeting in April 2017. 'First, it gives us a balance between mature and emerging economies. Over the years, we have seen our businesses in Spain, the United Kingdom and Brazil take turns as the major contributor to the Group's profits. Second, thanks to this balance, our results are more stable and predictable, which means we need less capital than our peers.'

Some critics say that being present in so many markets creates a risk of overextending. But unlike other banks with a global presence but with a small share in many markets, Santander seeks critical mass in its ten core markets, with market shares ranging from 10 per cent to 14 per cent. This allows it to maintain its focus and to achieve the economies of scale it needs to compete locally (the one exception is the United States, a very fragmented banking market where the bank's market share is still at 4 per cent in the northeast region).

This is the story of the international financial crisis. It began in the United States, and when things began to recover there, things started to get difficult in Europe, but Latin America continued to perform well. However, Banco Santander suffered disproportionately from the crisis because of its association with Spain. Despite its significant geographical diversification, markets saw the bank as a very Spanish institution. In 2012, at the height of the Spanish economic crisis, Santander's business in Spain represented just 10 per cent of its revenue stream. By 2017, with the economic recovery, Spain represented 14 per cent of its business. For this reason, the bank registered profits every quarter during the crisis and could continue paying dividends to its shareholders.

The other part of Santander's DNA is its customer-oriented approach: 'Our aim is to be the best retail and commercial bank, one that earns the lasting loyalty of our people, customers, shareholders and communities,' Ana Botín wrote in her 2016 letter to shareholders. 'In 2016, we earned the trust of 4 million new customers, raising our total number of customers to 125 million. We did this by improving the service and products we offer in every one of our ten core markets.' Compared to other banks of the same size, a very high proportion of Banco Santander's profits come from retail banking – 76 per cent. Another way to measure this is how much of its balance is made up of loans (about 75 per cent). In some large European banks, this figure can be below 50 per cent, as they engage in trading and other market activities.

PHOTO   9.1 *Ana   Botín,   Executive Chairman, Banco Santander (Spain).*

That said, the bank is financially conservative. Banco Santander has been growing slowly and only acquires another bank when strict financial and business criteria are met. Santander executives tell the story of a proposed merger with another large European bank in the early 2000s. Santander pulled out when it saw there were many derivative products not in line with Santander's conservative financial principles.

Simple, personal and fair

Banks around the world have been through a major crisis, and one that is not only economic, but also a crisis of values. Society in general has called into question the value of banks. In addition, the future is uncertain and changing: globalization may slow down with Trump in the White House. Ana Botín's question is, 'How do we want to be in this environment of change and mistrust?'

In 2014, when she took over, she brought with her new values acquired during her time in the United Kingdom as CEO: being simple, personal and fair. In 2016, she told shareholders:

> We worked hard to improve how we work: Our success at this time of exponential change will depend on an ever-stronger culture where customers come first, uniting our banks in Europe and the Americas. We want to gain customers' trust by acting in a way that it is simple, personal and fair. These are our main goals, today, tomorrow and as far into the future as we can see.

In addition, these values provide a common identity for Banco Santander's subsidiaries. The bank's international model is local at the same time because its subsidiaries in other countries are local banks. Banco Santander Brazil is a Brazilian bank subject to Brazilian law and is managed locally, not as a branch of a Spanish bank. The subsidiaries finance themselves and manage their business locally. The challenge for Ana Botín was how to unite banks from such differing cultures: this has been achieved through common values, hence the motto – Simple, Personal, Fair – which is recognized throughout the Group.

This motto serves as an umbrella for a common culture and brand within the Group. Based on this unique identity, the parent company provides common policies and the exchange of best practices, from human resources management to risk management and sustainability. The aim is to ensure that all subsidiaries comply with common principles, and rather than just meeting the Group's financial criteria, match its standards.

What role do values play in authentic leaders?

In recent years, leadership scholars have spent a great deal of time studying authentic leaders for the simple reason that they have moral standards and values that emphasize the collective interest of their groups or organizations within a greater society. Susan Michie and Janaki Gooty of Oklahoma State University[3] argue that a higher level of moral integrity is a key element of authentic leadership: 'Leadership scholars have suggested that authentic leaders are guided by a set of values that are oriented toward doing what's right and fair for all stakeholders.'

These values are known as 'self-transcendent' and include the values of benevolence (concern for immediate others) and universalism (concern for the welfare of all people). Consider this short quiz on self-transcendent values adapted from the Value Survey created by Shalom Schwartz at Hebrew University.[4] Think of the extent they are important to you, as compared to more self-enhancement values such as personal achievement or power, using 1, 'Not very important', to 5, 'Very important'.

Universal values are:
Social justice
Equality
Being broadminded

Benevolence values are:

Honesty

Loyalty

Responsibility

Michie and Gooty suggest that authentic leaders have both self-enhancement and self-transcendent values, but give a higher priority to self-transcendent values. They state:

> The two dimensions of self-transcendence reflect the notion that leaders must be concerned with the interest of both in-group and out-group stakeholders. Universalistic values emphasize understanding, appreciation, tolerance, and protection for the welfare of *all* people and for the environment. Benevolent values emphasize preserving and enhancing the welfare of people with whom the leader is in frequent personal contact.

Ana Botín's new values of being simple, personal and fair to all stakeholders clearly falls into the category of self-transcendent values.

The virtuous circle: stakeholders in cultural transformation

Simple, personal and fair are cross-cutting values to do with the interrelationship of the bank's multiple stakeholders, that is, the employees, clients, shareholders and society: the four quadrants of this virtuous circle.

If we start with the quadrant of *employees* in the virtuous circle, in the 2016 annual report Botín says, 'The talent, commitment and motivation of our 190,000 professionals are the basis of our success.' According to Santander's annual commitment survey, 'More than 75 per cent of our teams support the culture of simple, personal and fair.'

How does this manifest itself internally? Through greater transparency, more involvement and more feedback. For example, engagement surveys that used to be conducted every three years are now carried out annually, while other feedback channels are being considered for easier and more effective communication with employees. The redesign of the space at the Madrid headquarters will provide more open spaces and fewer offices, in line with the simple, personal and fair internal culture.

In addition, Santander is initiating flexi-work, implemented through team leaders. The team leader takes stock of the flexibility needs of each member of the group. For example, almost all employees have a laptop and can work from home; some need an afternoon or a day of teleworking a week. In addition, people can work from home from time to time if they need to do something in depth. The flexibility of the schedule includes alternatives such as working from 8am to 5pm, from 9am to 6pm, and from 9.30am to 6.30pm.

The other important aspect in managing people is training and development. Banco Santander has a corporate university with access to a wide variety of courses both in managerial skills and coaching on how to be a better boss, to more general and technical courses on banking strategy.

In addition, a diversity programme for women is implemented throughout the bank. This training, mentoring and network programme aims to boost the professional career of women. The board of directors has gone from 10 per cent female to 40 per cent. The latest addition is Homaira Akbari, an expert in innovative technologies, as the new independent director. Together, these new practices in people management have led Banco Santander to win the Top Employer Europe 2017 award.

Turning to the *customer* quadrant within the virtuous circle, the bank's focus is on increasing the number of loyal customers, digital customers and overall customer satisfaction. As Ana Botín points out, of Santander's 125 million customers, just 15.2 million are 'loyal', consuming multiple products and considering Santander their main bank. 'A loyal customer is four times more profitable than one that is not,' she told shareholders this year.

One way employed to increase the number of loyal customers has been through the 1/2/3 account, created in the UK, exported to Spain and spreading throughout the Group. The 1/2/3 formula rewards customers who use multiple products, for example through rebates on card purchases at 1 per cent, 2 per cent or 3 per cent, depending on the product consumed.

The bank also seeks digital clients, which requires a fluid relationship, more adjusted to the needs of the client and more efficient. The bank is investing in new technologies to meet the challenge. Botín points out in the annual report that 'Thanks to our investment in technology, the number of digital customers has increased by 25 per cent in 2016, to almost 21 million.' The goal is global customer satisfaction. 'Today Santander is among the top three banks for customer satisfaction in eight of its nine main countries. This was one of the goals for 2018 that we have already reached in 2016.'

Shareholders seems the most abstract quadrant in the virtuous circle, but they play an important role for the bank. Some 125 million customers drive profitable growth, coupled with geographic diversification and the subsidiaries model, generating stable profits and enabling a collaborative culture that promotes efficiency and benefits shareholders. 'When we do our job, our employees grow professionally, and our clients trust us more and they prosper together with our shareholders, and our communities,' Ana Botín told shareholders this year.

Unlike other banks, Santander has more than three million shareholders, most of them retail shareholders who are also loyal to the bank. For these shareholders, the bank's dividend is an income. Shareholder loyalty is a primary objective for Banco Santander, which is proud that it has always paid dividends, even during the recent economic crisis.

At the end of the virtuous circle are communities, the focus of the bank's sustainability plan. This aspect of Santander's corporate social responsibility is centred mainly on higher education, with agreements with more than 1,300 universities around the world. These agreements foster the exchange of students and teachers and promote digitalization and technology in universities. Santander's Impact Education blog includes the personal stories of scholarship recipients. The agreements also bring together universities, small businesses and entrepreneurs.

In 2016, Santander was named the best European bank for its commitment to sustainability, and its contribution to social progress and environmental protection was noted by the Dow Jones Sustainability Index. 'Corporate social responsibility projects include the award of more than 35,000 scholarships for higher education, 250,000 microcredit projects and participation in volunteer programs of more than 60,000 employees to support the most disadvantaged,' notes Botín in the 2016 annual report.

As part of its four-quadrant strategy, the bank has begun a more detailed measurement and tracking of how its community activities contribute to improving people's lives. Besides numerical targets, the bank is interested in knowing how it has benefited all these people and in sharing stories about the positive impact it is having on people. This effectively squares the virtuous circle by making employees feel proud of belonging to a bank that contributes to improving society.

Doing well by doing good: harmony in business and employees

Managerial thinking around the world has undergone a subtle but important shift in recent years about meeting employees' needs to express their true self through the work–life balance. It is now increasingly recognized that unless organizations provide a supportive environment, employees will find it difficult to meet their work and personal responsibilities. This line of thinking represents a significant shift from viewing employee issues as private concerns, to recognizing that managers play a critical role.

Santander is a pioneer of an important business shift towards meeting employees' psychological and social needs. In doing so, it is an example of the influence of senior leaders to create authentic organizations that care for employees' well-being. I conducted research to examine how building an authentic context is not only good for employees, but can also benefit the firm as a whole. My premise was that companies can 'do well by doing good'.

As part of a large research project in partnership with the Spanish government during 2007 and 2008, my research team examined the mechanism through which work–life policies (WLP) influence employees' authenticity within the organization and, ultimately, business competitiveness as indexed by sales growth.[5]

WLPs provide employees with time and resources to care for their personal lives: time off, leave of absence, reduced work hours, flexibility and ending rigid work times as well as in scheduling business trips, and online technology to facilitate telecommuting. Studies show that WLPs help employees reconcile their work and non-work identities and roles. These policies allow employees to customize their otherwise standard work schedules so that they can best express their true selves and carry on their roles in both the work and personal spheres.

Companies were recruited among participants in a nationwide award competition sponsored by the Spanish government. The award committee pre-screened the applicants and selected seventy companies to be eligible for the award. Organization-level information on the availability of WLPs along with company data were collected via a telephone interview with the human resource director of each organization. Next, a random sample of employees from each company completed a survey including all our employee-level measures. This procedure resulted in a multi-source data set of 3,262 employees in seventy organizations. In addition, we matched our sample of organizations with sales growth information available in the SABI database for three years.[6] We matched sales growth for thirty-nine companies for which we had a total of 1,872 employee responses. Firms represented a wide variety of industries.

Perhaps the most interesting finding is what might be called 'the business case for employees' authenticity'. Results, illustrated in Figure 9.1, show that employees working in companies that offer WLPs reported more moments of authenticity, as expressed by autonomy and satisfaction. They experienced 53 per cent more control over their work, and in turn expressed 16 per cent more satisfaction with their job. Furthermore, we demonstrated that a climate of authenticity as expressed by shared job satisfaction among employees benefits the organization, as reflected in an increase of 16 per cent in sales over three years. A shared sense of job satisfaction creates a climate of authenticity that helps employees express and enact their true selves, conserve their energy, use their time more efficiently and focus on important tasks. These positive

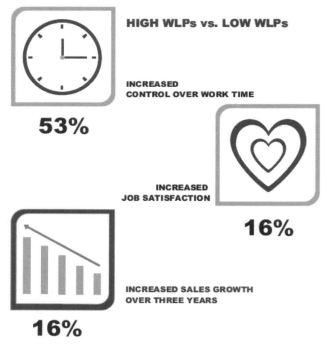

FIGURE 9.1 *Work–life policies (WLPs) increase employees' autonomy and job satisfaction as well as a firm's sales growth over three years.*

attitudes of the 'happy employee' can serve to create a culture of trust, collaboration, high morale and psychological safety that collectively leads to positive organizational outcomes.[7]

What this means is that leaders who build a welcoming context in which employees can express their authenticity managing work and personal roles may realize the maxim of 'doing well by doing good'. Companies will find harmony in agency and communion by focusing on both – the bottom line for the business; and the well-being of their employees.

The roots of authenticity: a territorial identity

Another ingredient of Santander's authentic leadership is its territorial identity. Banco Santander remains linked to the city in which it was founded and whose name it bears. The annual meeting is held there, as are some board meetings. Most managers make the 'pilgrimage' to Santander at least once a year.

This means that while the bank looks to the future, it does so with one foot always in the past. 'My father liked to say that Santander has the wisdom of experience and the spirit of youth,' Ana Botín said, referring to Emilio Botín, chairman of the bank from 1986 to 2014. Ana Botín regularly meets with representatives of local business, along with politicians and community leaders, underlining the bank's commitment to the region. The bank also contributes significantly to educational, cultural and social projects in the region. 'It is sometimes said that companies don't have feelings, or souls, or homes,' Ana Botín told a gathering earlier this year at the daily *El Diario Montañes* in Santander. 'That is wrong. In the bank, we owe much to Santander and to Cantabria. We wouldn't be where we are today without the work and efforts of so many executives, employees and shareholders of Santander and Cantabria. This is our home and will continue to be for the future.'

But it is Santander's headquarters in Boadilla del Monte, on the outskirts of Madrid, that best embodies this authentic leadership. Santander built the headquarters and moved here in 2004 after being spread across 21 buildings in the centre of the Spanish capital. Though employee surveys showed some initial misgivings about moving from the centre of the capital, the advantages of the new complex soon convinced most staff of the benefits of the move. Facilities include dining areas for all employees, sport facilities, a training and conference centre with classrooms and a 120-room residence, a medical centre, a store and many other amenities. It was a part of the transformation of the bank, and its physical expression was the new headquarters in the Financial City.

The brand logo is another important symbol for the Group. The Santander flame, adopted in Spain in 1989, has been the broader group's sole logo since 2007, the bank's 150th anniversary. At the same time, the group began advertising as an institution, not just as a local bank, using for the first time media such as the *Financial Times*, *The Economist* and the *Wall Street Journal*.

To further enhance the value of the brand, Santander set up sports sponsorships, notably a Formula 1 deal with Ferrari. Banco Santander also sponsors Spain's top-flight La Liga football division, which is followed by millions of spectators around the world. Banco Santander also hosts the Santander Triathlon Series. As a participant last year in several short-distance triathlons, I can assure you that they are one of the best organized. The simple, personal and fair motto also applies here. The Santander triathlon is simple and personal – it includes many distances and types like women's triathlon, and it's fair: prizes are given to all age categories.

Ana Botín always emphasizes how Banco Santander's purpose is to help people and businesses prosper by contributing to making society more sustainable and inclusive. That inclusion is both demographic, notably gender oriented, as well as financial; for example, through scholarships for the economically disadvantaged. Building on the success of micro-credit projects in Brazil, others are being launched in Mexico to promote social inclusion.

Santander's subsidiaries actively collaborate: senior managers from each country meet and the chairmen meet four times a year at what the organization calls 'Promontorios', a reference to the city of Santander.

The company is also focused on encouraging employees to meet corporate values through their behaviour. 'It's not just about what we do, but how we do it,' Ana Botín has told Santander employees. This is measured through evaluation surveys involving managers, peers and subordinates. The eight corporate behaviours that Santander wants its employees to apply include a commitment to truly listen, show respect, keep promises, embrace change and support people. Ana Botín emphasizes the importance of these behaviours for the sustainability of the bank in the 2016 Annual Report: 'As a management team, we are totally committed to adopting our corporate behaviours and leading by example. We know that we must attain outstanding financial results, but what will make us truly stand out will be our culture.'

Ana Botín projects a modern, digital and innovative approach. She has extensive international experience, including living and studying in the US and the UK. She also participates in several international forums where business leaders exchange ideas and insights.

Well-defined, well-communicated corporate governance provides for agility: the strategic lines of the political cultural transformation, including financial risk policies and corporate values work from the top down. However, key performance indicators (KPI) are decided via input from the heads of subsidiaries. Each quadrant of the virtuous circle has KPIs to facilitate the implementation of cultural changes in each of the subsidiaries' countries. For example, in the employees' quadrant, one KPI states, 'We want to be at least in the Top Three banks to work for.' Therefore, each country must ensure that it meets this goal. Botín concludes in the 2016 annual report, 'At the base of our transformation is a culture of being local in each one of our markets while also encouraging a shared way of doing things that is Simple and Personal and Fair; this culture binds us together across our 10 markets, fosters innovation and attracts the best talent.'

Beyond its digital transformation, Banco Santander is undertaking a cultural and human transformation. Storytelling is one of the tools that Botín has used to realize this transformation. One of her favourites is about Sandra:

> Sandra is a Brazilian, from a Sao Paulo favela called Paraisopolis. Her husband left her alone, except for $60,000 in debts. Rafael, the branch manager who told me about Sandra, said he had known her for years, and that she is a fighter – smart, honest, and could be trusted.
>
> We loaned Sandra $250, to launch her first shop. Now she has three, employing her sister and daughters. We follow the business closely, always taking into account the risk involved. There's no doubt that technology will play a large and growing role in our business. But no algorithm would have made that loan to Sandra. Personal contact with our 125 million customers and the 190,000 people on our teams is what makes the difference.

10 ways to stay authentic leaving a legacy

1 *Lead with a social purpose.* Set an example and show the way forward, finding a cause that provides direction, clarity, meaning and energy. For example, Banco Santander has been immersed in a major transformation for two years led by its executive chairman, Ana Botín, with a mission that provides a social purpose – 'to help people and businesses prosper'.

2 *Walk the talk.* Consistency between words and deeds gives exemplarity and justifies your leadership by serving a cause rather than personal interests. For instance, the transformation of Santander goes beyond achieving results to focus on the process of how to reach those results by considering the communion among its many stakeholders – customers, shareholders, employees and society.

3 *Sense and feel situations.* Listen to and respond to the group's needs, values and desires because their level of enthusiasm and satisfaction is the fuel that sparks your leadership. Values such as 'simple, personal and fair' reflect Santander's renewed identity in order to 'succeed in a world changing at exponential speed'.

4 *Manage geographical distance.* Personal identification with the leader and his/her values validate employees' identity as members of the organization when working from a distance. While Santander's geographic diversification in Europe and the Americas offers a highly attractive and differentiated profile, it also requires shared leadership values.

5 *Provide meaning to events.* Especially in times of crisis because employees' uncertainty elevates the need for explanation and the need for leadership. For instance, banks around the world have been through a major crisis of values. Society in general has called into question the value of banks. When Ana Botín took over as president of Santander she brought with her new values with the purpose to 'gain customers' trust by acting in a way that is Simple, Personal and Fair'.

6 *Be present, especially in difficult times.* Emotion-laden events like economic crises, downsizing, reorganization or rapid growth intensifies the need for leadership – people become hungry for charisma. Ensure visibility to address followers' hopes and fears. When Ana Botín visits Cantabria, she regularly meets with representatives of the local business, political and cultural communities, underlining the bank's commitment to the region.

7 *Make symbolic interactions.* Create a context for you to showcase your leadership purpose and vision. How does Santander's renewed identity manifest itself internally? Through greater transparency, more involvement and more feedback.

8 *Include everyone in your cause.* Inclusive leadership capitalizes on the benefits of diversity as a source of human and social capital while recognizing the challenges of conflict and tension among groups. The positive interrelationships of Santander's multiple stakeholders – employees, clients, shareholders and society – creating a virtuous circle is a good example.

9 *Serve the cause by serving the group.* Servant leadership on behalf of the common cause increases trust. For example, the new initiative of flexi-work shows that the company is responsive to employees' needs. These flexible work arrangements that foster employee welfare help at the same time to give the firm a positive image, and serve as an example to other organizations.

10 *Write your own legacy.* It is never too early to think of your contributions to others. Craft the message with humility: the use of humble rhetoric and transparency in your communication brings you close to the people.

Indra Nooyi writes letters to her employees' parents to express her gratitude for the contributions of their sons and daughters to Pepsico, reports CNBC.[8] The letters opened a 'floodgate of emotions', some of the executives telling her that 'this is the best thing that happened to my parents'. Ana Botín publically shows her appreciation of the commitment of her executives to the renewed values of Santander.

Conclusion to Part 3

Resolving the otherness-authenticity paradox in the social self

In resolving the tension between the self and otherness, we should remember that over the course of our lives it is inevitable that some of our experiences will be intimately linked to significant others like our partners, parents, family members, friends and colleagues. Here it is important to understand that authenticity is not about being 'oneself' *against* others; it is about being 'oneself' *in relation* to others. The true self develops though symbolic interactions.

In the 1930s, the psychologist and philosopher George Herbert Mead[1] championed the idea of symbolic interactionism, a revolutionary idea at the time because it argued that the self is socially constructed. That is, your true self is partially derived through your social interactions with others. Your relationships with others shape who you are. Thus, a dynamic and social self emerges from this dialectic between yourself and others through social interactions. This idea was the origin of what later was known as Social Identity Theory.

The pioneers of this social identity analysis – of what is called minimal group studies – are two social psychologists named Henri Tajfel and John Turner.[2] In a landmark set of experiments in the 1980s, they examined the implications of one's social identity – a person's sense of who they are based on their membership of social groups (e.g. organizations, family, religion, etc.). Belonging to high-status social groups is an important source of pride and self-esteem.

More recently, leadership scholars like Raymond Sparrowe[3] have recovered this idea of the social construction of the self, arguing that 'the true self is not discovered absent of others, but is constituted in relation to others' and that 'the hallmark of inauthentic leadership is unbridled self-interest that motivates leaders to treat followers as means to their own ends'. Similarly, Donna Ladkin and Steven Taylor argue that the social-self results from

> [s]ymbolic interactions occurring outside of the internal world. These symbols include the language people use to tell us about ourselves, our location in family and organizational structures, the gestures and facial expressions with which our behaviour is received and responded to, all of the many ways in which the world tells us 'who we are'.

If you look closely at authentic leaders, as often as not the attitudes that make them shine turn out to be not the focus on themselves but the focus on others. This is true of the three leaders I just discussed – Artur Schwörer, leader-to-be Francisco Rebelo and Ana Botín. We all want to believe that the key to authenticity lies in self-awareness and self-improvement of our personal qualities. But in none of these cases did the leader limited his or her leadership to self-enhancement. Instead, all these leaders became and stayed authentic by being true to others and leading by example through self-transcendent values and building structures that allowed others to shine.

It is no exaggeration to say that there is a strong communion between the values of PERI and the values of its employees. In the film *We are PERI*, employees emphasize repeatedly the *We* made up of many nationalities but only one organizational identity. Here is an example of a strong social identity of the self. As social architects, executives at PERI build scaffoldings out of social practices with a caring mindset that puts employees first. Walking the talk, they have in place progressive HR practices so that employees can express their authenticity and social identity through group activities like the bike team. The self-transcendent value of leaving something important behind keeps the Schwörer family with their head in today's problems and their heart in future generations.

Remember the community that Vista Alegre built for its employees with houses, schools, theatre and sport club? These social values are ingrained in the culture and history of the company and have been the cornerstone of its success for more than a century. Evolving with time to reflect the aesthetic of each age, leaders of Vista Alegre had to find creative ways to adapt without breaking its people-oriented culture. They decided to preserve rituals and symbols such as festivities, gala dinners and Christmas gifts that give employees 'moments of truth' that allow them to express their authentic social self. In this balancing act of agency and communion, Francisco Rebelo keeps his eyes and mind open to learn the nuances of authentic leadership within the constraints of organizational change in order to survive in a global and competitive environment.

Tempering my scepticism about the world of finance, it is clear that Santander is led by a competent and caring leader whose mission is 'to help people and business prosper'. Ana Botín strives in her leadership role to achieve virtuous harmony in agency and communion among the many stakeholders of the bank. And she is doing it. What is more important, she is doing it the right way – following the renewed self-transcendent values of being simple, personal and fair. The enactment of these authentic values creates a supportive environment for employees to fulfil both their work and non-work roles and identities. Santander is an example of the maxim 'doing well by doing good'.

Other great leaders teach us that to stay true to our authentic selves we have to care about others. To many, the rapid success of Sundra Pichai as CEO of Google is based on his ability to pull teams together and establish a culture of collaboration. As a pioneer, the former CEO of Southwest, Herb Kelleher, knew that when employees come first, they are happy; and happy employees means better business. And to build the future, Indra Nooyi, CEO of Pepsico, believes it is her obligation to pull others up so that one day they can take centre stage.

The Rhetoric of Authenticity: Felipe VI of Spain

Leadership is often less about leaders and more about shared aspirations and work. If leaders don't make it clear that they are acting in the best interests of the organization, their authority will be questioned. Seeing the bigger picture makes leaders more authentic and influential in the long run.

Perhaps more than any other Spanish institution, the royal family's success and survival depends on its reputation and solidarity with the populace. In his first speech as monarch after his low-key swearing-in ceremony on 19 June 2014, King Felipe VI said, 'The Crown must remain close to people, acquiring and maintaining their appreciation, their respect, and their trust.' In short, Spain's modern monarchy is in search of authenticity to build credibility and respect for the institution. But this authenticity cannot be created face to face. Instead, distant leaders like a monarch or the CEO of a multinational must project an image of authenticity mainly through speeches and public appearances.

A leader's oratory plays an important role in generating the attributes of authenticity and increasing trust and credibility in the leader. I conducted a thematic analysis of King Felipe's first speech to identify the themes of an authentic leader using the 3 Hs (heart, habit and harmony).

Heart

Expressing passion and vitality

At the beginning of the speech, Felipe says, 'I begin my reign with profound emotion at the honour of accepting the Crown, aware of the responsibility it entails and with the greatest hope for the future of Spain.' After making these references to emotion and hope, Felipe explicitly points out Spain's contribution to history: 'It is a nation forged over centuries of history by the shared endeavours of millions of people from all corners of our country and without whose participation the course of humanity cannot be properly understood.' This statement moves the speech into a 'higher order' of significance.

He then makes a personal connection to the country, referring to his emotional attachment to the nation: 'A great nation ... in which I believe and which I love and admire; a nation whose destiny has been bound to my own for all of my life, as Crown Prince and, from today, as King of Spain.' This personal touch carries over with his love for his mother: 'let me also thank my mother, Queen Sofía ... I trust that for many more years we shall continue to enjoy their support, their experience and their affection'.

Felipe's leadership is not only about positive feelings, but also about the emotional intensity and vitality required to move forward: 'And I undertake my task with energy, with enthusiasm and with the open and innovative spirit that has inspired the men and women of my generation.' This is a clear bid to energize those around him with his contagious passion. Felipe explicitly presents his vitality as emerging from his generation: 'The Spanish people, and especially the men and women of my generation, wish to revitalize our institutions.'

Reinforcing the humility of unsung heroes

Felipe's leadership is about much more than mere compliance with formal functions; his speech is a call to view him as an approachable person who identifies with his followers. 'I shall be a head of state who is loyal and willing to listen; ready to understand, to warn and to advise; and always vigilant to defend the general interest.' Thus, his leadership creates a context to achieve collective goals.

Authentic leaders constantly raise the importance of a common purpose in the minds of those around them: 'The parliamentary monarchy must be open to and engaged with the society it serves; it must be a faithful and loyal interpreter of people's aspirations and hopes, and must share – and feel as its own – their successes and their failures.' Implied in this message is also a duty of service towards followers and a shared sense of ownership for leadership outcomes. The use of humble rhetoric is elegantly illustrated at the end of the speech, when Felipe quotes Spain's greatest novelist: 'Cervantes, speaking through Don Quixote, said, "One man is no more than another if he does no more than another".'

Storytelling to bridge the past and the future

Felipe's leadership is based on his royal identity. However, to transcend the confines of this position and become an independent leader who can make a name for himself he must develop a unique, personal identity. But he must do this without undermining the contribution of his predecessor, his father. This is what he tries to do in the following passages – to emphasize a positive legacy: 'I wish to pay a tribute of gratitude to, and respect for, my father, King Juan Carlos I. From today, an exceptional reign becomes part of our history, one that has left an extraordinary political legacy.' Felipe explicitly points out that this positive legacy is not only a link to the person of the previous king; it is also a tribute to the success of his contemporaries: 'Today we render to the person of King Juan Carlos the appreciation he deserves, from a generation of citizens who paved the way for democracy, for understanding among Spaniards and for their coexistence in a climate of freedom.' Thus, this statement also emphasizes the personal identification between the figure of the king and his contemporaries.

Felipe explicitly presents his own leadership as emerging from past generations, but at the same time, departing from them by emphasizing the characteristics of new times. He makes a call to his own generation to take the baton: 'The men and women of my generation are heirs to that great collective success which has been admired worldwide and of which we are so proud. It is now up to us to pass it on to the coming generations.' This historical view creates a sense of progress among people and serves to take ownership and responsibility for the future. Implied in these passages is Felipe's attempt to bridge a generational gap showing gratitude and pride for past achievements while building on them to move forward towards a better future.

Habit

Renewal to evolve and adapt to new times

In his speech, Felipe places a lot of emphasis on the need for change. He uses the word 'new' nine times: new times, new reign, new century, new opportunities, new challenges, new technologies, new actors, new risks and a new king. The reference to renewal is also implied in the phrase 'a renewed monarchy for new times,' which is also repeated towards the end of his speech: 'these are my convictions about the Crown, which from today I shall embody: a renewed monarchy for new times'. The need for change implied in this statement is further strengthened by the above-mentioned embodiment of these beliefs to adapt to the new circumstances which he continues to emphasize: 'today I should like us to look forward to the future; toward the renewed Spain that, in unison, we must continue to build, from the beginning of this new reign'.

The references to change are balanced between the challenges and the opportunities that the new times represent: 'As we are all aware, profound changes are taking place in our lives, bearing us away from traditional ways of seeing the world and our place within it. And while this may provoke disquiet, uncertainty or fear, it also opens up new opportunities for progress.' At the same time, Felipe attempts to empower citizens by looking back to past successes: 'History has shown us that all the great advances have taken place in Spain when we have evolved and adapted to the reality of our times.' These statements are paving the way for his uplifting vision for a future filled with hope and confidence.

Building confidence in the leader and his/her mission

Felipe's vision revolves around common values and an attempt to raise hope and instil faith in Spaniards at a time when the opinion polls show that people are disenchanted with the country's institutions, including the monarchy. 'We hope for a Spain in which people regain and retain confidence in their institutions, and for a society based on civic values, tolerance, honesty and rigour, one that is open minded and constructive and that acts in a spirit of solidarity.' This phrase is addressed especially to people whose scepticism towards the monarchy and other public institutions has been growing due to past mistakes. To meet the new challenges, Felipe calls for a 'profound change in the mentalities and attitudes of many people and, of course, great determination and courage, vision and responsibility'. Thus, these references, in addition to raising awareness for the need of change, can also serve to increase the confidence of people in Spain's institutions.

Overcoming adversity with resilience

The reference to history follows a progressive pattern in which positive outcomes have followed periods of adversity: 'Today, if we were to look to the past, I hope it would be not with nostalgia, but with great respect for our history; with the will to overcome whatever may have separated or divided us; and thus, remember and appreciate everything that unites and gives us strength and solidity for the future.' Spain's recent history is also used to emphasize the same point: 'Over recent years, and not without difficulties, we have lived together in a democracy, having finally overcome past eras of tragedy, silence and darkness. Preserving the principles and ideals on which this coexistence is based, and to which I referred earlier, is not only an act of justice to the generations that have preceded us, but a source of inspiration and example at all times in our public life.' This sequence of success after failure reinforces a sense of collective efficacy – a strength achieved by uniting forces and working together to overcome difficulties.

Harmony

Leading by example and virtue

The hallmark of authentic leadership lies in presenting moral principles of conduct and an embodiment of these moral codes. 'The Crown must safeguard the dignity of the institution, maintain its prestige and conduct itself straightforwardly, honestly and transparently, in accordance with its institutional role and its social responsibility. Because only in this way will it possess the necessary moral authority for the exercise of its functions.' In addition, Felipe refers in the speech to many people's wish for their leaders to set an example. He tells his audience, 'Today, more than ever, and quite rightly, people are calling for moral and ethical principles to inspire our public life and for behaviour to be exemplary in this respect.' He also makes clear that this starts with the monarchy: 'And the king, as head of state, must not only lead, but also be at the service of this fair and legitimate demand by the people.'

Creating a collective identity and community

Felipe wants to use the figure of the king as a symbol of unity. In his speech, he tries to provide a sense of community and to crystallize a shared collective identity despite great cultural diversity. There are several references in his speech to the value-added dimension of diversity: 'Spain is a nation forged over centuries of history by the shared endeavours of millions of people from all corners of our country'; 'diversity stems from our history, exalting us and giving strength'; and 'Historically, Spain has been home to diverse traditions and cultures, which have enriched all its peoples throughout the ages.'

This emphasis on finding strength in diversity appears in many other parts of the speech. Felipe appeals to his followers:

> Let us all work together, each with their own personality, enriching the whole; let us do so with loyalty, to achieve the new goals before us all in the twenty-first century. Because a nation is not only its history, it is an all-encompassing project, one that is felt and shared by all, one that looks to the future ... [P]olitical values are essential for our coexistence and for the organization and development of our life in common.

These passages on diversity not only call for a shared collective identity, but also for Spain's political institutions to set aside differences and coordinate collective action.

Reinforcing sustainability and transformation

Authentic leaders make explicit reference to certain values to raise the relevance of them in people's minds. Towards the end of his speech, Felipe explicitly refers to key values such as innovation, entrepreneurship, ethics, the environment and equality: 'We now face the great challenge of promoting new technologies, science and research, which are the real energizers of wealth today; the challenge is to promote and encourage innovation, creativity and entrepreneurship as essential attitudes for development and growth.' He continues, 'The twenty-first century, which is also the century of the environment, must be one in which humanistic and ethical values – which we must recover and maintain – are exercised to help eliminate discrimination, secure the role of women and further promote peace and international cooperation.' With such statements, Felipe is trying to align his followers' progressive values with his own. These shared values help people to identify with the leader.

This emphasis on authenticity involves mutual trust if a better future for everyone is to be built. Felipe shows this positive vision to his listeners: 'My belief in our future is based on my faith in Spanish society; it is mature and vigorous, responsible and caring, a society that is showing great fortitude and one that has a laudable spirit to prevail over its difficulties.' He concludes the speech with a strong emotional appeal to national pride: 'I am proud of the Spanish people and nothing would honour me more than if, through my work and my effort, day by day, I could make the people of Spain proud of their new king.'

Bringing everything together, the themes outlined above are representative of how authentic leaders speak. This is a speech whose main elements illustrate the 3 Hs of authentic leadership: heart, habit and harmony. The heart themes include references to passion, humility and storytelling. The speech expresses positive feelings and emotional intensity and is crafted with passion and vitality to revitalize the institutions and the nation. This emotional appeal is transmitted with humility, which reinforces personal identification with the leader. Furthermore, storytelling is used to bridge past and future generations.

The habit of learning themes revolved around renewal, confidence and resilience. The emphasis on the need to evolve and adapt to the new times is present in many parts of the speech. This renewal is further coupled with the need to build confidence in the leader and in the institutions which he represents. Specifically, Felipe showcases examples in history when the country overcame adversity through resilience and by working together.

Finally, the harmony themes contain the hallmarks of authentic leadership: setting an example, community, and legacy. Given some Spaniards' scepticism about the monarchy, Felipe's oratory emphasizes integrity and virtue and leading by example. His speech is also an attempt to create a collective identity, unifying forces around differences. He views diversity as a source of strength in building a successful community. His concluding statements are examples of his goal to have a positive impact in the future by reinforcing sustainability and leaving a legacy. The proclamation speech transmitted a message of hope for the future and for change.

On 15 June 2015, a survey carried out for leading Spanish daily *El Mundo* on the first anniversary of the proclamation showed that 74.7 per cent of Spaniards held a favourable (52 per cent) or highly favourable (22.7 per cent) opinion of King Felipe VI. And this is a growing trend. His personal endorsement has spilled over to the institution he leads. At the beginning of 2017, another survey revealed that 'Felipe places the monarchy in its best standing in twenty years.' Just over two years into his reign, the new king had managed to restore the prestige of the monarchy with his personal reputation and authenticity.

Agenda for Change

Change with authenticity: lessons from
12 Angry Men

The VP of finance at a large European bank in Portugal told me that, once, the night before a very important meeting, he happened to watch the 1957 classic *12 Angry Men*. The movie, which won an Oscar and stars Henry Fonda, is about a jury that must decide whether a defendant is guilty or innocent based on reasonable doubt. It is a great noir thriller that touches on the power of influence and consensus building. The finance executive mentioned that these lessons were fresh in his mind when dealing with his boss and colleagues that next day. It was clearer to him how to get people to buy-in to the changes he wanted to implement in the company.

I have included this movie in my leadership development classes ever since to illustrate effective influence using the 3 Hs framework of authentic leadership. The lessons remain even more relevant today. The main challenge CEOs face is gaining trust, credibility and respect from their peers. The script of *12 Angry Men* is a masterpiece on change management using influence without power.

Let's divide the movie into three parts. Part 1 teaches lessons on how to be influential *unfreezing* and mobilizing the group and winning their *hearts*. Part 2 centres on the lessons of how to *change* the group and create movement by making learning a *habit*. Finally, Part 3 focuses on lessons regarding *freezing* the change, consolidating the created momentum and finding social *harmony*.

Part 1: Win their hearts

After a preliminary vote, the initial verdict of the jury is eleven guilty and one not-guilty. Henry Fonda's character votes not-guilty and he proposes a secret vote and to further discuss the case if someone else votes non-guilty.

- Move slowly by observing and listening to others to understand their inner motivations and personality. For example, the salesman and Yankees fan simply wants to get away in time for the baseball game. Understanding the motivations of others will help you win their hearts and customize your tactics of influence later.

- Begin with a small request, such as 'I guess we talk' and avoid big requests such as 'I'm not trying to change your mind.' Reframe your purpose with modesty. For instance, in response to the question of 'Why are we here?' the assumption is that they just need to vote guilty in what seems a clear case of murder. Yet, he answers 'I don't know, maybe no reason . . .' and then, 'We owe him a few words . . . let's take an hour.'

- Gain the trust of others by revealing your own weaknesses; for example, 'It's not easy to raise my hand.' Sharing your doubts and being humble make you closer to your peers. For example, 'I don't have anything brilliant, I only know as much as you do.' But, by the same token, question assumptions by pointing out inconsistencies in others' arguments. For example, Henry Fonda questions the logic of the garage owner about the woman who saw the killing coming from the same background as the boy – 'How come you believe the woman; she's "one" of them too, isn't she?'

Part 2: set the habit of learning

After a secret vote, the old man changed his vote to not-guilty to support Henry Fonda. Then four additional jurors changed their vote in favour of acquittal, ending this second part of the movie with six for guilty and six for not-guilty.

- Be alert to new ideas and use new evidence coming from your early supporters to advance your case. For instance, the man from the slums' remarks about the old man who testified against the boy was a turning point in the movie. It raises the idea that 'witnesses can make mistakes'. This made Henry Fonda say, 'I'd like to know if an old man who drags one foot because he had a stroke can get from his bedroom to his front door in fifteen seconds.' He requested the map of the apartment and recreated the scene of the old man going to the door, creating doubts about this critical testimony.

- Your main role as an agent of change is making sense of things and helping others learn. For example, when Henry Fonda recreates the scene of the old man going to the door, he concludes, 'I know what happened' and 'we have proved the old man couldn't have heard what the boy said'. This generates movement by identifying small wins that illustrate how general support is on his side. Then, make learning tangible, he suggests, 'I think we ought to have an open ballot.'

- Allow your opponents to reveal their own inconsistencies. For example, one member of the jury says, 'He was an old man, he was confused.' The garage owner also remarks, 'he don't even speak good English'. These two examples have an impact on the plot of the movie, showing how these two jurors lose credibility in front of the others. They are then socially isolated because other jurors do not want to be associated with them.

Part 3: build social harmony

The six remaining jurors who still think the boy is guilty change their mind one by one as Henry Fonda uses three different influencing techniques to support him in the final part.

- Focus on bonding with the people who are likely to go with the flow. They are easily convinced when they see that the momentum is on your side. In the movie, the baseball fan, the foreman and the advertising man belong to this neutral group. For example, Henry Fonda listens to the foreman's personal story as an assistant coach.

- Move your case forward with rational people, such as the broker – put yourself in their shoes. Provide them with an empathetic experience to 'feel' the arguments. For example, Henry Fonda asks the broker to remember details about a movie he watched with his wife – 'put yourself into the boy's shoes, could you remember details under those circumstances?' – and when the broker failed the test, he concluded '. . . and you were not under an emotional stress, were you?'

- Finally, socially isolate those who show strong negative emotions towards your goals. For example, the garage owner is rejected by the rest of the group. At the same time, save your opponents' face to assure that yesterday's enemies will be your friends of tomorrow. For example, after he points out the stereotyping statements, Henry Fonda remarks, 'It's always difficult to keep personal prejudice out of a thing like this.' Then show politeness to provide emotional comfort to former opponents in order to start building and repairing a positive relationship. For example, Henry Fonda helps another member of the jury on with his coat.

In *the end*, do not forget to celebrate your success with your first follower. He/she was the one who started the movement. Remember the last scene on the stairs between the architect and the old man.

Feel, learn and build

The stories in *Yours Truly* have one thing in common: the emotional investment of their protagonists. Rafael de la Rubia is not motivated by a big salary; nor does he have a well-thought strategic plan. He is passionate about living as an athlete, an entrepreneur and a rock star, and is authentic outside the authenticity script. Hiroko Samejima was a designer at Chanel and decided to start her own company, andu amet, to fulfil her dream of creating authentic quality products by combining the elegance of the best of global fashion brands, African taste and Japanese craftsmanship.

This is the first lesson of *Yours Truly*. Being an authentic leader requires finding passion and motivation within yourself and your own idiosyncratic life story to win the *hearts* of your followers. If you are interested in developing your authenticity, your motivation ought to be concentrated on your feelings and what makes you tick. Carlo Volpi's feelings towards his winery made him see what others could not; so he did what his business partner at the time could not do. Carlo started a process of internationalization by seeing his wine as part of Italy's heritage that needed to be known around the world. His passion took him to a route that put Volpi's wine on the map. Resolving the *protean–authenticity paradox* requires a balance between the 'true' selves and the 'multiple' selves.

A critical analysis of these courageous leaders shows that the core characteristic of authentic leaders is a willingness to experiment with their 'possible' selves. This is the second lesson of *Yours Truly*. Authentic leaders are in a constant motion of learning to set new *habits*. In an entrepreneurial narrative punctuated by potential crisis, Rakesh Aggarwal 'faked' self-confidence to transform his milk company. During the process, he developed the necessary tenacity and flexibility to adapt and progress. Dena Schlutz learned how to become a top executive and a successful entrepreneur, flourishing after adversity. And Angel Ruiz took control of his destiny by overcoming the many obstacles he faced. Yet we have an instinctive bias for consistency and continuity, wanting to be able to predict the social world around us. The problem, of course, is that personal transformation involves a certain degree of contradiction. Embracing this contradiction and its inevitable anxieties brings the greater good of enriched authenticity and that is what the process of *Yours Truly*, in the end, is all about. Resolving the *growth–authenticity paradox* requires a balance between one's behavioural integrity and one's growth.

Authentic leadership is a collaborative choreography – great leaders embrace *harmony* and develop a context to make followers shine. This is the final lesson of *Yours Truly*. The success of companies like PERI-Group, Vista Alegre and Santander, and even the Spanish royal family, relies, in large part, on creating a context for others to grow. Resolving the *otherness–authenticity paradox* requires a balance between one's agency and one's communion.

In conclusion, illustrated with real-world examples, throughout *Yours Truly* we have identified the pivotal role of focusing on the 3 Hs of authenticity: Heart, Habit and Harmony.

First, *feel* and activate the passion in your Heart and those of your followers – to experience emotional authenticity. Second, *learn* and consolidate the Habit of Learning – to experience behavioural authenticity. Third, *build* harmonious relationships with others – to experience social authenticity. This is a practical and powerful tool for anyone with a desire to better him/herself and advance the world. Be yourself with passionate humility, cultivate the habit of learning and find harmony between your own and others' interests.

Heart, habit and harmony is a comprehensive framework for authenticity that responds to the questions of who you are, what you do and how you do it, respectively. The heart factor refers to self-awareness and unbiased processing which result in positive emotions. The habit of learning refers to behaving consistently in relation to one's values, preferences and needs, while being open to new experiences and growing into your best self. Finally, the harmony in agency and communion is achieved through a harmonious unity between one's true self and one's relationships with others.

In sum, authentic leaders are aware of who they are and embrace their personal identity with passion. They have a growth mindset that helps them adopt the habit of changing and expanding their behavioural repertoire. And finally, authentic leaders build harmonious relationships with others and enrich the social environment so that others can shine and develop.

Remember, to stay true to your authentic *protean, possible and social* self in leadership and life, embrace your multiple selves with passionate humility, stay true to your authentic self while changing over time, and enrich your social context. Authentic leaders are passionate actors, avid learners and memorable architects. They have many faces but one heart. They better themselves but become humble over time. They build projects that live beyond their time.

NOTES AND REFERENCES

Introduction

1   Sparrowe, R. (2005). 'Authentic leadership and the narrative self'. *Leadership Quarterly* 16(3): 419–39.

2   http://www.edelman.com/trust2017/ (accessed 17 March 2017).

Chapter 1

1   https://www.inc.com/jeff-haden/why-richard-branson-is-the-most-important-living-entrepreneur.html (accessed 17 March 2017).

2   Vannini, P. (2006). 'Dead poet's society: Teaching, publish-or-perish, and professors' experiences of authenticity'. *Symbolic Interaction* 29: 235–57.

3   Rogers, C. (1961). *On Becoming a Person: A Therapist's View of Psychotherapy*. Boston: Houghton Mifflin.

4   This 10-item scale of stress is published in Cohen, S. and Williamson, G. (1988). 'Perceived stress in a probability sample of the United States'. In S. Spacapan and S. Oskamp (eds), *The Social Psychology of Health*, 31–67. Newbury Park, CA: Sage.

5   Lyubomirsky, S. and Lepper, H. S. (1999). 'A measure of subjective happiness: Preliminary reliability and construct validation'. *Social Indicators Research* 46: 137–55.

6   The original 20-item scales are included in Ryff (1989). 'Happiness is everything, or is it? Explorations on the meaning of psychological well-being'. *Journal of Personality and Social Psychology* 57: 1069–81. The authors used the short versions of the six subscales which contain three items. We used the 14-item scales currently recommended by the Institute of Aging of the University of Wisconsin with permission from the authors.

7   Scoring key for authenticity: low: 4 to 14; average: 15 to 25; and high: 26 to 28.

8   Scoring key for inauthenticity: low: 4 to 7; average: 8 to 18; and high: 19 to 28.

9   We used the 14-item scales currently recommended by Ryff at the Institute of Aging of the University of Wisconsin with permission from the authors.

10 This relationship between psychological well-being and social capital is limited to the advice network and they are not central in the 'friendship network' (e.g. people

with whom they go out for social activities outside the class, such as going out for informal lunch, dinner or drinks).

11   Sheldon, K. M., Ryan, R. M., Rawsthorne, L. J. and Ilardi, B. (1997). 'Trait self and true self: Cross-role variation in the Big-Five personality traits and its relations with psychological authenticity and subjective well-being'. *Journal of Personality and Social Psychology* 73: 1380–93.

12   The Big-Five personality traits is measured by the NEO Personality Inventory and include Extraversion, Neuroticism, Agreeableness, Conscientiousness and Openness to Experience.

13   Synder, M. (1974). 'Self-monitoring of expressive behavior'. *Journal of Personality and Social Psychology* 30(4): 526.

14   In response to the criticisms of Snyder's original scale, Lennox and Wolfe in 1984 developed a revised self-monitoring scale of 13 items using a six-point Likert scale rating from 'certainly always false' to 'certainly always true.' Seven of their items measure individuals' ability to modify self-presentation and six items involve their sensitivity to the expressive behaviours of others. Here I include only the first dimension.

15   Scoring key for self-monitoring: take into account that items 4 and 5 are reversed code.

16   Kakarika, M., Biniari, M. and Mayo, M. (2013). 'Where does the heart lie? Harmonious versus obsessive entrepreneurial passion and role identity transitions'. Academy of Management Annual Meeting, Orlando, Florida.

Chapter 2

1   Christakis, N. A. and Fowler, J. H. (2009). *Connected: The Surprising Power of Our Social Networks and How They Shape Our Lives*. New York: Little Brown and Company.

2   Larsen, R. J. and Diener, E. (1992). 'Promises and problems with the circumplex model of emotions'. In M. S. Clark (ed.), *Emotion*. Newbury Park, CA: Sage Publications.

3   Scoring key: the first-line adjective refers to the activated pleasant emotions; the second refers to the inactivated pleasant emotions; the third refers to the activated unpleasant emotions; and the fourth refers to inactivated unpleasant emotions.

4   Ou, A. Y., Waldman, D. A. and Peterson, S. J. (2015). 'Do humble CEOs matter? An examination of CEO humility and firm outcomes'. *Journal of Management*.

5   Owens, B. P., Johnson, M. D. and Mitchell, T. R. (2013). 'Expressed humility in organizations: Implications for performance, teams and leadership'. *Organization Science* 24(5): 1517–38.

6   Owens, B. P. and Hekman, D. R. (2016). 'How does leader humility influence team performance? Exploring the mechanisms of contagion and collective promotion focus'. *Academy of Management Journal* 59(3): 1088–111.

7   Scoring key: sum up the points and divide by 9.

8   Jones, D. N. and Paulhus, D. L. (2014). 'Introducing the short Dark Triad (SD3): A brief measure of dark personality traits'. *Assessment* 21(1): 28–41.

9   Scoring Key: sum up the points and divide by 9.

10   Mayo, M. (April 2017). 'If humble people make better leaders, why do we fall for charismatic narcissists?' *Harvard Business Review*.

11   Conger, J. A. and Kanungo, R. N. (1998). *Charismatic Leadership in Organizations*. Thousand Oaks, CA, and London: Sage Publications.

12   Galvin, B. M., Waldman, D. A. and Balthazard, P. (2010). 'Visionary communication qualities as mediators of the relationship between narcissism and attributions of leader charisma'. *Personnel Psychology* 63(3): 509–39.

13   Pastor, J., Mayo, M. and Shamir, B. (2007). 'Adding fuel to fire: The impact of followers' arousal on ratings of charisma'. *Journal of Applied Psychology* 92(6): 1584–96.

14   Martin, S. R., Côté, S. and Woodruff, T. (2016). 'Echoes of our upbringing: How growing up wealthy or poor relates to narcissism, leader behaviour, and leader effectiveness'. *Academy of Management Journal* 59(6): 2157–77.

Chapter 3

1   Shamir, B., Dayn-Horesh, H. and Adler, D. (2005). 'Leading by biography: Toward a life-story approach to the study of leadership'. *Leadership* 1: 13–29.

     Shamir, B. and Eilam, G. (2005). 'What's your story? Toward a life-story approach to authentic leadership'. *Leadership Quarterly* 16: 395–417.

2   http://www.sesp.northwestern.edu/masters-learning-and-organizational-change/knowledge-lens/stories/2013/the-story-of-my-life-developing-authentic-leaders.html (accessed 17 March 2017).

3   Zak, Paul J. (October 2014). 'Why your brain loves good storytelling'. *Harvard Business Review*.

4   McAdams, D. P., Diamond, A., Aubin, E. S. and Mansfield, E. (1997). 'Stories of commitment: The psychosocial construction of generative lives'. *Journal of Personality and Social Psychology* 72(3): 678–94.

5   Mayo, M. and Kark, R. (2013). 'The psychosocial construction of leadership identity: A life story approach'. In the symposium *Who is a Leader? A Follower? New Research on Leadership Identity in Organizations* by R. Piccolo and S. DeRue. Academy of Management Annual Meeting, Orlando, Florida.

6   Goffee, R. and Jones, G. (2006). *Why Should Anyone Be Led by You? What It Takes to Be an Authentic Leader.* Cambridge, MA: Harvard Business Review Press.

Chapter 4

1   Mischel, W., Shoda, Y. and Peake, P. K. (1988). 'The nature of adolescent competencies predicted by preschool delay of gratification'. *Journal of Personality and Social Psychology* 54: 687–96.

2   Shoda, Y., Mischel, W. and Peake, P. K. (1990). 'Predicting adolescent cognitive and self-regulatory competences from preschool delay of gratification: Identifying diagnostic conditions'. *Developmental Psychology* 26(6): 978–86.

3   Adapted from Lockwood, P., Jordan, C. and Ziva, K. (2002). 'Motivation by positive or negative role models: Regulatory focus determines who will best inspire us'. *Journal of Personality and Social Psychology* 83: 854–64.

4   Score of promotion is the total sum of these items: 3, 5, 6, 8, 12, 14, 16, 17, 18. Scores range from 9 to 81. A high score indicates promotion self-regulation with a focus on ideals, hopes and considering new possibilities. Score of prevention is the total sum of these items: 1, 2, 4, 7, 9, 10, 11, 13, 15. Scores range from 9 to 81. A high score indicates prevention self-regulation with a focus on duties, responsibilities and meeting obligations.

5   Guillen, L., Mayo, M., Whitman, D. and Korotov, K. (2016). 'Understanding visionary leadership perceptions: A leader identity perspective'. Academy of Management Annual Meeting. Anaheim, California.

6   Dweck, C. (2017). *Mindsets: The New Technology of Success.* New York: Ballantine Books.

7   https://www.mindsetkit.org/static/files/YCLA_LessonPlan_v10.pdf (accessed 17 March 2017).

Chapter 5

1   http://content.time.com/time/magazine/article/0,9171,988512–2,00.html (accessed 17 March 2017).

2   http://www.nytimes.com/2005/09/23/books/oprahs-book-club-toadd-contemporary-writers.html (accessed 17 March 2017).

3   http://www.huffingtonpost.com/2008/08/08/the-oprah-effect-one-mill_n_117685.html (accessed 17 March 2017).

4   Mayo, M., Kakarika, M., Pastor, J. and Brutus, S. (2012). 'Aligning or inflating your leadership self-image? A longitudinal study of responses to peer feedback in MBA teams'. *Academy of Management Learning & Education* 11(4): 631–52.

5   https://hbr.org/2016/08/the-gender-gap-in-feedback-and-self-perception (accessed 17 March 2017).

6   https://hbr.org/video/5159470991001/even-after-criticism-men-think-highly-of-themselves (accessed 17 March 2017).

7   Gable, S. L., Reis, H. T., Impett, E. and Asher, E. R. (2004). 'What do you do when things go right? The intrapersonal and interpersonal benefits of sharing positive events'. *Journal of Personality and Social Psychology* 87: 228–45.

8   Wang, Y. N. (2016). 'Balanced authenticity predicts optimal well-being: Theoretical conceptualization and empirical development of the authenticity in relationships scale'. *Personality and Individual Differences* 94: 316–23.

9   Scoring key: balanced authenticity (mean = 12.15, SD = 1.39), ego-centric authenticity (mean = 7.14, SD = 2.62), and other-distorted authenticity (mean = 9.35, SD = 2.50).

10   Guillen, L., Mayo, M. and Karelaia, N. (forthcoming). 'Appearing self-confident and getting credit for it: Why it may be easier for men than women to gain influence at work'. *Human Resource Management.*

11   Mayo, M. (July 2016). 'To seem confident, women have to be seen as warm'. *Harvard Business Review.*

Chapter 6

1   http://www.businessinsider.com/interview-with-starbucks-new-ceo-kevin-johnson–2017–4 (accessed 17 March 2017).

2   Seligman, M. E. P. (April 2011). 'Building resilience: What business can learn from a pioneering army program for fostering post-traumatic growth'. *Harvard Business Review.*

3   To take the complete survey you can go to https://www.authentichappiness.sas.upenn.edu/user/login?destination=node/504 (accessed 17 March 2017).

4   Meevissen, Y., Peters, M. L. and Alberts, H. (2011). 'Become more optimistic by imagining a best possible self: Effects of a two-week intervention'. *Journal of Behaviour Therapy and Experimental Psychiatry* 42(3): 371–8.

5   Rotter, J. B. (1966). 'Generalized expectancies for internal versus external control of reinforcement'. *Psychological Monographs* 80(1): 1–28.

6   Score is number of these items: 1b, 2a, 3a, 4a, 5b, 6b, 7b, 8a, 9a, 10a, 11a, 12a, 13a. Scores range from 0 to 13. A high score indicates an internal locus of control, while a low score indicates an external locus of control.

7   Zhou Koval, C., vanDellen, M. R., Fitzsimons, G. M. and Ranby, K. W. (2015). 'The burden of responsibility: Interpersonal costs of high self-control'. *Journal of Personality and Social Psychology* 108(5): 750–66.

8   Mayo, M., Pastor, J., Gómez-Mejia, L. and Cruz, C. (2016). 'Why some firms adopt telecommuting while others do not: A contingency perspective'. *Human Resource Management* 48(6): 917–39.

9   Watson, M., Greer, S., Pruyn, J. and Van der Borne, B. (1990). 'Locus of control and adjustment to cancer'. *Psychological Reports* 66(1): 39–48.

10   Mayo, M., Gómez-Mejia, L., Firfiray, S., Berrone, P. and Villena, V. H. (2016). 'Leader beliefs and CSR for employees: The case of telework provision'. *Leadership & Organization Development Journal* 37(5): 609–34.

11   Brown, B. (2012). *Daring Greatly: The Courage To Be Vulnerable Transforms the Way to Live, Love, Parent and Lead.* London: Penguin.

Part 2 Conclusion

1   Ibarra, H. (January–February 2015). 'The authenticity paradox'. *Harvard Business Review.*

Chapter 7

1   Gladwell, M. (2000). *The Tipping Point: How Little Things Can Make a Big Difference.* London: Abacus.

2   Pastor, J., Meindl, J. and Mayo, M. (2002). 'A network effects model of charisma attributions'. *Academy of Management Journal* 45(2): 410–20.

3   Mayo, M. and Kakarika, M. (2014). 'Cross-boundary team social capital and team effectiveness'. In the symposium *Exploring the Social Foundations of Effective Team Process and Outcomes* by A. Richter. Society of Industrial and Organizational Psychology (SIOP), Hawaii.

4   Mayo, M., Kakarika, M., Mainemelis, C. and Deuschel, N. (2017). 'A metatheoretical framework of diversity in teams'. *Human Relations* 70(8): 1–29.

5   Mayo, M., van Knippenberg, D., Guillen, L. and Firfiray, S. (2016). 'Team diversity and categorization salience: Capturing diversity-blind, inter-group biased, and multiple perceptions'. *Organizational Research Methods* 19(3): 433–74.

6   https://www.ft.com/content/c5c577f8–75ce–11e6-b60a-de4532d5ea35 (accessed 17 March 2017).

7   Hackman, R., Gonzalez, A. and Lehman, E. (2002). 'Nobody on the podium: Lessons about leadership from the Orpheus Chamber Orchestra'. *Harvard Business Review.*

8   Kernis, M. H. and Goldman, B. M. (2006). 'A multicomponent conceptualization of authenticity: Theory and research'. *Advances in Experimental Social Psychology* 38. DOI: 10.1016/S0065–2601(06)38006–9.

Chapter 8

1   http://www.washingtontimes.com/news/2016/nov/9/millennials-prefer-authenticity/ (accessed 17 March 2017).

2   Firfiray, S. and Mayo, M. (2016). 'The lure of work–life benefits: Perceived person–organization fit as a mechanism for explaining job seeker attraction to organizations'. *Human Resource Management.*

3   This study was partially funded by a research grant from the Ministry of Economy and Competitiveness, Spain, #ECO2012–33081, to Margarita Mayo as principal investigator.

4   Adaption of the scale by Cabe, D. M. and DeRue, D. S. (2002). 'The convergent and discriminant validity of subjective fit perceptions'. *Journal of Applied Psychology* 87: 875–84.

5   Ladkin, D. and Taylor, S. (2010). 'Enacting the "true self": Towards a theory of embodied authentic leadership'. *Leadership Quarterly* 21: 64–74.

6   Weischer, A. E., Weibler, J. and Petersen, M. (2013). '"To thine own self be true": The effects of enactment and life storytellings on perceived leader authenticity'. *Leadership Quarterly* 24(4): 477–95.

7   Yagil, D. and Medler-Liraz, H. (2013). 'Moments of truth: Examining transient authenticity and identity in service encounters'. *Academy of Management Journal* 56(2): 473–97.

8   Guillen, L., Mayo, M. and Korotov, K. (2015). 'Is leadership a part of me? A leader identity approach to understanding the motivation to lead'. *Leadership Quarterly* 26: 802–20.

9   https://www.youtube.com/watch?v=8_CeFiUkV7s (accessed 17 March 2017).

Chapter 9

1   https://www.youtube.com/watch?v=24d4rfnsOxg (accessed 17 March 2017).

2   https://www.youtube.com/watch?v=AVq_tZOtW78 (accessed 17 March 2017).

3   Michie, S. and Gooty, J. (2005). 'Values, emotions and authenticity: Will the real leader please stand up?' *Leadership Quarterly* 16: 441–57.

4   Schwartz, S. H. (1994). 'Are there universal aspects in the structure and contents of human values?' *Journal of Social Issues* 50: 19–45.

5   Mayo, M., Cao, J., Firfiray, S. and Sanchez, J. (2015). 'Modeling employee and business outcomes of work–family support policies'. Academy of Management Annual Meeting. Vancouver, Canada.

6   SABI is similar to COMPUSTAT in the United States, except that it also includes firms that are not publicly traded. Since nearly all participating public companies are local branches of large multinational companies listed in various stock exchange markets all over the world, they follow different financial reporting rules. Therefore, we selected only non-public companies in order to achieve a more consistent comparison of sales growth measures.

7   Mayo, M. (April 2016). 'Don't call it the end of the siesta. What Spain's new work hours really mean'. *Harvard Business Review*.

8   http://www.cnbc.com/2017/02/01/why-pepsico-ceo-indra-nooyi-writes-letters-to-her-employees-parents.html (accessed 17 March 2017).

Part 3 Conclusion

1   Mead, G. H. (1934). *Mind, Self, and Society*. Chicago: University of Chicago Press.

2   Tajfel, H. and Turner, J. C. (1986). 'The social identity theory of intergroup behaviour'. In S. Worchel and W. G. Austin (eds), *Psychology of Intergroup Relations*, 7–24. Chicago: Nelson Hall.

3   Sparrowe, R. (2005). 'Authentic leadership and the narrative self'. *Leadership Quarterly* 16(3): 419–39.

INDEX

Page numbers in *italics* refer to figures and photographs.